P9-CQM-117

Romantic Religion

Romantic Religion

❀ A Study of Barfield, Lewis, Williams, and Tolkien

R. J. Reilly

University of Georgia Press, Athens

Library of Congress Catalog Card Number: 70–145886
Standard Book Number: 8203–0267–8

The University of Georgia Press, Athens 30601

Printed in the United States of America
by The Kingsport Press, Inc., Kingsport, Tennessee 37662

The author acknowledges permission to quote passages from the following material: "For the Time Being" in *Collected Longer Poems* by W. H. Auden, by permission of Random House, Inc.; *History in English Words* by Owen Barfield, by permission of Faber & Faber (English edition) and Eerdmans Publishing Company (American edition); *Poetic Diction* by Owen Barfield, by permission of Faber & Faber; *Saving the Appearances* by Owen Barfield, by permission of Harcourt Brace Jovanovich, Inc. All other quotations from Owen Barfield's works are reprinted by permission of Wesleyan University Press and Faber & Faber. Also, *The Mind and Heart of Love* by Martin C. D'Arcy, S.J., by permission of Holt, Rinehart and Winston, Inc.; *Charles Williams* (1955) by John Heath-Stubbs, reprinted by permission of Longman Group Ltd., for the British Council; *Interpretation: The Poetry of Meaning* edited by Stanley Romaine Hopper and David L. Miller, reprinted by permission of Harcourt Brace Jovanovich, Inc.; *The Four Loves, Letters to Malcolm,* and *Till We Have Faces,* by C. S. Lewis reprinted by permission of Harcourt Brace Jovanovich, Inc.; *Surprised by Joy* by C. S. Lewis, reprinted by permission of Harcourt Brace Jovanovich, Inc. (American edition) and Geoffrey Bles Ltd. (English edition); Preface by C. S. Lewis in *Essays Presented in Honor of Charles Williams,* by permission of Oxford University Press; *Pilgrim's Regress* by C. S. Lewis, published by Sheed and Ward, Inc. New York; "Tolkien and the Fairy Story" by R. J. Reilly, in *Thought* (Spring 1963) by permission from Rev. Joseph E. O'Neill, S.J.; "On Fairy Stories" by J. R. R. Tolkien, in *Essays Presented to Charles Williams* by permission of Oxford University Press; *He Came Down from Heaven* and *The Forgiveness of Sins* by Charles Williams, reprinted by permission of Faber & Faber; *The Image of the City* (1958) and *Taliessin through Logres* (1938) by Charles Williams, by permission of Clarendon Press, Oxford; *Religion and Love in Dante* by Charles Williams, by permission of Dacre Press: A. & C. Black Ltd., London.

For my father, my late mother,
and my daughters, Kathleen and Mary

Contents

Foreword

Many people have helped me write this book, though no one but myself is responsible for its deficiencies.

First, I should like to extend special thanks to Mr. Owen Barfield, who, by a happy accident, read the book in its manuscript form and most graciously suggested several ways of improving it.

I am also indebted to many friends and colleagues at the University of Detroit, especially to Professor Edward Wolff for his sympathetic attention over a long period of time, for his careful readings of many versions of the manuscript, and for his generous yet pointed criticisms. I owe thanks also to other colleagues, Professors John Mahoney, Thomas Porter, and Norman McKendrick, for help of various kinds—particularly for simply telling me things that I did not know. I thank also Miss Mary Jo Lynch of the University of Detroit Library, whose bibliographical help has been immense, and Mrs. Claire Tanase, the English Department secretary, who has helped me (as she has helped so many others) in a hundred ways.

I owe a long-standing debt of thanks to Professor C. C. Hollis of the University of North Carolina, whose interest in the subject of the book has helped to bring it into print. And I am grateful to Professor Howard Fulweiler of the University of Missouri for reading the manuscript and making many incisive comments on it. Others to whom I should like to extend my thanks for help and advice of many kinds are Professor T. J. J. Altizer of Emory University, Professor John Yunck of Michigan State University, Professor Bernard Duffey of Duke University, Professor Hazard Adams of the University of California at Irvine, Mrs. Marjorie Slater of Drew University, and Dr. C. M. Klyman.

Finally, my thanks are due the administration of the University of Detroit for the research leave that allowed me to work on this book.

Chapter One

Introduction

To use Sir Herbert Grierson's metaphor, what I have tried to do in this study is to examine one of the crosscurrents in contemporary literature. The metaphor suggests the fact that the complete history of any given time is like a body of moving water: events, ideas, religious attitudes, social ideologies, literary theories, and a thousand other things flow together like currents and eddies in a river, or perhaps an ocean. And even the mere literary history of a given time deals not only with literature but with at least some of these other currents and eddies as well—ideas, movements, religious attitudes—which literature has assumed to itself. The content of literature is everything except literature; literature, it may be said, gives a form to the "everything except." I have not, like Grierson, tried to depict an age, only one of the crosscurrents of our age: the fusion of a certain literary form with a certain subject matter, the romantic manner applied to religious matter. Inevitably, I have had to separate the form from the content in order to discuss them, though (as I shall often repeat) the two things are not really separable, but form a single current which I have called "romantic religion."

The four men in whose work I have found this peculiar fusion are Owen Barfield (an Anglican and an Anthroposophist), C. S.

Lewis and Charles Williams (also Anglicans), and J. R. R. Tolkien (a Roman Catholic). The last three need little introduction, perhaps only a reminder that all are (or were) critics and scholars who also have worked in "creative" forms. Lewis is well known for his scholarly work, his Christian apologetics, and his fiction—especially his "inter-planetary" trilogy and *Till We Have Faces.* Williams was a prolific critic, a poet, a novelist, a dramatist, and a theologian. Tolkien was for years known only within the small world of medieval and linguistic scholarship for such things as his work on *Beowulf* and *Sir Gawain and the Green Knight,* but he has come into such recent prominence with his "fairy story for adults," *The Lord of the Rings,* that reviewers are now speaking casually of certain books as being in "the Tolkien tradition." The fourth man, Barfield, is the least known to the general reader, and his work is hardest to describe briefly. Until his recent retirement he was a solicitor in London, having no formal association with any university, an "amateur" in the world of English thought and letters—relatively unknown in England and almost completely unknown in America. His early book *Poetic Diction* (1927) for years enjoyed a kind of underground reputation among such critics and poets as R. P. Blackmur and Howard Nemerov, who were concerned with poetic theory; and in view of Barfield's recently growing influence the book seems likely to become a standard work in the field. But it was *Saving the Appearances* (1957) that began to draw wider attention to Barfield's work. Till then he had existed in the public mind largely as someone whom Lewis insisted on citing in his own work. Now, in his later years, he is finally becoming a figure of some consequence, both in England and America. A recent reviewer referred to him as "one of the major and insufficiently appreciated prophets of the time,"[1] and T. J. J. Altizer has called *Saving the Appearances* not only a "fascinating and deeply illuminating book"[2] but has even said that it is "potentially one of the truly seminal works of our time."[3]

Since Barfield's retirement he has lectured at various American universities—Brandeis University, Drew University, Hamilton College, the University of Missouri—and has published in rapid order *Worlds Apart, A Dialogue of the 1960's* (1963), *Unancestral*

Voice (1965), and *Speaker's Meaning* (1967). His work is difficult to categorize. The early books, *History in English Words* (1926) and *Poetic Diction,* are primarily philological, though full of implications about subjects larger than the history of language and the making of poetry. The later books nearly defy classification. They are basically religious, in the sense that they advance a religious view of the universe, but they are not primarily theological. They reveal a startling breadth of mind: their arguments move at breakneck speed in such disciplines as linguistics, anthropology, philosophy, historiography, biblical exegesis, depth psychology—even modern physics and astronomy. Of the four men Barfield is the only one who has not written any seriously creative work. Though the dialectic of *Worlds Apart* and *Unancestral Voice* is given a nominal fictional scaffolding, the books are no more fiction than the Platonic dialogues which they imitate in form. Because Barfield's work is complex and relatively unknown to the general reader I have discussed it in some detail, and the chapter on Barfield is the longest of the book.

A literary historian looking for obvious affinities among the four men might well focus on Oxford, for in one way or another all have been connected with each other there as students or professors. It was there that Lewis and Barfield met as students shortly after the first world war; it was there that Tolkien and Lewis met when both taught there; and it was there that Williams came and occasionally lectured when his employer, Oxford University Press, moved there from London during the Battle of Britain. During those last years of the war, the four men and some few others "argued, drank, and talked together" until Williams's sudden death in 1945. Two years later, Oxford University Press published a collection of essays honoring Williams, the collection including pieces by the remaining three of the group and a few others.

Thus there is no little biographical justification for thinking of the four men as a group. But there is also a meeting of minds among the four, as is clear from their published references to each other. Lewis dedicated his *Allegory of Love* to Barfield and Barfield his *Poetic Diction* to Lewis. Lewis cited Tolkien's trilogy approvingly while it was still in manuscript, and reviewed it enthusiastically on publication. Williams has cited Lewis's work, Barfield has praised Williams's work on Dante and commended his theology, and so on. My reason for grouping the four men together is this meeting of minds, and in fact the reason for the grouping is the argument of this study. I hope to show that the work of the four men is best understood when seen as a fairly homogeneous body of both critical and creative literature written for a specific purpose and from a specific point of view: in short, when seen as romantic religion.

I do not mean by the term only that the four men are romantic writers who have an interest of some sort in religion; I mean (as I have said) that their romanticism is hardly separable from their religion. It may be argued that any deeply-felt romantic conviction is intrinsically religious—that the romanticism of Shelley and Coleridge and Melville, for example, is not only a literary point of view but a religious one as well. I do not quarrel with that view. It seems to me quite likely that Melville's vast and incomprehensible ocean, his Job's whale, and the various Gothic elements of the book, such as the spirit spout and the Parsee's prophecies, are objective correlatives for his romantic agnosticism, for his religious point of view. But that is a very large argument in itself, and leads to the further hypothesis that *any* deeply held artistic view—such as that of James, or Zola, or Brecht—also implies a religious view. My argument is simpler and less speculative. I wish to show that the work of these four men reveals itself, on analysis, as a deliberate and conscious attempt to revive certain well-known doctrines and attitudes of romanticism and to justify these doctrines and attitudes by showing that they have not merely literary but religious validity. In short, I want to demonstrate that the result of their work is a literary and religious construct whose purpose is to defend romanticism by showing it to be religious, and to defend religion by traditionally romantic means. This construct is what I mean by the term romantic religion. Thus the romanticism of the four men is both scholarly and combative. It is necessarily scholarly and even antiquarian because of the mere lapse of time between the early nineteenth-century romantics and themselves. It is necessarily combative because their purpose is not literary criticism—or literary creation—as such: it is the revival and use of romantic doctrine for present ideological and religious disputation. The romanticism that they advocate is what Williams calls "corrected romanticism" and what Barfield means by romanticism that has "come of age"; it is romantic doctrine lifted into the realm of formal doctrinal religion and justified as being part of that religion.

Specifically, I shall argue that both Barfield and Tolkien revive Coleridge's doctrine of the creative imagination and defend its validity by showing that it leads (for Barfield) to truths about God and man and the relationship between them and (for Tolkien) to a state of soul essentially the same as that of the soul that has achieved the Christian beatitude. I shall show that Lewis has revived the Kant-Coleridge distinction between the Practical and the Speculative Intellect in order to apprehend and then defend the truths of the Christian faith. And I shall show that Lewis, Williams, and Tolkien in various ways affirm that the experiences which we generally call romantic—*Sehnsucht,* sexual love, *faerie* —are also, or can be, religious experiences.

On this last point—the way that Lewis, Williams, and Tolkien make use of subjective experience for religious purposes—a word should be said in advance. We live in the age of analytical philosophy, what one writer has called "the ghost of logical positivism."[4] As a result, all of us have become aware of Wittgenstein's "language game." We have become wary and cautious about the words we use, afraid of making statements—especially about religious matters—that have no verifiable meanings and which therefore (we are afraid) mean nothing. We may be hesitant, then, about accepting at face value religious assertions which spring from such wholly subjective experiences as Tolkien's "thrill," or Williams's "falling-in-love" experience, or Lewis's "longing." This may well be a prudent approach, yet unless we wish to dismiss the work of these three men out of hand, we ought to remember that not all verification is the same, since not all statements are of the same kind. John Wilson reminds us of this: to the question "How are religious statements ultimately verified?" his answer is "By religious experience."[5] And he goes on to show that religious experiences cannot be verified in the usual empirical way, any more than esthetic experiences can be so verified, yet both are real.

> Ability to make scientific tests of our experience is not necessary. . . . It is not necessary that the experience should be shared by a majority of people. . . . It is not necessary that the experience should be . . . whole and complete. It may be true of an experience both that it is cognitive, and that we have to learn how to have it. . . . It is not necessary that the testing-system for assertions should be universally adopted, or that the terms figuring in the assertions should have a meaning constant for all groups of people who make them. . . . Prediction of a sophisticated or scientific nature—or any prediction beyond what is implied by the assertion itself—is not a necessary condition.[6]

To this it might be added that Christian theology itself springs from a "given," an experience—not an idea but a happening, or a series of happenings.

To return to the subject of the revival of the elements of nineteenth-century romanticism: this revival will be clear enough, I believe, in spite of the confusion surrounding the word *romanticism,* though a writer who deals with romanticism and religion together may fairly be accused of recklessness. In either matter, much less both, he may feel, like Sir Thomas Browne, that he is "not a proper Champion for Truth, nor fit to take up the Gauntlet in the cause of Verity." I do not intend to darken counsel on the subject of romanticism by attempting to define or even describe it. Everyone knows Lovejoy's famous comment that we must have a "discrimination of romanticisms" before the word loses reference completely. A defining word that can be applied equally to Satan, Plato, St. Paul, and Kant is no doubt close to meaning nothing. But as Northrop Frye has pointed out, it is because Lovejoy abstracted the word from its historical context that he was able to show its amazing variety and its seeming ubiquity in all the ages of literary history. But romanticism is not an idea, Frye insists, it is an event with "a historical center of gravity, which falls somewhere around the 1790–1830 period." To deal with it as an idea is to commit "the fallacy of timeless characterization" and do as Lovejoy did:

break the single idea down into component ideas, many of which conflict with each other. The real historical characteristic—and therefore identity—of romanticism, Frye argues, is not in the ideas but in the poetic imagery to be found in romantic poetry. In general, the imagery indicates what has often been noted as a romantic characteristic: it is "subjective" in the sense that it tends to turn inward into man's own conscious and unconscious mind in order to establish the meaning of the "outer" world. Frye aptly quotes Coleridge from the Notebooks: " 'In looking at objects of Nature, I seem rather to be seeking, as it were *asking* for, a symbolical language for something within me that already and forever exists, than observing anything new.' " The "something within," Frye notes, is a sense, common to most of the romantic poets, that they were in touch with something other than themselves—"a creative power greater than his own because it includes his own"[7]—and this can be seen in the work of Wordsworth, Coleridge, Keats, Blake, and Shelley. This sense of the meaning of things coming from within the human mind—and from something greater with which the human mind is in touch—is not an idea but a historical attitude brought about by the romantic reaction to Newtonian mechanical laws, so that the romantics were historically induced to see the outer world as dead and mechanical without the "organic" and life-giving processes of the human imagination.

René Wellek has also defended the notion of romanticism as an entity rather than a conglomeration of ideas nominally yoked by violence together. Like Frye he sees the common denominator of romanticism as "one central and valid concept: the reconciling, synthetic imagination" with "its rootedness in a sense of the continuity between man and nature and the presence of God." Not only English romanticism but that of the continent as well was "the concern for the reconciliation of subject and object, man and nature, consciousness and unconsciousness. . . ."[8]

Frye's and Wellek's depiction of romanticism seems to me an accurate one, and one that applies not only to nineteenth-century romanticism but also to the romanticism which is the subject of this study. In fact, as I hope will be clear from the romantic revival I describe, Barfield may "stand for" Coleridge, while Williams may stand for Wordsworth, and Lewis and Tolkien may stand for—or at least suggest—Shelley and Keats respectively. (I hasten to add that I mean these comparisons only in what Thomas Browne called "a soft and tropical sense," and am not making value judgments.) In any case, in the following pages I use the words *romantic* and *romanticism* dozens of times but never, I hope, in such a way as to cause confusion. Generally I have used them in the obvious senses in which they are applied to Coleridge and Wordsworth. Thus I call Kant's "transcendental" philosophy romantic; I call Coleridge's doctrine of the primary and secondary imagination romantic; I call Wordsworth's view of Nature romantic. Beyond these rather doctrinaire uses, I occasionally use the terms to describe attitudes and phenomena which most of us would, I believe, agree to call romantic. Thus I speak of "romantic longing" in connection with Lewis, partly because he himself uses the phrase, partly because the desire for what is over the hills and far away (either in this world or in some other) seems to me at least intelligible as it is explained by transcendental philosophy. I call imagined worlds romantic when it is clear that they are imagined not only for satirical or didactic purposes but also for their own sake, because I believe that in such imaginings some sort of agreement with Coleridge's notion of the secondary imagination is implicit. In no case do I equate the word *romantic* with unreason or irrationality, though I believe that in the romantic attitudes of Coleridge, Wordsworth, and the four men to be discussed, reason in the sense of discursive or inferential thought usually plays a secondary part to something else—intuition, imagination, or religious faith.

Finally, one last word on the subject of romanticism: I do not intend to show (in fact, I could not) that the four men I am concerned with are identical in their romanticism. It would be untrue to characterize them as all equally indebted to Coleridge, or as all equally sure that Wordsworth's belief in Nature is valid. In far better organized religions than the romantic one I describe, some latitude is permissible. By calling the Oxford group romantics, I do not suggest that they are carbon copies of one original, any more than Keats is a carbon copy of Shelley.

I have not tried to make this study a "source" study or an "influence" study, much less a "history of ideas" study; I have simply tried to keep my eye fixed on the phenomenon and describe it as accurately as possible. There is no doubt that the four men influenced each other in various ways; often, as in the case of Lewis's debt to Barfield, the influence is admitted. But I have not tried to emphasize influences so much as similarities and resemblances. It is true, of course, that no intellectual group exists isolated in time, that every group and every man has roots. The ultimate source of the Oxford romantics is nineteenth-century romanticism; but I shall note here some other obvious sources and suggest others more conjectural.

Of Barfield I shall say nothing now, because the nature of his work has led me to discuss in the next chapter his debt to Rudolf Steiner and Anthroposophy. Williams presents a problem to the critic concerned with the sources of a man's thought. Lewis has mentioned Williams's vast reading:[9] he was acquainted with the church fathers and with much of the literature of Western mysticism; he had a broad if unsystematic knowledge of technical philosophy—ancient, medieval, and modern; he seems really to have read all the important critical and creative literature from the time of the English romantics on, and a great deal before that time as well. There is also the possible influence of certain occult studies, which certainly produced at least the trappings of most of his fiction. And in his publishing position at the Oxford University Press he had easy access to at least cursory knowledge of ideas and disciplines beyond enumeration. Anyone acquainted with Williams's work can point out certain writers and bodies of ideas which seem to have been special favorites of his: Wordsworth, Dante, the pseudo-Dionysius, Malory and the Arthurian legend, Milton. He draws on all these and more, but there is no obvious pattern to his choices. As Lewis said, Williams will not be pigeon-holed. He certainly admired the work of Evelyn Underhill, whose letters he edited. John Heath-Stubbs has pointed out[10] that Miss Underhill's early novel *The Pillar of Dust* seems to have served as a model for much of his fiction. More important than her fiction, perhaps, is her work in mysticism and the history of worship. Williams's *The Descent of the Dove, A History of the Holy Spirit in the Church,* echoes Miss Underhill's view of the Church as fundamentally a mystical experience translated, and in part distorted, by the necessary institution and organization in which it is embodied. And her work in mysticism shows a broad and tolerant view of medieval occultists, many of whom she holds to have been quite close to genuine mystical experience. This latter view, I believe, Williams must have found more than palatable. Yet, even granting a certain indebtedness to Miss Underhill, there is more to Williams than that. I have suggested in my discussion of his "romantic theology" that he tried to subsume under the heading of the "romantic experience" many seemingly disparate values drawn from his reading in literature, philosophy, and religion. Like Coleridge he was forever aiming at synthesis. My own belief is that his work, like Coleridge's, is inconclusive. But I freely admit also that, like Coleridge, he requires a Lowes to follow his attempt.

With Lewis there is, first of all, the obvious influence of George Macdonald. In dozens of places Lewis has praised Macdonald, and has even spoken of himself as a kind of disciple. His debt to Macdonald's *Unspoken Sermons,* he has said, "is almost as great as one man can owe to another. . . ."[11] In *The Great Divorce* the hero, venturing into the afterlife, meets Macdonald, as Dante met Virgil; and it is Macdonald who explains to him the nature of heaven and hell. In the later discussion of Lewis we shall see that he credits Macdonald's books with bringing about his reconversion to Christianity. Such clear and present influence, one would think, should be easy to describe. In fact, however, it is very difficult. If one turns from Lewis's praise of *Phantastes,* for example, to the book itself (which was published in 1858), one can guess readily enough that Lewis was attracted by the Spenserian quality of the story. The hero moves through fairy landscapes much like those of *The Faerie Queene;* but there is no allegory in *Phantastes,* and though there is a kind of quest, neither the hero nor the reader is quite certain of its real nature. At the end of the book the hero thinks he has heard a voice proclaiming a great truth: "Yet I know that good is coming to me—that good is always coming; though few have at all times the simplicity and the courage to believe it. What we call evil, is the only and best shape, which, for the person and his condition at the time, could be assumed by the best good."[12] Perhaps the best way of describing the book and some of Macdonald's other novels, such as *Lilith,* is to say they are fairy romances, without any special doctrine, but with a "feel" of holiness to them. For Lewis they seem to have combined in a special way his early tastes for *faerie* and a desire to bring these tastes into a moral realm. Later, as we shall see, he could attribute to Macdonald's work the qualities to be found in the great myths—the generalized meaning, what Tolkien calls the "inherent morality," and the impact on the reader that takes place on a non-rational level. In his own fiction, particularly in *Till We Have Faces,* he tries to recapture that peculiar blend of fairy romance and generalized religious feeling that he found in Macdonald.

In trying to describe the influence one is finally driven to paraphrasing Lewis's description of it, and to concluding that each man takes something different to the books he reads. I believe the nature of the influence is best understood by seeing Macdonald as an early advocate of romantic religion, which can exist as a corollary to a man's professed formal religion. And this is also true of the other man on whom Lewis greatly depends, Chesterton. Like Lewis, Chesterton had high praise for Macdonald, and a strong case could be made for a line of inheritance running from Macdonald to Chesterton to Lewis and Tolkien. All these men meet on that middle ground between *faerie* and formal religion which is the subject of this study.

A final word should be said about the organization of this study. I have begun with Barfield because I believe that many of the romantic notions common to the members of the group exist in their most basic and radical form in his work. I have dealt with Lewis next because much of his work is best seen in relation to Barfield's. I have discussed Williams next and then Tolkien because I believe that much of what Lewis and Williams have to say is brought into sharper focus by Tolkien's view of the religious implications of the fairy story. In the concluding chapter I have tried to "place" romantic religion in the context of the current religious situation. It is a tentative and perhaps somewhat fumbling attempt; but I have made it in the belief that the literary and religious crosscurrent I have dealt with is of some significance, that it suggests partial answers to the perennial question—which is basically religious, but which all serious literature and literary theory implies—the question of what it means to be a man alive today.

Chapter Two

Owen Barfield and Anthroposophical Romanticism

Anything like a general recognition of Barfield's work has been a long time coming, and since he does not work in such popular forms as fiction or poetry, it is unlikely that he will ever be as well known as Lewis, Williams, and Tolkien. His reputation, if it grows—as it surely should—is likely to be in the areas of literary theory, philology, and theology. A recent writer, for example, has discussed his work in connection with that of Wittgenstein and Heidegger, and theologian Robert W. Funk has cited his work often and approvingly in a discussion of the New Testament parables. To my knowledge Barfield has made only one real attempt to popularize his general views, an essay entitled "The Rediscovery of Meaning" which he contributed to the *Saturday Evening Post* series entitled "Adventures of the Mind." It is a remarkably readable and condensed version of arguments he has been advancing for some forty years, but even so it did not create a Tribe of Owen. Barfield's work, even when popularized, remains, as Huck Finn said of *Pilgrim's Progress,* interesting but tough.[1]

Probably most readers who know Barfield were first led to read him from Lewis's remarks about him in *Surprised By Joy* and other books. In trying to assess his own intellectual development, Lewis places Barfield along with Chesterton and Macdonald as among the most important conscious influences on him. They studied together at Oxford after World War I, and he notes that Barfield and he carried on what he calls a "Great War," but that Barfield "changed me a good deal more than I him. Much of the thought which he afterwards put into *Poetic Diction* had already become mine before that important little book appeared. It would be strange if it had not. He was of course not so learned as he has since become; but the genius was already there."[2] And Lewis's *Allegory of Love* is dedicated to Barfield, the "wisest and best of my unofficial teachers." This is indeed high praise from one of the most respected of modern scholars, and perhaps many readers of Lewis turn to Barfield with some anticipation at the thought of finding the Real Lewis or the Man Behind Lewis, as a generation ago they might have turned with some eagerness to find the Real Kittredge or the Man Behind Lowes.

What they find, probably to their dismay, is an Anthroposophist, a man who insists on referring to Rudolf Steiner as his master: in short, an "occultist." It is no doubt Barfield's unabashed association of himself with the Anthroposophical movement that has helped to keep him relatively unread until quite recently. The general reader, once he has assimilated the almost unpronounceable name, very likely connects Anthroposophy with Theosophy, and thus with Madame Blavatsky, automatic writing, seances, ectoplasm, and so on, and dismisses the whole thing with a shrug and a superior smile. Barfield has said little about his own relative obscurity, but he has commented on that of Steiner, and his comments indicate his belief that a great mind has been left largely unexplored. People who have been willing to listen to what they thought were Barfield's ideas have simply stopped listening when he began to speak of Steiner. Even Lewis, "who was meticulous, if ever a man was, about passing on hearsay judgments," simply rejected Steiner out of hand. The resistance to Steiner has been a "combination of a refusal to investigate with a readiness to dismiss." It may be the very word *occult,* Barfield thinks, which has played a great part in this rejection, since the "principal source-book" of Anthroposophy is entitled *Occult Science: An Outline.* And yet any fair-minded scholar concerned with the history of thought would soon discover on reading Steiner that the word *occult* "signifies no more than what a more conventionally phrased cosmogony would determine as 'non-phenomenal,' 'noumenal,' 'transcendental.'" However, the word, connoting as it does for the contemporary mind secrecy and concealment, even magic and witchery, has helped to seal Steiner's work off from the larger public. But this will not always remain the case, Barfield believes: "future historians of Western thought will interpret the appearance of Romantic philosophy towards the close of the eighteenth century as foreshadowing the advent of Rudolf Steiner towards the close of the nineteenth. . . ."[3]

To readers who react to occultism as Lewis did—that is, to most of us—Barfield's comments on the word *occult* itself may seem merely an *ad hoc* argument for Steiner's work. Yet it is worth reminding ourselves that perfectly respectable and even "great" writers have not disdained certain forms of occultism—we think at once of Blake and Emerson and Yeats, perhaps of Milton, and Thomas Browne and his love of "the Hermetic Philosophy." We may assume that we can separate the occult elements in these men's work from the "legitimate" elements, but this is surely an illusion. Further, as Evelyn Underhill has pointed out, it has always been difficult to draw a clear line between mystical experience and certain occult writings. It is also a truism that we live in an age of empirical science and are thus suspicious of anything not verifiable by empirical evidence. Depth psychology, for example, has achieved respectability by assuming the status of empirical science; this scientific position, particularly in clinical psychiatry, has been buttressed by the popular analogy between mental and physical illness. Yet, recalling Barfield's synonyms for *occult,* we may say with real truth that the psychiatrist deals with "noumenal" or "transcendental" realities—with invisible forces that he calls the Id or the Ego or the Super-Ego—that these things are not verifiable or demonstrable as the phenomena of the botanist or biologist are verifiable and demonstrable. The Id or the Ego or the unconscious mind itself are not things at all in the empirical sense; they are mental constructs—what Barfield might call "notional models"—in short, "occult" phenomena, if we can forget the connotations of the adjective. I am not marshalling an argument for occultism in general, but a last point should be made about Anthroposophy. If it is not a religion itself, it surely has religious implications. Chesterton long ago pointed out that religion of its very nature will produce cranks and fanatics; and the observation is true of any religion that has not been reduced to sheer rational theology, such as eighteenth-century Deism or nineteenth-century Unitarianism. In any system of worship that produces what Jonathan Edwards called "religious affections," there will be some who go too near the fire, and there will be mystics—and fanatics and cranks—whether the religion is Anglicanism, Catholicism, or Buddhism. Anthroposophy no doubt has its share of cranks and eccentrics, but that fact of itself proves nothing one way or the other except that the movement helps shape one's religion. That Barfield himself is not a crank or eccentric will be clear to anyone who reads him.

Barfield's clearest assessment of his debt to Steiner occurs in the book I have been citing, in the introduction to *Romanticism Comes of Age*. Here Barfield speaks of two early "discoveries" that he had made for himself about literature. The first was that there is something "magic" about certain combinations of words, that they have a power not easily explained. "It seemed there was some magic in it; and a magic which not only gave me pleasure, but also reacted on and expanded the meanings of the individual words concerned" (p. 9). The second discovery was connected with the first; it was

> the way in which any intense experience of poetry reacted on my apprehension of the outer world. The face of nature, the objects of art, the events of history and human intercourse betrayed significances hitherto unknown as the result of precisely these poetic or imaginative combinations of words. . . . I found I knew things about them which I had not known before. (p. 10)

The beliefs about poetic combinations of words led him at once to the romantic poets and their doctrines of imagination and then to the general conclusion that romanticism had never fulfilled itself, that in spite of Coleridge and Goethe, it had never been philosophically "justified." It was at this point in his studies that he discovered Steiner's work, and particularly three things about it. "The first was that many of the statements and ideas which I found there produced an effect very similar to the combinations of words to which I have already alluded . . . . Something happened: one felt wiser. This was a fact" (p. 13). The second thing was that Steiner's scattered remarks on language showed that he had anticipated Barfield's own philological theories. And the third thing was "that anthroposophy included and transcended not only my own poor stammering theory of poetry as knowledge, but the whole Romantic philosophy. It was nothing less than Romanticism grown up" (p. 14).

Since what I hope to do in the following pages is to examine Barfield's avowedly romantic notions about poetry and language and imagination, and to show their religious implications, it will be best to begin with a sketch of his "world view," his basic vision of being or things in general. But such a sketch, as we have seen, will have to be preceded by some brief examination of Steiner's thought. I am not competent to conduct more than a cursory examination of Anthroposophy, and for the most part I shall cite Barfield's own comments on Steiner's work. Occasionally I shall cite Steiner himself—his *Mystics of the Renaissance* and one of his major books, *The Philosophy of Spiritual Activity*—a book which (as Lewis said about Anthroposophy in general) has "a re-assuring Germanic dullness about it."[4]

Anthroposophy is usually described as an offshoot of the older Theosophical movement popularized about the turn of the century by Madame Blavatsky; and one of the ways of distinguishing between the two schools is to say that they differ in their philosophical orientation or background. Theosophy stresses Eastern elements of thought, mostly Buddhist, while Anthroposophy (at least, so far as Steiner is its spokesman) works largely within the framework of German nineteenth-century Idealism. But a better distinction is that Theosophy is hardly philosophical at all, but is rather a mystery religion, a modern Gnosticism—in short, it is "occult" in the usual modern sense of that term. Anthroposophy does not ignore Eastern thought—in fact, it does not ignore Idealistic thought of whatever kind—but it attempts to systematize it. The Buddhist doctrine of *maya*—of the phenomenal world as illusion, or of matter itself as unreal—contains an element of truth for the Anthroposophist, as it did for romantics like Emerson and Coleridge and

Goethe, who often described the phenomenal world as spiritual in essence but perceived under the mode of matter. The romantic imagination, in fact, as Barfield says, was "the emergence in the West . . . of an experience which the East had cultivated for ages." And he quotes Sir Walter Raleigh: " 'Time and again, when East meets West, the spirit of Romance has been born.' "

Now Steiner's philosophy, as Barfield notes, is primarily epistemology. It begins with the process of thinking itself, not with the concepts which are the results of this process. Steiner refers to his philosophy interchangeably as Monism or Objective Idealism; it differs from Subjective Idealism in that a Subjective Idealist like Hegel, for example, " 'regards the concept as something primary and ultimate.' " But the concept cannot be the primary phenomenon; nothing in fact can be the primary phenomenon except thinking itself. As Barfield says, the epistemologist must start from zero, with no a priori assumptions. When this is done, when one begins with thinking itself, one finds that "thinking is anterior even to the elementary distinction between subject and object," because, as Steiner says, thinking " 'produces these two concepts just as it produces all others.' " Steiner elaborates:

> "When . . . I, as thinking subject, refer a concept to an object, we must not regard this reference as something purely subjective. It is not the subject, but thinking, which makes the reference. The subject does not think because it is a subject, rather it conceives itself to be a subject because it can think. The activity performed by man as a thinking being is thus not merely subjective. Rather it is neither subjective nor objective; it transcends both these concepts. I ought never to say that I, as an individual subject, think, but rather that I, as subject, exist myself by the grace of thinking. Thinking is thus an element which leads me beyond myself and relates me to objects." (pp. 244–45)

When this process of thinking is combined with the percepts—what is taken in by the senses—then real subjectivity is achieved: "my separate existence apart from nature and apart from my fellow human beings."

It would seem then that we can make a neat division between

the subjective human entity and the phenomenal world outside him, since, though thinking itself is not subjective, at least the percepts are. But this division cannot be that sharp, since the percepts themselves are meaningless without the concepts which thinking attaches to them. A phenomenon perceived but not thought about cannot really be said to be perceived at all; perception without thought would be only what William James called " 'blooming, buzzing confusion.' " As Steiner puts it: "The percept . . . is not something finished and self-contained, but one side only of the total reality. The other side is the concept. The act of cognition is the synthesis of percept and concept. Only the percept and concept together constitute the whole thing."[5] Thus, if we regard the phenomenal world as the "Given," then we must suppose that " 'If there is to be knowledge, everything depends on there being, somewhere within the Given, a field in which our cognitive activity does not merely presuppose the Given, but is at work in the very heart of the Given itself.' " The link between phenomena and the perceiving-thinking subject supposes that " 'the object of observation is qualitatively identical with the activity directed upon it.' " And that activity, Barfield adds, is thinking itself.

Barfield clarifies the issue by distinguishing between the "net Given" and the "specious Given," borrowing from William James's distinction between the "real" and "specious" present. The net Given is what is really "out there," what Kant meant by the noumenal world; the specious Given is what we experience by the synthesis of perceiving and thinking, Kant's phenomenal world. We never experience the net Given as such, only the specious Given. The net Given is "saturated at all points with the activity of thinking, past and present." The empirical methods of science, to the extent that they confuse the net Given (which is independent of human thought) with the specious Given, are thus fallacious. Any "edifice of knowledge or science erected on the specious Given is incomplete and unreliable—for we know that the latter already includes the results of thinking—and may well, therefore, be tainted with subjectivity and error." What, then, would a truer and more accurate method be for the achievement of knowledge? The answer comes by analyzing that link between phenomena and knower, that process which is qualitatively the same as the object known: thinking.

> If we are determined to eliminate all subjectivity and to be uncompromisingly empirical, if we insist on verifying from experience at all points, from the very start onwards, our only course is to find some way of penetrating with full consciousness into that unconscious no-man's-land (or should one say "every-man's-land"?) which lies between the net Given and the specious Given. This is the realm where thinking performs the function of Coleridge's "primary imagination," or what Susanne Langer calls "formulation." It is, incidentally, the realm where language is born. (p. 253)

It is in this realm where language is born, the imagination, that Barfield has been working for forty years. In fact, as we shall see, his work may really be called Anthroposophy philologically considered.

One of the most important elements of Barfield's thought is his view of evolution, a view which is in many respects the reverse of the commonly held post-Darwinian notion, no matter how much that basic notion is modified. In fact, it is possible to give a rough outline of Barfield's thought based on just this point of evolution; in effect, that is what he himself did in the *Saturday Evening Post* article already mentioned. Here, however, I wish to discuss as briefly as possible Steiner's view of evolution, again using Barfield himself as my Virgil. The closeness of Steiner's and Barfield's views will be clear from later discussions. Steiner speaks of the "moral" aspect of Anthroposophy as "spiritualized Evolutionism applied to the moral life,"[6] and refers to his thought as supplemental to that of Darwin. Barfield has remarked that if one had to say in a few words what Anthroposophy is, he might well say "*the concept of man's self-consciousness as a process in time*—with all that this implies." The concept implies a great deal indeed. It implies an evolution of human consciousness which Barfield never tires of establishing on philological grounds but which, I believe, for Steiner must have been basically a religious dogma. "Through Rudolf Steiner," as Barfield says, "there was revealed the process of that gradual entrusting of the Cosmic Intelligence to man, of which the Incarnation of the Word was the central event, and which is the meaning of history." And again, "In language, as it develops and changes through the course of its history, we can watch a cosmic intelligence gradually descending and incarnating as human intelligence. We behold the microcosm emerging from the macrocosm. . . ."[7] We have seen Steiner's argument that thinking as such is neither subjective nor objective but a process which precedes both classifications, and, further, that it is not thinking which makes man a subjective being but rather the combination of thinking with the subjective percepts. The implication is that thinking is not personal, not of itself subjective, but a part of a larger extrapersonal process. As Steiner puts it, plainly and repetitively:

> Paradoxical as it may sound, it is the truth: the Idea which Plato conceived and the like idea which I conceive are not two ideas. It is one and the same idea. And there are not two ideas: one in Plato's head and one in mine; but in the higher sense Plato's head and mine interpenetrate each other; all heads interpenetrate which grasp one and the same idea; and this idea is only once there as a single idea. It is there; and the heads all go to one and the same place in order to have this idea in them.[8]

Where all the heads "go" is into the Logos, the Cosmic Intelligence. Barfield reminds us that Steiner once said by way of illustration, " 'The mind is related to thought, as the eye is to light.' " And to this Barfield adds, "Everyone accepts the very special relation that exists between the eye and light; but no one suggests that light is simply something that goes on in the eye."[9] The reader will no doubt feel at this point that he is not very far from Plato's World of Ideas, nor perhaps from Jung's race memory, and certainly close to Yeats's *Spiritus Mundi.* In 1901, after Yeats had studied with Madame Blavatsky, he wrote in an essay on magic that he believed

> (1) That the borders of our mind are ever shifting, and that many minds can flow into one another, as it were, and create or reveal a single mind, a single energy.
>
> (2) That the borders of our memories are as shifting, and that our memories are a part of one great memory, the memory of Nature herself.

(3) That this great mind and great memory can be evoked by symbols.[10]

But it is important to distinguish between resemblances and real similarities. Steiner's and Barfield's ideas (and perhaps Yeats's) are more akin to Plato's than to Jung's. Jung assumes the general postulate of Darwinian evolution, the ascent of matter up to mind. Steiner and Barfield do not.

For Steiner, evolution was not, as it was for Darwin, simply a process by which matter grew ever more complex and highly organized until it finally produced human consciousness. It was rather, as Barfield says, "a descent, an involution of the Spirit into the Material, which it, the Spirit, organises and transforms, and through which it acquires a new intensity, a new level of self-awareness." But is was not only a descent. At a certain point in time—the time of the historical Incarnation of Christ and His subsequent death—the process became one of ascent, or re-ascent. Diagrammatically, Barfield says, the process of evolution appears not as a straight line sloping always upward but more as a capital "U."

> If you move down the left-hand side, or limb, of a letter u, round the curve at the bottom and up the right-hand limb, you will keep on reaching points on the right side, which are at the same level as corresponding points on the left; and these levels you certainly did pass on your way down. The journey on will, by its nature—to that extent—involve a journey back, or a return.[11]

This journey "down" Steiner elsewhere calls a "flight from Nature" and comments that "we must find our way back to her again," presumably as we ascend the right-hand limb of the u.[12] Spirit, then, or God—sooner or later I think we must make the equation—progressively incarnates itself in the phenomenal world, then narrows itself into human consciousness, and at the point of the Incarnation begins a movement back upward toward Spirit again, having assumed, or subdued, all things to itself. Barfield sums up the cyclic movement by speaking of it as

> that metaphysical conception of the human being which sees him as a "microcosm" evolving from a "macrocosm" and finally return-

> ing, in a sense, to the great whole from which he took his birth; which sees him reposing at first unconscious in the bosom of the Father, then, like a shed seed, separating himself from this unity and finally regaining in some remote future his "at-one-ment" with the Father principle, only now in full self-consciousness, as a self-poised, self-contained "Ego."[13]

Here the reader may be reminded of Chardin's belief that all things are evolving upward toward ultimate spirit, the Omega point of Christ. Barfield clearly has some sympathy with Chardin's view, but his criticism of it is that it begins as Darwin's does, with inanimate matter, not spirit, and thus misses the whole beginning of the story. One may think, too, of other views of the evolution of human consciousness, such as that of Richard Bucke, who believed he had found evidence that man was evolving toward what he called "cosmic consciousness," and that such people as St. Paul and Whitman were forerunners of this ultimate state. But Steiner has defined the phases of man's evolution of consciousness with some precision. I mention only the two stages which I think have most relevance to Barfield's work: the age of the Intellectual Soul and the age of the Consciousness Soul. The Age of the Intellectual Soul is what Barfield calls the Graeco-Roman period and extends roughly from B.C. 750 to A.D. 1450. It is the age in which conceptual thinking begins and develops, and with it the slowly growing sense of the subjectivity of human thought. Thus in the Platonic dialogues, as Barfield says, it is possible to feel the sense of the speakers that their thoughts are not precisely inside them but both inside and out, partly fused with a process other than that going on in their own minds. But by the end of this period the sense of the subjectivity of human thought is complete, and it is just this sense of complete subjectivity that leads man into the next phase, that of the Consciousness Soul. That is the time from A.D. 1450 to our own time and beyond; and the time of the Consciousness Soul may be described as the time when the "severance, or birth, of the human microcosm from the macrocosm has just been completed. The consciousness soul, we may say, *is* 'the having been cut off.' "

As over-simple as the preceding analysis is, I hope it may serve to make Barfield's own arguments seem less strange, may serve as a frame of reference which the general reader often needs when reading Barfield. Barfield is a philologist, among other things; most of his philosophical and religious arguments are supported by philological evidence. His "proofs" are frequently philological proofs, and if one does not carefully follow his linguistic dialectic one is likely to feel that he has flown from alpha to omega on viewless wings. Steiner's notion of God as a kind of Hegelian cosmic thought, for example, Barfield documents by philological evidence, and in Barfield's terms God (on this level) becomes Meaning. Steiner's "process God" becomes for Barfield the evolution of Meaning from Unconsciousness to Consciousness in the human mind and imagination, and this too Barfield establishes by an analysis of language. T. J. J. Altizer has referred to "Steiner's mystical thesis that nature is man's unconscious being,"[14] and Barfield arrives at this conclusion by tracing the evolution of language, which originated in the interaction between the human mind and nature. The dissolving of the subject-object relationship between man and phenomena, which in Steiner seems alternately Kantian and then mystical, is a conclusion that Barfield uses explicitly as a major thesis in *Saving the Appearances*—where his arguments echo those of Kant and Steiner—but he has also satisfied himself elsewhere on linguistic grounds that the relationship is only an apparent one. All these arguments, and others, I shall examine more closely later on, but here, as a means of moving from Steiner's thought to Barfield's, I shall briefly recapitulate what I have already called the best introduction to Barfield's thought, his argument against Darwinian evolution. Inevitably it repeats much of what has just been said about Steiner's thought, but the angle of vision is just different enough, just philological enough, to show the difference of approach.

Barfield objects even to Chardin's "mystical" evolution, as I have said, just because it begins with the old Darwinian assumption that matter preceded mind, that, over aeons, matter evolved into ever more complex organisms, and that eventually the increasing complexity of structure in matter produced consciousness. With the arrival of consciousness in man—so the Darwinian argument goes—there came the correlative subject-object dichotomy between man and phenomena, and that is as it must be: it is a true and inevitable relation. Man, detached from and essentially different from, natural phenomena, can now study phenomena scientifically and can even bring much of nature under his control. He can do this because mind is essentially different from matter; that is where its power lies. Matter cannot meaningfully control matter: landslides, earthquakes, and floods are phenomena that man can understand, but they are not phenomena that the phenomena themselves can understand. Now Barfield's argument—conducted in great part on philological grounds—is that all the facts are present in this usual idea of evolution but that the perspective from which they are seen is wrong and, further, undemonstrable. And to the extent that this perspective has been taken over from biology by anthropology, philology, and religion it has caused great confusion. The historical study of language shows that mind (or spirit, or meaning) preceded matter; as the tutelary spirit in Barfield's *Unancestral Voice* tells the hero categorically, "Interior is anterior." All the evidence buried in language shows that *in illo tempore*, as the mythologists say, in the beginning, man participated in, was part of, the phenomenal world, and that this phenomenal world was mental, not material. Primitive or "mythic" thinking suggests the same organic connection; there was no subject-object relationship. In the beginning was the Word (thought and speech, potential language), what Barfield calls "unindividuated meaning." The true evolution that has taken place, and is taking place, is the evolution of meaning in the human imagination. By analogy, we may say that unconscious meaning is gradually becoming conscious. It is this evolution of self-consciousness that leads to the notion of personal subjectivity which we assume today, and the corollary sense that we are cut off from the phenomenal world. But in man evolution has become conscious of itself. Applying the corrective of Kantian epistemology, we can become aware that our independence of the phenomenal world is only a seeming one, that really we are still part of it, in the obvious sense that by our perceiving processes we help to create it. We are distinct from the phenomenal world only as the conscious mind is distinct from the unconscious.

But even this realization that we unconsciously participate in the creation of our phenomenal world is only the penultimate step.

If, to repeat Altizer's comment, nature is man's unconscious being, then the phenomena that man creates, he creates out of the depths of his own mind, and "what he let loose over Hiroshima, after fiddling with its exterior for three centuries like a mechanical toy, was the forces of his own unconscious mind."[15] But if nature is man's unconscious being—or, in other terms, generalized Meaning which is yet to be concretized in phenomena—it should be possible for man to choose more carefully the meaning he realizes; it should be possible just because man *has* become conscious of his creative powers, *has* become aware that he can make new meanings and thus ultimately new phenomena. Since it is the imagination which makes new meanings by new and different combinations of words that lead to new knowledge, it follows that if man could become more fully aware of the workings of the imagination he would, or could, more consciously individuate new meaning from the vast well of potential meaning that is both nature and his unconscious being. And this hypothesis necessarily involves a systematic study of the imagination and a willingness to put the imagination to work in the fields of science. The primary people whom Barfield usually cites at this point in the argument are Steiner, Coleridge, and Goethe. Coleridge held that the Primary and Secondary Imagination are parts of a single power. It is by means of the Primary Imagination that we "create" the phenomenal world by our unconscious structuring of the Kantian noumena. It is by means of the Secondary Imagination that we create new metaphors and thus new meaning. But as we have some control over the Secondary Imagination, so we have some control over the Primary. When we have understood how a poet creates new knowledge in a poem, we will have begun to understand how a scientist can create new phenomena. Barfield believes that Goethe came closest to this sort of imaginative science in his work on the morphology of plants. Committed by his poetic theory to a belief that there is an "inside" to nature, that natural phenomena have meaning, he did not approach his subject empirically but imaginatively. He saw what the plant "stood for" or "meant" or what it "symbolized." It meant "metamorphosis," he said; all the disparate parts of the plant are explainable as metamorphoses of the leaf; from seed to leaf is a process of sameness in difference, or transformation. The empirical approach can only show change from one thing to another—what Barfield calls substitution. In the same way the empirical approach to evolution can only show the same sort of substitution, not continuity, not sameness in difference. Darwinian evolution is committed to saying that matter evolved into something wholly different from matter: mind. But Barfield's notion of evolution is one of transformation, not substitution; it is a process of essentially the same thing metamorphosing into many forms but yet remaining itself: mind, meaning, spirit. And here Barfield's argument turns finally to the "mystic": for the systematic training of the imagination is really a religious matter, involving certain forms of introspection and meditation. It is, perhaps, a form of the contemplative life. And for instruction in the contemplative way we are usually sent to the masters of that way—the Zen masters, or St. Theresa. Barfield at this point usually directs the reader to Steiner.

I shall now examine Barfield's argument in some detail, an argument that has been remarkably consistent from its beginning in *History in English Words* (1926) to its present stage in *Speaker's Meaning* (1967). I believe it is obvious from what has been said up to this point that Barfield's romanticism is closely allied with his religious views, that in fact romanticism and religion are for him almost interchangeable terms. A closer look at his argument, and the evidence for his argument, will demonstrate this union even more clearly.

Barfield has called *History in English Words* a "slight attempt at a semantic approach to Western history."[16] The book introduces two of Barfield's basic notions which I have already discussed in very general terms. The two notions—they are really two aspects of a single notion—are the "evolution of consciousness" and "internalization." They are both arrived at and demonstrated by means of philology. As the title indicates, the book is not an ordinary "history of the language" text; it is an attempt to construct a history of humanity (beginning with pre-history, actually) from the history of the changing meanings of words. There are, according to Barfield, "secrets which are hidden in language" which only an evaluation of the shifting meanings of words can reveal to us. Other kinds of history can give us other kinds of information: geology, for example, can give us a "knowledge of outward, dead things—such as the forgotten seas and the bodily shapes of pre-historic animals and primitive men." But the study of language gives us the inner secrets, for "language has preserved for us the inner, living history of man's soul. It reveals the evolution of consciousness." What the book attempts to do, then, is to formulate a history of the development of the soul of western man, the history being based largely (though not entirely) on evidence gained from philology. For philology, combined with the findings of anthropology, can do more than tell us what the past was; it enables us to "feel how the past is." Language is a window in the soul of man, and as man looks out by means of it, so the philologist looks in.[17]

Abstracting the idea from the documentation in which it is embedded, we see that it comes to something like this: the history of meanings shows an evolution of the human mind from relative unself-consciousness to relatively complete self-consciousness. It shows a progression away from the aboriginal unity of man and nature and toward a human consciousness of self as distinct from things. In short, the history of meanings reveals Steiner's "flight from Nature." Recognizable consciousness of self as a matter of importance arrives (approximately) only in the period of the Reformation. With the arrival of self-consciousness comes the corollary belief that the meanings of things (what might be called the essences of things) are not in the things themselves, as primitive and early man presumably thought, but in the minds of men. The progression toward this belief Barfield calls the "internalization" of meaning. The romantic poets, especially Wordsworth and Coleridge in England and Goethe in Germany, were the first to sense this process and its significance; they were the first to use, or at least to use well and artistically, a means of coming to terms with this process: imagination.

The first part of the book, entitled "The English Nation," is devoted to an imaginative retelling of the story of the Aryans (Indo-Europeans), which of course is nearly the story of western civilization. The second part, "The Western Outlook," begins the real thesis, and we begin to see the philological evidence for the evolution of consciousness, evidence which indicates that language pictures a "vast, age-long metamorphosis from the kind of outlook which we loosely describe as 'mythological' to the kind which we may describe equally loosely as 'intellectual thought' " (p. 84). Approaching the level of the Aryan pre-historical consciousness from the point of view of religious thought, Barfield notes that the words *diurnal, diary,* and *dial* derive from the Latin *dies,* and that *journal* comes to us through French from the same source. "These syllables," according to Barfield,

> conceal among themselves the central religious conception common to the Aryan nations. As far back as we can trace them, the Sanskrit word "dyaus," the Greek "zeus" . . . and the Teutonic "tiu" were all used in contexts where we should use the word *sky;* but the same words were also used to mean *God,* the Supreme Being, the Father of all the other gods—Sanskrit "Dyaus pitar," Greek "Zeus pater," Illyrian "Deipaturos," Latin "Juppiter" (old form "Diespiter"). We can best understand what this means if we consider how the English word *heaven* and the French *ciel* are still used for a similar double purpose, and how it was once not a double purpose at all . . . if we are to judge from language, we must assume that when our earliest ancestors looked up to the blue vault they felt that they saw not merely a place, whether heavenly or earthly, but the bodily vesture . . . of a living Being. And this fact is still extant in the formal resemblance between such words as *diary* and *divine.* (pp. 84–85)

This is, in part, Barfield's picture of the pre-historic Aryan consciousness. It is not a consciousness dwelling in some distant age of metaphor, although the way the consciousness operates inevitably suggests metaphor. It is rather a consciousness which has not yet become aware of the distinction—or more accurately, in Barfield's terms—has not yet *made* the distinction between literal and figurative. It is a consciousness for which the thought, or perception, of sky is the equivalent of the thought or perception of God. It is a dreaming consciousness which does not make metaphors but which is the substance out of which later metaphors must come. For it is the basis of western language, and embedded in it are the "natural" metaphors of later consciousness—the equation of good with light and evil with dark, of height with power and depth with wretchedness. (We must put on the armor of light, and *facilis descensus Averno*).

Barfield, through the scattered hints and insights of language, traces the evolution away from this sort of consciousness up as far as the pre-Homeric Greeks, where he pauses over the word *panic*. The word, he says, "marks a discovery in the inner world of consciousness" (p. 82). Before the word itself came into being, the thing we call panic must have been, not perhaps a different thing, but a thing differently perceived by humanity. He sees in the word a miniature of the whole process from mythological to intellectual thinking:

> The word enables us to realize that the early Greeks could become conscious of this phenomenon, and thus name it, because they felt the presence of an invisible being who swayed the emotions of flocks and herds. And it also reveals how this kind of outlook changed slowly into the abstract idea which the modern individual strives to express when *he* uses the word *panic*. (pp. 82–83)

And he goes on to note that with the Romans this consciousness of a real being, a god or presence, becomes much less real; the analytical mind, a product of Aristotle and later Greek philosophy, is moving toward fruition, and the "mythical world" of the Romans is more like "a world of mental abstractions."[18]

One of the clearest examples of the evolution of consciousness is to be found in the traditions and beliefs of medieval science. Medieval logic, says Barfield, is Aristotelian, but medieval science is based on pre-Aristotelian Greek science. The important point is that medieval science was content to build on Greek foundations because there remained in the Middle Ages enough of the ancient Greek consciousness to make the Greek medicine seem worth continuing. "In spite of that strong and growing sense of the individual soul, man was not yet felt, either physically or psychically, to be isolated from his surroundings in the way that he is to-day. Conversely, his mind and soul were not felt to be imprisoned within, and dependent upon, his body." Barfield then lists a group of words taken from medieval science: *ascendant, atmosphere, complexion, cordial, disaster, disposition* and *indisposed, influence, temperament* and *temper*. These, he says, "give us more than a glimpse into the relations between body, soul, and cosmos, as they were felt by the medieval scientist" (p. 136). He next reviews the general tenets of medieval science. The body contained four humours (moistures). Diseases (distempers) and character traits were connected with the temperament (mixture). Through the arteries flowed three different kinds of ether (Greek, the upper air) or spirits—the animal, vital, and natural.

> But the stars and the planets were also living bodies; they were composed of that "fifth essence" . . . which was likewise latent in all terrestrial things, so that the character and the fate of men were determined by the *influence* . . . which came from them. The Earth had its *atmosphere* (a kind of breath which it exhaled from itself); the Moon . . . had a special connection with *lunacy*, and according as the planet Jupiter, or Saturn, or Mercury was *predominant* or in the *ascendant* in the general *disposition* of stars at a man's birth, he would be *jovial, saturnine,* or *mercurial*. Finally, things or persons which were susceptible to the same *influences*, or which *influenced* each other in this occult way, were said to be in *sympathy* or *sympathetic*. (p. 137)

What has happened to the meanings of the terms of medieval science, says Barfield, is evidence of the process (corollary to the evolution of consciousness) which he calls internalization. Man is no longer thought to have any connection with the world beyond himself. Conscious of himself now as distinct from what is not himself, he has retained the former terms by rooting them out of their objective phenomena and transferring them to himself. So he is perhaps still saturnine, but no longer "influenced" by anything beyond the confines of his own will and imagination. That transferring, says Barfield, is the penultimate step in the evolution toward intellectual thought.

> When we reflect on the history of such notions as *humour, influence, melancholy, temper,* and the rest, it seems for the moment as though some invisible sorcerer had been conjuring them all inside ourselves—sucking them away from the planets, away from the out-

> side world, away from our own warm flesh and blood, down into the shadowy realm of thoughts and feelings. There they still repose; astrology has changed to astronomy; alchemy to chemistry; to-day the cold stars glitter unapproachable overhead, and with a naive detachment mind watches matter moving incomprehensibly in the void. At last, after four centuries, thought has shaken herself free. (p. 138)

(Here, as elsewhere in Barfield, there are echoes of Emerson, especially *Nature,* which Barfield praises highly in *Poetic Diction.* In the sixth chapter of *Nature,* Emerson wrote of the changing relationship between mind and matter: "The astronomer, the geometer, rely on their irrefragable analysis, and disdain the results of observation. The sublime remark of Euler on his law of arches, 'This will be found contrary to all experience, yet is true,' had already transferred nature into the mind, and left matter like an outcast corpse.")

Barfield then takes the same argument into another area—the rise of astronomy. The three Arabic words *azimuth, nadir,* and *zenith* appear in English for the first time towards the end of the fourteenth century (two of them are to be found in Chaucer's *Treatise on the Astrolabe*). But they appear as a new part of the old context of classical astronomy; for the most part, the astronomers of the Dark Ages had relied on the Greek zodiac, and had mapped out the heavens into twelve signs. But the three Arabic words "express something which the ancients had, apparently, never felt the need of expressing—that is, an abstracted geometrical way of mapping out the visible heavens" (p. 140). The new words express a new concept, and the new concept is possible only because human consciousness has taken another forward step. "It is probable that, with the use of these words, there came for the first time into the consciousness of man the possibility of seeing himself purely as a solid object situated among solid objects" (p. 140). Anticipating the argument that Plato and other early Greeks formulated geometrical laws, Barfield points out that these "laws" were not so much intellectual generalizations; they were rather felt to be "real activities of the soul—that human soul which . . . the philosopher could not yet feel to be wholly separate from a larger world Soul or planetary Soul" (p. 141). The progress of astronomy through the sixteenth and seventeenth centuries, then, may be seen as an illustration of that same process of internalization which we have already seen in astrology and medicine. The notion that mathematics had its origin in the observing of the movements of the stars may well be true if we can account for its later progress by means of internalization.

> Is it too fanciful to picture to ourselves how, drawn into the minds of a few men, the relative positions and movements of the stars gradually developed a more and more independent life there until, with the rise in Europe first of trigonometry and then of algebra, they detached themselves from the outside world altogether? And then by a few great men like Copernicus, Kepler, Galileo, Newton, these abstract mathematics were re-fitted to the stars which had given them birth, and the result was that cosmogony of infinite spaces and a tiny earth in which our imaginations roam to-day? When the Aryan imagination had at last succeeded in so detaching its "ideas" about the phenomena of the universe that these could be "played with," as mathematicians say, in the form of an equation, then, no doubt, it was a fairly easy matter to turn them inside out. (pp. 141–42)

The preceding arguments lead us to a rough statement of the chronology of the evolution of western consciousness. Modern consciousness began roughly about the time of the Reformation and became fairly widespread only in the seventeenth century. The Reformation, "with its insistence on the *inwardness* of all true grace," Barfield sees as "another manifestation of that steady shifting inwards of the centre of gravity of human consciousness" (p. 153). But until the days of the revival of learning this progress towards self-consciousness is an unconscious one. "Up to the seventeenth century the outlook of the European mind upon the world . . . has yet always felt itself to be at rest, just as men have hitherto believed that the earth on which they trod was a solid and motionless body" (p. 161). But with Bacon we get the first real historical distinction between the ancients and moderns, and the beginning of historical perspective. The seventeenth century first gives us words that indicate this perspective: *progressive, anti-*

quated, century, decade, epoch, out-of-date, primeval. Also, as an aftermath of the Reformation, we begin to find words hyphenated with *self* appearing in the language: *self-conceit, self-confidence, self-contempt, self-pity*—the centre of gravity has shifted from phenomena to self. The seventeenth century provides us with the most spectacular of proofs that man has arrived at something like total awareness of self in Descartes, who thought of himself as starting philosophy anew; nearly all philosophy since his time has been fundamentally the same, beginning with a kind of *cogito ergo sum,* moving from the mind outward rather than from phenomena to the mind. Locke adopts the word *consciousness* itself, and gives the newer term *self-consciousness* its "distinctive modern meaning" (p. 166).

The last argument for the evolution of consciousness and the consequent internalization of meanings concerns the changing views of the emotions, what the medieval writers called "the passions." The philological evidence shows, says Barfield, that even in respect to the passions, which might be supposed a fortress of subjectivity, the shift from outer to inner has taken place. "The nomenclature of the Middle Ages generally views them from without, hinting always at their results or their moral significance. . . ." As evidence of this Barfield lists such medieval terms as *envy, greedy, happy, malice, mercy, peace, pity, remorse, rue, sin.* Not until the seventeenth century do we find words that express "that sympathetic or 'introspective' attitude to the feelings," words such as *aversion, dissatisfaction, discomposure,* "while *depression* and *emotion*—further lenient names for human weakness—were used till then of material objects." The eighteenth century gives us words which indicate attempts to "portray character or feeling from within": *apathy, chagrin, ennui,* the expression *the feelings.* The same century transfers words like *agitation, constraint, disappointment, embarrassment,* and *excitement* from the outer world to the inner. It also gives a class of words which depict phenomena not as they are but as they affect us: *affecting, amusing, boring, charming, diverting, entrancing, interesting, pathetic.* And Barfield concludes the argument:

These adjectives can be distinguished sharply—indeed they are in a sense the very opposite of those older words, which can also be said . . . to describe external objects "from the human point of view." Thus, when a Roman spoke of events as *auspicious* or *sinister,* or when some natural object was said in the Middle Ages to be *baleful,* or *benign,* or *malign,* a herb to possess such and such a *virtue,* an eye to be *evil,* or the bones of a saint to be holy, or even, probably, when Gower wrote:

> The day was *merry* and *fair* enough,

it is true that these things were described from the human point of view, but the activity was felt to emanate from the object itself. When we speak of an object or event as *amusing,* on the contrary, we know that the process indicated by the word *amuse* takes place within ourselves; and this is none the less obvious because some of the adjectives recorded above, such as *charming, enchanting,* and *fascinating,* are the present participles of verbs which had implied genuine, occult activity. (pp. 170–71)

Having established the reality of the evolution of consciousness and the internalization of meanings, Barfield finds that two results follow from these processes. First, the "peculiar freedom" of man is felt to derive largely from within himself; it is a product of those "*spontaneous* impulses which control human behavior and destiny." This is seen in the semantic evolution of such words as *conscience, disposition, spirit,* and *temper;* in the transferring of words like *dissent, gentle, perceive,* and *religion* from the outer world to the inner; and in the Protestant Reformation which, as was noted above, stresses the inwardness of all true grace. Second, the spiritual life which had been assumed to be immanent in phenomena fades: the life "in star and planet, in herb and animal, in the juices and 'humours' of the body, and in the outward ritual of the Church—these grow feebler." There arises the concept of impersonal laws which govern the world: "words like *consistency, pressure, tension* . . . are found to describe matter 'objectively' and disinterestedly, and at the same time the earth ceases to be the centre round which the cosmos revolves." The European mind has cut itself loose from its environment (fled from Nature); it has become "less and less of the actor, more and more of both the author and spectator" (pp. 166–67).

Now Barfield sees the romantic movement as essentially a triumph because, utilizing the end product of the long evolution of consciousness (the end product is, of course, self-consciousness), the romantic poets saw the fatality of a dead world moving in a void, a world drained of its immanent life by the very evolution which enabled them to perceive its deadness. They may not have understood how the world came to be dead, but they saw the necessity of somehow revitalizing it, of bringing it back to some kind of life. There had been some stumbling poetic attempts before them, evidence that the poet at least cannot deal with a world of Hobbes's matter in motion. Both Denham and Milton had taken up the new word *conscious* and had applied it to inanimate things. Denham had written: "Thence to the coverts and the conscious Groves . . ."; and Milton: "So all ere day-spring, under conscious Night / Secret they finished. . . ." Barfield comments that

> we can almost fancy, by their readiness to seize upon the new word, that our poets were beginning, even so soon, to feel the need of restoring "subjectively" to external Nature—of "projecting into" her, as we are now inclined to say—a fanciful substitute for that voluntary life and inner connection with human affairs which Descartes and Hobbes were draining from her in reality. (pp. 175–76)

But it was left to the romantics and their theories of the power of the imagination really to resuscitate the lifeless world. Coleridge, in his distinction between the Fancy and the Imagination, is largely responsible for their success; for Coleridge defined Imagination (in Barfield's words) as "the power of creating from within forms which themselves become a part of Nature—'Forms,' as Shelley put it,

> more real than living man,
> Nurslings of immortality."

For Wordsworth and Coleridge, Nature is not only what we perceive but also what we half-create; "the perception of Nature . . .

depends upon what is brought to it by the observer. Deep must call unto deep." Coleridge had said that Imagination was "essentially vital, even as all objects (*as* objects) are essentially fixed and dead" (p. 211). The world as perceived by the senses and evaluated by the Understanding was indeed dead; but the world as "perceived" by the Imagination was alive, for the Imagination as much created it as perceived it. Imagination, for Coleridge, was "organic"; as it was alive itself, so what it bodied forth was also alive. In Kantian terms, it created phenomena, not *ex nihilo,* but out of the noumena. It gave shape, form, existence itself to the phenomenal world.

> And this re-animation of Nature was possible because the imagination was felt as *creative* in the full religious sense of the word. It had itself assisted in creating the natural forms which the senses were now contemplating. It had moved upon the face of the waters. For it was "the repetition in the finite mind of the eternal act of creation" —the Word made human. (p. 213)

The book ends on this curious and rather challenging note; any explicit conclusion is left for the reader to draw. At the risk of being obvious, I shall draw it briefly. Barfield's book culminates with the romantics because the romantics were the first to do consciously what ancient and early man had done unconsciously—that is, participate actively in the construction of the very world itself. And conscious participation in the world-process, as Steiner says in his praise of Angelus Silesius, is at least analogous to divine creation.

Poetic Diction (1928, 1952), is dedicated to Lewis (" 'Opposition is true friendship' "). It is Barfield's closest approach to purely "literary" criticism, and it is as a theory of poetry that it has achieved its reputation. But it is really a part of, or an application of, Barfield's larger argument which I have tried to summarize some pages back. It presents a philological theory of poetry and in so doing assumes the evidence and conclusions of *History in English Words.* But there is more than a theory of poetry involved; as the subtitle, *A Study in Meaning,* indicates, the book is also a theory of knowledge, as Barfield admits in the Preface to the second edition.[19] This preface is long and combative. Since one of the main arguments of the book is that it is the poetic and metaphoric element in language that leads to new knowledge, I. A. Richards, the logical positivists and later linguistic analysts, and modern empirical science bear the brunt of Barfield's attack. Richards, in his distinction between "emotive" (poetic) language and "referential" language of course argued that poetic language never "communicates" anything, but is simply "expressive." The linguistic analysts, insisting on the principle of empirical verification in order for a statement to be meaningful, have attempted to reduce language to the state which the logician desires: a state in which the words used have a fixed and unchangeable meaning or referent. Their abhorrence of metaphor is actually a fear that the language will change under their hands and thus render their logic meaningless: ". . . logical judgements, by their nature, can only *render more explicit* some one part of a truth *already implicit in their terms. . . .*" The logician "is continually seeking to reduce the meaning of his terms . . . he could only evolve a language whose propositions would really obey the laws of thought by eliminating meaning altogether." (p. 16). And the empirical scientist, blind to the evidence of the history of language and the lessons of Kant, insists on dealing with the phenomenal world as if it were the net given and man played no part in constructing it:

> Science deals with the world it perceives but, seeking more and more to penetrate the veil of naive perception, progresses only towards the goal of nothing, because it still does not accept in practice (whatever it may admit theoretically) that the mind first creates what it perceives as objects, including the instruments which Science uses for that very penetration. It insists on dealing with "data," but there shall no data be given, save the bare percept. The rest is imagination. Only by imagination therefore can the world be known. And what is needed is, not only that larger and larger telescopes and more and more sensitive calipers should be constructed, but that the human mind should become increasingly aware of its own creative activity. (p. 28)

In brief, the book is a double edged argument for the validity of the creative imagination; or rather it is an argument for both Coleridge's primary and secondary imagination. In its simplest form, the argument goes: "as the secondary imagination makes meaning, so the primary imagination makes 'things'" (p. 31).

I have already mentioned Barfield's early discovery of the "magic" of certain combinations of words and the belief that they not only give pleasure but lead to new knowledge. He begins his argument proper in *Poetic Diction* from the same absolutely subjective state, the reactions of the individual reader to the individual poem. There must be an emotional reaction; if not, then for that reader what he is reading is not poetry. But the reaction, when it occurs, may be analyzed, and thus Barfield finds that "appreciation of poetry involves a 'felt change of consciousness.'" It is precisely at this moment of change that the pleasure occurs. Further, a significant new metaphor enables us to see the phenomenal world differently; it modifies the meaning of the phenomena for us. In this sense it repeats what language in general does for us on the perceptual level. If a man were somehow deprived of all the stored knowledge in his language, all his power of recognition would disappear as well. The phenomenal world would dissolve into chaos: colors would blur, sounds would fuse into a meaningless roar. Thus both language in general and the striking new metaphor in particular may truly be described as "'an expansion of consciousness'"; in the first case an ordering, in the second case a re-ordering of the phenomenal world. When this new knowledge of the world remains with us as a permanent possession it may be called wisdom (pp. 52–57).

Having asserted that metaphor may lead to knowledge and wisdom, and even that metaphor is the only way that meaning comes into being in language, Barfield turns to the problem of metaphor itself, really the problem of language itself. Max Müller and many other nineteenth century philologists advanced a view of language that is still, with some modifications, widely held today. Briefly, it is this: all language is dead metaphor; even when we speak most literally, the words we use bear traces of a metaphorical origin. The fallacy of Ogden and Richards's book *The Meaning of Meaning,* for example, is that they attempted to be scientific about language but did not realize that their own terminology—cause, reference, organism, stimulus—was not "miraculously exempt" from the nature of language itself; thus the book is "a ghastly tissue of empty abstractions" (p. 135). Müller and others supposed that metaphor came into language always as a conscious imaginative attempt on the part of an individual speaker to convey an abstract meaning by using the words at hand in a new way; and the words at hand for "primitive man" were assumed to be "literal" words, names for material objects or for discernible physical processes. But this is an absurd assumption, Barfield argues. If the etymological evidence suggests that the farther back one goes in language, the more metaphorical it is, then how can one posit a period when it was not metaphorical at all, but perfectly literal? Such an argument does not proceed from linguistic evidence but from a different assumption entirely, the assumption of Darwinian evolution. When that assumption is brought over into the history of language it has to posit a primitive mentality to go with its picture of primitive man; it has to assume that early man evolved mentally as well as physically, and that as he did so his language had to change in order to express the abstract notions now becoming possible for him to conceive. Thus he began to use language as a tool, just as he used flint and bone as tools. But if we stay within the limits of the evidence in language itself, we see that Emerson's view must be more nearly right: language is fossil poetry. Early language is all metaphor, in the sense that an early word never meant *simply* a physical object or a discernible physical process. We recall from *History in English Words* that the Aryan word for "sky" included the meaning "God," or vice versa. And linguistic evidence will take us to no other conclusion about the nature of early language. The individual word always had multiple related meanings, or rather had what Barfield calls "an old single meaning" (p. 91) which had as its referents a number of disparate phenomena, both interior and exterior to man, both mental and material. The natural tendency of language is to move "from homogeneity towards dissociation and multiplicity" (p. 81). Müller's view of the origin of metaphor ignores this fact and is thus an example of what Barfield calls "logomorphism," which is "projecting post-logical thoughts back into a pre-logical age" (p. 90). Barfield takes as an example the Latin *spiritus* (Greek *pneuma*). Müller would have it that the word originally meant "breath" or "wind" and that there then came a time when man felt the need to express the abstract notion of "the principle of life within man or animal" (p. 80). But Barfield argues that

> such an hypothesis is contrary to every indication presented by the study of the history of meaning; which assures us definitely that such a purely material content as "wind" . . . and . . . such a purely abstract content as "the principle of life within man or animal" are both *late* arrivals in human consciousness. Their abstractness and their simplicity are alike evidence of long ages of intellectual evolution. So far from the psychic meaning of "spiritus" having arisen because someone had the idea, "principle of life . . ." and wanted a word for it, the abstract idea "principle of life" is itself a *product* of the old concrete *meaning* "spiritus," which contained within itself the germs of both later significations. We must, therefore, imagine a time when "spiritus" or πνεῦμα, or older words from which these had descended, meant neither *breath*, nor *wind*, nor *spirit*, nor yet all three of these things, but when they simply had *their own old peculiar meaning,* which has since, in the course of the evolution of consciousness, crystallized into the three meanings specified—and no doubt into others also, for which separate words had already been found by Greek and Roman times. (pp. 80–81)

The natural tendency of language, Barfield holds, is toward division, toward a splitting up of original singular meaning into later diverse meanings. This is what Shelley sensed when he said that "Every original language near to its source is itself the chaos of a cyclic poem" (p. 58). We have, says Barfield, a possible example of meaning in the transition stage from old to new (from singularity to diversity) in the phrases which associate emotions with certain parts of the body. Nowadays we make "a purely verbal allotment" of emotions to the liver, the bowels, and the heart; previously, such allotment was more nearly literal than verbal. In the case of the current use of the word *heart,* "an old single meaning survives as two separate references of the same word—a physical and a psychic" (p. 80). But in our phrase "I have no stomach for that," we have an expression which is

> still by no means purely psychic in its content. It describes a very real physical sensation, or rather one which cannot be classified as either physical or psychic. Yet . . . it is reasonable to suppose that,

> when a sufficient number of years has elapsed, the meaning of this word also may have been split by the evolution of our consciousness into two; and the physico-psychic experience in question will have become as incomprehensible to our posterity, as it is incomprehensible to most of us today that anyone should literally feel his "bowels" moved by compassion. (p. 80)

What looks to us like a metaphor, then, is simply a meaning that was "latent in meaning from the beginning." In earlier consciousness, the material things which served as referents for words were not only sensible and material objects; they were not, "as they appear to be at present, isolated, or detached, from thinking and feeling" (p. 85). There could not have existed the subjective-objective antithesis, for the antithesis presupposes self-consciousness. And self-consciousness "is inseparable . . . from rational or discursive thought operating in abstract ideas" (p. 204). In a prelogical time, then, a time when meaning originates, man is incapable of feeling himself as distinct and cut off from the rest of the universe; or, in plain terms, he is *not* thus isolated and cut off. This is the state of man before Steiner's "flight from Nature," the preconscious stage of man-Nature unity.

> In order to form a conception of the consciousness of primitive man, we have really . . . to "unthink," not merely our now half-instinctive logical processes, but even the seemingly fundamental distinction between self and world. And with this, the distinction between thinking and perceiving begins to vanish too. For perception, unlike the pure concept, is inconceivable without a distinct perceiving subject on which the percepts, the soul-and-sense-data, can impinge. (p. 206)

How then can we describe the kind of thinking done by primitive man? As "a kind of thinking which is at the same time perceiving, a picture-thinking, a figurative, or imaginative, consciousness, which we can only grasp today by true analogy with the imagery of our poets, and, to some extent, with our own dreams" (pp. 206–7).

The development of consciousness shows us two opposing principles in language. The first is the principle according to which single meanings tend to divide; the second is "the nature of lan-

es Sam help grow?

es the sun warm up?

en plants too.

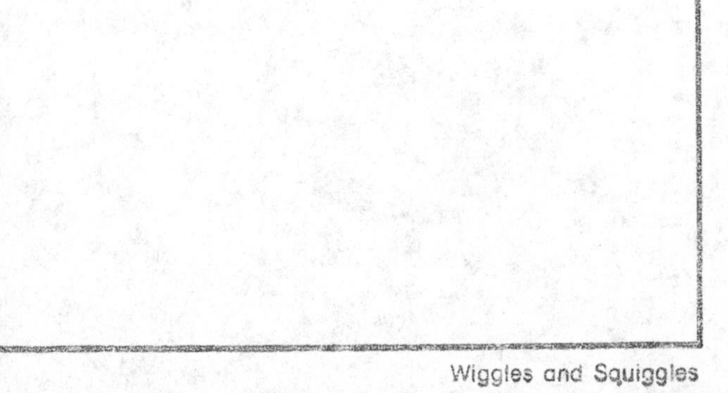

guage itself at its birth. It is the principle of living unity" (p. 87). The principle of division indicates the differences between things; the second indicates the resemblances. We find this second principle operative in the metaphors of the poets. It enables them

> to intuit relationships which their fellows have forgotten—relationships which they must *now* express as metaphor. Reality, once self-evident, and therefore not conceptually experienced, but which can *now* only be reached by an effort of the individual mind—this is what is contained in a true poetic metaphor; and every metaphor is "true" only in so far as it contains such a reality, or hints at it. The world, like Dionysus, is torn to pieces by pure intellect; but the poet is Zeus; he has swallowed the heart of the world; and he can reproduce it as a living body. (p. 88)

What the true poet grasps, then, and expresses by metaphor, is the ancient unity of thought and perception. (The "false" poet, then, is presumably one whose imagination does not perceive the essential unity and who thus must rely on fancy—which makes only superficial or "artificial" metaphor, such as Donne's compass.) And this ancient unity, this pre-conceptual mixture which included both the percept and its significance, is well called "figurative" or "pictorial." For the percept and the meaning were one and the same apprehension; the whole of reality, not only the percept or only the concept, was taken in as a kind of meaning figure. The ancient single meaning of the verb *to shine,* for example, was "the same definite spiritual reality which was beheld on the one hand in what has since become pure human thinking; and on the other hand, what has since become physical light; not an abstract conception, but the echoing footsteps of the goddess Natura—not a metaphor but a living Figure" (pp. 88–89).

In short, ancient man apprehended total reality; or, rather, total reality lived within him and he within it. What existed (and all that existed) was Mind; it existed "as Life, and Meaning, before it became conscious of itself, as knowledge . . ." (p. 179). What we call thinking "was not merely *of* Nature, but was Nature herself" (p. 147). At this point we see that Barfield's view of metaphor and meaning has led us back to the larger framework of his thought previously described. We see that philological evidence has taken us back to a time preceding the Intellectual Soul, when the distinction between subject and object did not exist in the human mind—or, simply, did not exist at all.

For Barfield, then, we may say that language is a tension between the original unity of meaning inherent in language from the beginning and the tendency toward the splitting up of this meaning, "the natural decline of language into abstraction." Since language is correlative with human consciousness, the same two tendencies exist in tension in the human mind: the imagination and the discursive intellect, the unconscious and the conscious mind. The work of the imagination, or the poetic principle, is "the bringing farther into consciousness of something which already exists as unconscious life." The imagination infuses meaning, or discovers it by metaphor; in relation to the intellect it is the "maker," and the intellect is the "user." This interaction between the two principles is the basis of all knowledge, whether "poetic" or "scientific." It is the way that the human entity arrives at truth. The empirical techniques of the experimental sciences are not ways of knowing, only ways of testing or verifying.

> Language does indeed appear historically as an endless process of metaphor transforming itself into meaning. Seeking for material in which to incarnate its last inspiration, imagination seizes on a suitable word or phrase, uses it as a metaphor, and so creates a meaning. The progress is from Meaning, through inspiration to imagination, and from imagination, through metaphor, to meaning; inspiration grasping the hitherto unapprehended, and imagination relating it to the already known. (pp. 140–41)

And science advances by means of the same process. Barfield quotes approvingly the book *Thought and Things* by the American psychologist J. M. Baldwin:

> the development of thought . . . is by a method essentially of trial and error, of experimentation, *of the use of meanings as worth more than they are as yet recognized to be worth.* The individual must use his own thoughts, his established knowledges, his grounded judgements, for the embodiment of his new inventive constructions.

> He erects his thought as we say "schematically" . . . projecting into the world an opinion still peculiar to himself, as if it were true. *Thus all discovery proceeds.* (p. 142)

At the purely literary level, as we have seen, esthetic appreciation comes from the "felt change of consciousness." Thus in all poetry that is so appreciated, there is an element of "strangeness," which "arises from contact with a different kind of *consciousness* from our own, yet not so remote that we cannot partly share it. . . ." But the greatest poetry—or the greatest reaction to poetry—comes from the closest possible interaction between the imagination and the intellect, when the two momentarily fuse. This kind of reaction

> depends, not so much upon the difference between two kinds of consciousness or outlook, as on the act of becoming conscious itself. It is the momentary apprehension of the poetic by the rational, into which the former is for ever transmuting itself—which it is itself for ever in process of becoming. This is what I would call pure poetry. This is the very moonlight of our experience, true and ever-recurring begetter of strangeness; it is the pure idea of strangeness, to which all the others are but imperfect approximations. . . . (p. 178)

Historically, great poetry is likely to occur when a given language has not yet become grammatically and syntactically "fixed," when it is still relatively fluid and malleable, as in the cases of Homer and Shakespeare. But what may be called the efficient cause of great poetry is the contact of a fine intellect, such as that of Keats or Shakespeare, with a current of "living meaning, such as that contained in Greek myth itself—Platonism—Esoteric Christianity. . . ." In such poetry, which is "the progressive incarnation of life in consciousness," we best see at work the two great principles of imagination and intellect in the act of creative tension: creating and using meaning. And these two principles, we recall, are principles of language itself, and therefore principles of the World-Soul or Logos itself. But though Barfield has called these two forces "principles," that is not the right word:

> The Greeks had no such word as "principle"; they called what I have been speaking of—with that divine concreteness which makes the

> mere language a fountain of strength for the exhausted modern intelligence—simply ποιεῖν and πάσχειν—Do and Suffer.
>
> But to ordinary abstract thought a *principle* can never be anything more than an *idea,* induced from observations of what *has* happened. . . . Yet all conclusions of this nature could be no more than subjective shadows of the forces themselves, of the two living realities, which can actually be *known,* once our intellect has brought us to the point of looking out for them; being themselves neither subjective nor objective, but as concrete and self-sustaining in every way as the Sun and Moon—which may well be their proper names. (pp. 210–11)

Barfield's next major work, *Saving the Appearances* (1957), is the one which began to draw more general attention to him. By way of preamble I may say that it is less philological than the work we have been examining so far and more directly concerned with religion and epistemology—the Steiner-Kant-Coleridge epistemology we have already briefly seen. Yet it is the mixture as before: the arguments from Steiner, from *History in English Words,* and from *Poetic Diction* turned now to a specifically religious application. The book takes its title from Simplicius's sixth-century commentary on Aristotle's *De Caelo.* The phrase meant that a hypothesis could explain phenomena but was not on that basis necessarily true; even two contradictory hypotheses could explain the appearances, as did the Ptolemaic and Copernican versions of the movements of the planets. Galileo's trouble with the Church, says Barfield, stemmed from the fact that he and Copernicus and Kepler came to think that the Copernican version not only saved the appearances (that is, satisfactorily explained phenomena) but was on that account true. What the Church feared was not a new theory of celestial movements but "a new theory of the nature of theory; namely, that, if a hypothesis saves all the appearances, it is identical with truth."[20] Barfield's book is an attempt to explain not merely celestial movements or other phenomena but the reality underlying *all* phenomena. It is literally an attempt to explain the nature of things, to save *all* the appearances, by an extension of the theories we have already examined in the earlier books.

The book (the foreword to which thanks Lewis for help and advice) begins with a statement of intention: to look at the world in a new perspective and to see what follows from so doing. The new perspective consists of a "sustained acceptance by the reader of the relation assumed by physical science to subsist between human consciousness on the one hand and, on the other, the familiar world of which that consciousness is aware" (p. 11). Modern physics especially has taught us that the actual structure of the universe—what is really "out there" and distinct from us—is nothing like the phenomena which we see or hear or smell or even touch. Realizing this, most post-Kantian philosophers have dealt at length with the extent to which man participates in the constructing of the phenomena which he perceives. Barfield intends, he says, to keep in mind this psychological relationship between man and nature, and also to point out (what we have already seen) that this relationship has not remained static through the centuries but has changed, and will continue to change, as a corollary of the evolution of consciousness. Barfield describes the overall intention of the book:

> The greater part of this book consists . . . of a rudimentary attempt to remedy the omission [of the man-nature relationship]. But this involves . . . challenging the assumption [that the relationship has remained static]. . . . The result—and really the substance of the book—is a sort of outline sketch . . . for a history of human consciousness; particularly the consciousness of western humanity during the last three thousand years or so.
>
> Finally, the consequences which flow from abandoning the assumption are found to be very far-reaching; and the last three chapters are concerned, theologically, with the bearing of "participation"—viewed now as an historical process—upon the origin, the predicament, and the destiny of man. (p. 13)

The opening chapters of the book deal largely with epistemology. Barfield uses the example of a rainbow to illustrate the fact that man participates in the creation or evoking of the phenomena that he perceives. The rainbow is not really "there"; it is simply "the outcome of the sun, the raindrops and your own vision." The analogy between the rainbow and seemingly "real" phenomena is very close. Science tells us that the phenomenal world consists of atoms, protons, and electrons—that even these are perhaps only "notional models or symbols of an unknown supersensible or subsensible base." Now the tree, unlike the rainbow, can be touched, smelled, etc.; but if science is right about the composition of phenomena—if they consist of "particles" (as Barfield calls them)—"then, since the 'particles' are no more like the thing I call a tree than the raindrops are like the thing I call a rainbow, it follows . . . that—just as the rainbow is the outcome of the raindrops and my vision—so, a tree is the outcome of the particles and my vision and my other sense-perceptions" (pp. 16–17). The tree that I perceive, then, is what Barfield calls a "representation." Phenomena consist of my sensational and mental construction of the particles or the "unrepresented." (The particles, or unrepresented, seem close to Kant's noumena, the representations to his phenomena.) The tree that I perceive is not a dream tree or a private hallucination, since both you and I perceive it—that is, you and I construct a similar representation of the unrepresented. Thus phenomenal nature—the nature studied, weighed and measured, the nature experimented with by scientists—is what Barfield calls a "system of collective representations." We have the same view of the universe because we have arrived at the same (or approximately the same) level of consciousness. "The time comes when one must either accept this as the truth about the world or reject the theories of physics as an elaborate delusion. We cannot have it both ways" (p. 18).

Now a representation consists of the activity of the senses (perception) plus another process. We do not hear a thrush singing, says Barfield, nor do we smell coffee. Another activity must take place before we can say that we hear a thrush or smell coffee, or even be aware that we are perceiving these things. It is the activity that identifies, or puts in their proper places, these raw sensations. This activity Barfield calls "figuration," and the activity recalls to us Steiner's belief that thinking fills out the percept, that objects undergo a "rebirth" in mind or spirit.

> On the assumption that the world whose existence is independent of our sensation and perception consists solely of "particles," two operations are necessary (and whether they are successive or simul-

> taneous is of no consequence), in order to produce the familiar world we know. First, the sense-organs must be related to the particles in such a way as to give rise to sensations; and secondly, those mere sensations must be combined and constructed by the percipient mind into the recognizable and nameable objects we call "things." It is this work of construction which will here be called *figuration.* (p. 24)

Barfield next goes on to make a distinction drawn from the work of Steiner. He distinguishes between two kinds of thinking: "alpha-thinking" and "beta-thinking." Alpha-thinking is thinking about phenomena as if they were really objective and independent of our minds; it is thinking which assumes the naively realistic view of the universe; it is the thinking characteristic of the physical sciences (excepting modern physics). Beta-thinking is thinking about thinking and perception; it is reflective thinking, the result of which is that we become conscious of the fact that phenomena are not independent and totally outside us. It is not a different kind of thinking from alpha-thinking; the two kinds of thinking are the same, but their subject matters are different. Barfield is concerned with "the interaction between figuration and alpha-thinking" (p. 26), and is thus himself beta-thinking.

The next step in the theory introduces the most difficult concept of the book, that of "participation." Barfield begins his discussion of participation by citing the anthropological work of Levy-Bruhl and Durkheim among primitive societies. In effect he uses their work as evidence to support his earlier assertions about primitive mentality—its lack of conceptual thinking, its relative lack of self-consciousness. This mentality, Levy-Bruhl holds, is "essentially synthetic . . . the syntheses which compose it do not imply previous analyses of which the result has been registered in definite concepts . . . the connecting links of the representations are given . . . in the representations themselves" (pp. 29–30). Levy-Bruhl maintains that such thought has nothing to do with the earlier anthropological theory of animism; the primitive does not *associate* his beliefs with his phenomena (representations). "The mystic properties with which things are imbued form an integral part of the idea to the primitive who views it as a synthetic whole." The primitive does not "dissociate" himself from phenomena, does not perceive himself as distinct from them. And "as long as this 'dissociation' does not take place, perception remains an undifferentiated whole" (p. 31). Turned around the other way, the lack of dissociation may positively be termed "participation." For us, the only link between ourselves and phenomena—except through beta-thinking—is through the senses. For the primitive, however, there is another link, an extra- or super-sensory one, not only between the percipient and the phenomena (representations) but between the representations themselves and between the percipients themselves. Thus the primitive mind achieves a kind of unity of reality (through synthesis) by means of participation or lack of dissociation. Barfield concludes the anthropological evidence for his assumption that the psychological relationship between man and nature has not remained static, that the primitive outlook is essentially different from ours:

> It is not only a different alpha-thinking but a different figuration, with which we have to do, and therefore the phenomena are treated as collective representations produced by that different figuration. . . . the most striking difference between primitive figuration and ours is, that the primitive involves "participation," that is, an awareness which we no longer have, of an extra-sensory link between the percipient and the representations. This involves, not only that we think differently, but that the phenomena (collective representations) themselves are different. (pp. 34–35)

There is a fundamental difference between not only primitive thinking and our own but between primitive phenomena and our own; and the difference in both cases is due to the fact that the primitive participates in both his thinking and in his phenomena as an active experience, while our participation in our phenomena is largely unconscious.[21]

From the preceding evidence about primitive mentality, it follows, says Barfield, that the general view of pre-history is a myth. We can have no real knowledge, for example, of the evolution of the earth before the arrival of man—and not only of man, but of relatively modern man. For the evolution of phenomena (including the earth) is correlative to the evolution of consciousness, since phenomena are no more than representations on the part of that consciousness. So the pre-historic evolution of the earth as described, for example, in Wells's *Outline of History* "was not merely never seen. It never occurred" (p. 37). Something may have been going on in the "unrepresented," but what it was would depend on the level of consciousness which perceived—and thus constructed—it. In so far as we really think we know what was going on in pre-historic times, we are simply projecting our own collective representations into "the dark backward and abysm of time"; we are creating what Bacon called "idols of the study."

Having come thus far in the argument, Barfield stops and points out the possible alternatives if his view is not accepted. We may adopt the "super-naive realism" of Dr. Johnson; we may kick our stone and say, "Nature is nature, and the earth is the earth, and always has been since it all began." But this involves rejecting the findings of physics. Or we may do what Orwell called "double-think": we may ignore the findings of physics except when we are engaged in a physics problem; we may pretend that the discoveries of physics have no relation to the subject matters of other sciences such as botany, zoology, and geology. Or finally we may adopt the view of radical idealism: that the representations which we call phenomena "are sustained by God in the absence of human beings." This last alternative involves believing that God has chosen our own particular set of collective representations out of all the possible others of ancient and medieval consciousness.

Barfield then resumes the discussion of the real evolution (of consciousness) as distinct from the false (as it is assumed in Wells). Evolution as we ordinarily understand the term, says Barfield, is an evolution of idols of the study. The theory reached its peak of popularity in the nineteenth century because the original participation of man in his perception was not sufficiently realized, though Kant and Steiner had taught it. Thus phenomena were held to have an independent and objective existence which they do not really have: Darwinian evolutionists were alpha-thinkers. "But a representation, which is collectively mistaken for an ultimate, ought not to be called a representation. It is an idol. Thus the phenomena themselves are idols, when they are imagined as enjoying that independence of human perception which can in fact only pertain to the unrepresented" (p. 62). (Here the subtitle of the book may be mentioned: "A Study in Idolatry.") And the Darwinian evolution of idols is not only wrong itself but begets wrong in other fields—in etymology, mythology, anthropology. The doctrine of animism is a direct result of the failure to perceive that the only meaningful evolution can be the evolution of phenomena following on the evolution of consciousness. The early anthropologists accepted Darwinian evolution as a framework within which all their results must fit. Thus they postulated a primitive man who was simply a modern man "with his mind *tabula rasa,*" faced with phenomena (collective representations) the same as our own.

> The development of human consciousness was thus presented as a history of alpha-thinking beginning from zero and applied always to the same phenomena, at first in the form of erroneous beliefs about them and, as time went on, in the form of more and more correct and scientific beliefs. In short, the evolution of human consciousness was reduced to a bare history of ideas. (p. 66)

When we understand the true evolution, however, as distinct from the evolution of idols, then history takes for us a different and a truer shape. The evolution of consciousness is correlative with the rise of conceptual reasoning (as we saw earlier) and with the decline of "original" participation. We have seen, from the philological evidence presented in *History in English Words,* that participation lasted into the late Middle Ages. Indeed, says Barfield, the "whole basis of epistemology from Aristotle to Aquinas assumed participation, and the problem was merely the precise manner in which the participation operated." As Aristotle is more subjective in his thought than Plato (further along in the process of internalization), so Aquinas is more subjective than Aristotle; yet even in the rise of subjectivity which goes with increased self-consciousness we can see that for Aquinas, as for Aristotle, the principle of original participation is assumed. "The *nous* of which Aristotle spoke and thought was clearly less subjective than Aquinas's *in-*

tellectus; and when he deals with the problem of perception, he polarizes not merely the mind, but the world itself, without explanation or apology, into the two verbs . . . *poiein* and *paschein:* 'to do' and 'to suffer' . . . these two words alone are as untranslatable as the mentality which they reveal is remote from our own" (p. 100). And the whole of Aquinas's work is shot through with the same assumption; for Aquinas the assumption is so obvious that only once does he bother to explain it, and then by analogy: "Suppose we say that air participates the light of the sun, because it does not receive it in that clarity in which it is in the sun" (quoted from *De Hebdomadibus,* cap. 2). Aquinas assumed participation as much in logic as in the ladder of being itself:

> At one end of the scale the subject participates its predicate; at the other end, a formal or hierarchical participation *per similitudinem* was the foundation of the whole structure of the universe; for all creatures were in a greater or lesser degree images or representations, or "names" of God, and their likeness or unlikeness did not merely measure, but *was* the nearer or more distant emanation of His Being and Goodness in them. (p. 90)

We should read the history of western consciousness, then, as the gradual decline of original participation, the gradual increase of self-consciousness and awareness of self as distinct from phenomena which has (unfortunately, Barfield thinks) culminated in idolatry—the granting of objective existence to our collective representations. The glaring and wonderful exception to this historical trend is the case of Israel, which must be noted because Israel's religion is in many ways analogous to Barfield's final religious conclusion.

The Israelites in Egypt received from Moses "the unheard of injunction" "not to make unto thee any graven image or any likeness of anything that is in heaven above, or that is in the earth beneath, or that is in the water under the earth." They were enjoined not to make images when the people of every nation around them practiced the prevailing original participation. And "participation and the experience of phenomena as representations go hand in hand; . . . the experience of representations, as such, is closely linked with the making of images." For in original participation the link between self and phenomena is *experienced,* not arrived at (as in our case) by beta-thinking. "Original participation is . . . the sense that there stands behind the phenomena, and on the other side of them from man, a represented, which is of the same nature as man. It was against this that Israel's face was set" (p. 109).

Participation thus began to die for Israel as the result of a moral injunction, while for western man in general it dies only as a natural process. This Jewish progress away from participation Barfield traces by the Jewish reference to the name of God Himself. The Old Testament tells us that the Jews, before they left Egypt, were told by Moses the real name of their God. The name, says Barfield, was thought to be "too holy to be communicable." It may be found written in the Psalms, for instance, but by the third century B.C. it was never read aloud; other word such as "Adonai" or "Elohim" were substituted. "The Name itself was pronounced only by the priests in the Temple when blessing the people or by the High Priest on the Day of Atonement. Other precautions and uses emphasized and preserved its ineffable quality." The Name is written in four consonants and is taken from a verb which means both "to be" and "to breathe."

> The Hebrew word for "Jew" is derived from the same verb; so that a devout Jew could not name his race without recalling, nor affirm his own existence without tending to utter, the Tetragrammaton. Written . . . without vowels, when any true child of Israel perused the unspoken Name, יהוה must have seemed to come whispering up, as it were, from the depths of his own being! (p. 112)

This Jewish "ingathering withdrawal from participation" (p. 114) Barfield sees illustrated in two encounters with God recorded in the Old Testament. The first shows God as still thought to be "outer" and somehow in or behind the phenomena; the second shows Him to be considered "within." The Lord appeared to Moses from the phenomenon of a burning bush; but "by the time of Elijah the withdrawal . . . was already far advanced. . . ." Barfield then quotes the famous verses which catalogue the natural beauties which do *not* contain God: He was not in the wind, nor in the earthquake, nor in the fire—"and after the fire a still small voice."

> He had now only one Name—I AM—and that was participated by every being who had eyes that saw and ears that heard and who spoke through his throat. But it was incommunicable, because its participation by the particular self which is at this moment uttering it was an inseparable part of its meaning. Everyone can call his idol GOD, and many do; but no being who speaks through his throat can call a wholly other and outer Being I. (p. 114)

And Rabbi Maimonides, about 1190, repeated "the mystery of the Divine Name. It was 'that name in which there is no participation between the creator and any *thing* else.' "

Now if the rise of self-consciousness and the decline of original participation (aided by God, in the case of the Jews) have led to the state of things that Barfield calls idolatry, what hope is there for the future? Idolatry is clearly wrong: aside from being forbidden to the chosen people, it does not square with the nature of things. But what is to be done about it? The answer to this question is the crux of the argument.

There have occurred, according to Barfield, certain "symptoms of iconoclasm," the major one of which (as we saw in *History in English Words*) was the romantic movement. The romantic movement was possible because, as consciousness evolved toward self-consciousness and thus gave rise to "phenomena on the one side and consciousness on the other," the thing that we call *memory* came into being.

> As consciousness develops into self-consciousness, the remembered phenomena become detached or liberated from their originals and so, as images, are in some measure at man's disposal. The more thoroughly participation has been eliminated, the more they are at the disposal of his imagination to employ as it chooses. If it chooses to impart its own meaning, it is doing, *pro tanto,* with the remembered phenomena what their Creator once did with the phenomena themselves. Thus there *is* a real analogy between metaphorical usage and original participation; but it is one which can only be acknowledged if the crude conception of an evolution of idols . . . is finally abandoned, or at all events is enlightened by one more in line with

> the old teaching of the Logos. There is a valid analogy *if*, but only if, we admit that, in the course of the earth's history, something like a Divine Word has been gradually clothing itself with the humanity it first gradually created—so that what was first spoken by God may eventually be re-spoken by man. (pp. 126–28)

The process of internalization has taken the meanings of the phenomena inside man, and meaning has now become available for his own "creative 'speech'—using 'speech' now in the wide sense of Aquinas's 'word.' " The decline of participation in the west has had as its complement a "growing awareness . . . of this capacity of man for creative speech." The more man comes to believe that phenomena are wholly distinct from himself and have no immanent life, the more he comes to see that he can manipulate his memory-images of them in any way he chooses. For the artist, so long as Nature contained immanent life akin to that of the artist himself, it was enough to imitate Nature because "the life or spirit in the object lived on in his imitation, if it was a faithful one." The artifact was more than imitation because the artist and the object imitated shared the same immanent life of the universe. But with the decline of participation, imitation of Nature became purely mechanical, to be replaced ultimately by photography. Thus men, sensing the loss of life in phenomena, began to formulate doctrines of "creative" art, in which the artist (in whom there was still life) infused life into the objects which he imitated from dead Nature. Barfield traces the beginnings of these doctrines of creative art back as far as Chrysostom in the first century, and through Philostratus in the second and Plotinus in the third. The doctrines continued up through Scaliger and Sidney in the sixteenth century, and reached their climax in Coleridge in the nineteenth.

But the romantic theory of the imagination went a step beyond its forebears. Properly speaking, the theory as it is stated by Sidney means little more than that the artist manipulates the images of things for his own moral ends. Literature can teach where Nature cannot because literature uses the images of Nature purposefully. It is in this sense that, as Sidney says, "the truest poetry is the most feigning." And it is in this sense only that the Renaissance neo-Platonists spoke of man as a creator. But Coleridge's doctrine of the primary and secondary imagination radically changed the older view. For Coleridge affirmed that the artist does not manipulate images of dead things outside of himself, but images of live things which he himself has partly created by means of the primary imagination. Thus the artist was doubly a creator, both in the making of his objects and in the manipulating of images of them for his own purposes. Now all of this Coleridge knew as doctrine; but it was Wordsworth who *experienced* the truth of the doctrine. Coleridge knew that Nature is alive because his philosophy told him that he himself put life into it. But Wordsworth *felt* the life in Nature, felt somehow that the life immanent in himself was also immanent in Nature. He tried to explain it by theories verging on pantheism, and pantheism, Barfield says, is a "nostalgic hankering after *original* participation."

As Barfield points out, the distinction between the creativity of the primary imagination and the manipulation of the secondary may be seen in the division of labor between Coleridge and Wordsworth in the *Lyrical Ballads*.[22] In the well known section from Chapter XIV of the *Biographia Literaria,* Coleridge describes the two kinds of poetry to be included in the *Lyrical Ballads*. Wordsworth was to write poetry that would have "the power of exciting the sympathy of the reader by a faithful adherence to the truth of nature," while Coleridge was to write poetry that had "the power of giving the interest of novelty by the modifying colours of imagination." Coleridge's poetry would be the work primarily of the secondary imagination; though he knew of the immanent life in Nature, he did not feel it, and thus he would be reduced to manipulating the images of what he *felt* to be things merely dead and objective. Thus he would "make up" the "incidents and agents" and feign that they were "supernatural"; his aim was, like Sidney's, no more than to show his readers "the dramatic truth of such emotions, as would naturally accompany such situations, supposing them real." But Wordsworth, who felt common life in himself and Nature, would minimize the inventiveness of the secondary imagination, because it would be sufficient for him merely to "imitate Nature." He would write of subjects from "ordinary life," for something of the life of Nature would linger on in his poems.

Wordsworth would not have to concern himself with the workings of the secondary imagination so long as he experienced the workings of the primary imagination, in which sounding cataracts haunted him like a passion. He would be practicing original participation.

Thus the romantics were symbols of iconoclasm in the sense that Coleridge knew and Wordsworth felt that Nature was not an "idol," not something fixed and dead, but alive. Wordsworth, the pantheist, supposed what primitive man supposed, that God is immanent in all things, and thus Wordsworth misinterpreted his experience. Coleridge, saved from pantheism by his knowledge of Kantian philosophy, knew that the life in Nature is the life that we give it through the primary imagination. Coleridge knew that man stands in what Barfield calls "a directionally creator" relationship to Nature; man half creates what he sees and then manipulates images of phenomena. But what Coleridge did not know is the true nature of man the creator. Thus "the true . . . impulse underlying the Romantic movement has never grown to maturity; and, after adolescence, the alternative to maturity is puerility." The romantic movement might well have borne great fruit if Coleridge had known the kind of being he was as well as he knew the way that his mind operated. For what stands in this "directionally creator" relationship to Nature "is not my poor temporal personality, but the Divine Name in the unfathomable depths behind it." What stands in this relationship is the Logos, the World-Process, working its way through and out of man's unconscious mind.

And here, having reminded ourselves of the nature of man (in Barfield's view), we may also remind ourselves of the nature of Nature. In speaking of Wordsworth as one who experienced the immanent life in Nature we may have allowed ourselves to slip back into the position of naive realism. But such a position, we recall, is radically wrong. The Nature that we have been talking about exists in a world of thought. Barfield finds it ironic that modern man, prone to see the phenomenal world as objective and "out there," should have become so fond of Jung's theory of the collective unconscious. Our "literal minded generation," he says, "began to accept the actuality of a 'collective unconscious' before it could even admit the possibility of a 'collective conscious'—in the shape of the phenomenal world." For the phenomena are "collective representations," as has been already established. Thus of the hypothetical evolution that we are so fond of positing of the phenomenal world—our talk of "pre-historic" phenomena—the most that we can accurately say is that the phenomena which we posit for those times are "potential phenomena." But we must keep in mind that "the phenomenal world arises from the relation between a conscious and an unconscious and that evolution is the story of the changes that relation has undergone and is undergoing." So it follows that it is at the least "highly fanciful . . . to think of any unperceived process in terms of potential phenomena, unless we also assume an unconscious, ready to light up into actual phenomena at any moment of the process." The concept of the potentially phenomenal as existing in the unconscious is the answer to the difficulty, now that the old act-potency relationship of Aristotle and Aquinas (arrived at through original participation) has faded away. As was the case with participation itself for Aristotle and Aquinas, so "potential" meant something much more for Aristotle than *possibilis* did for Aquinas, though Aquinas still meant much more than our mere "possible." We have difficulty in "grasping *process* as such" because we are "hamstrung by the lack of just such a concept of the potentially phenomenal and the actually phenomenal." For us, "to ask whether a thing 'is' or 'is not' is . . . to ask whether it is or is not a phenomenon. . . ." And this is to be expected so long as we remain idolaters. But once we admit the possibility of the unconscious we have a basis for reaffirming the *actus-potentia* distinction; it need no longer be for us, as it was for Bacon (who did so much to help turn the representations into idols), a *frigida distinctio* (pp. 135–136).

Now in so far as we realize conceptually (by beta-thinking) that we participate in our phenomena "with the unconscious part of ourselves," we perceive as a fact what may be called "final" participation as distinct from original participation. That is, we apprehend by conceptual thinking what primitive, ancient, and (to some extent) medieval man felt as an actual experience. But this mere intellectual awareness has no epistemological significance; our representations are no different for our being aware that we in effect create them. There can only be epistemological significance "to the extent that final participation is consciously experienced. Perhaps . . . we may say that final participation must itself be raised from potentiality to act." But we can raise our final participation only by sustained effort: "it is a matter, not of theorizing, but of the imagination in the genial or creative sense. A systematic approach towards final participation may therefore be expected to be an attempt to use imagination systematically" (p. 137).

I said much earlier in this discussion that when Barfield's argument reaches the stage where he must presume some sort of systematic use or training of the imagination he usually refers the reader to Steiner. So he does at this point—to Steiner and to Goethe. Steiner both practiced this systematic use of the imagination and described the process in *The Philosophy of Spiritual Activity:*

> Steiner showed that imagination, and the final participation that it leads to, involve, unlike hypothetical thinking, the whole man—thought, feeling, will, and character—and his own revelations were clearly drawn from those further stages of participation—Inspiration and Intuition—to which the systematic use of imagination may lead. (p. 141)

At this point we might turn to Steiner's discussion, which is certainly full, if not as lucid as Barfield asserts. Unfortunately, that is like turning to Aquinas on angelology or Jonathan Edwards on the freedom of the will. Steiner's discussion presupposes a good deal more knowledge of Anthroposophy as a whole than I have so far supplied. The reader will be aware, in fact, that throughout the preceding pages I have tried to deal primarily with Barfield, with as little direct reference to Anthroposophy as is possible. In a way this is of course unfair and bears out Barfield's earlier complaint about Steiner's obscurity. But, whether for good or ill, Barfield's analysis of his relationship to Steiner is true, at least for the present: it is Barfield that people want to read, not Steiner. In any case, though I am sure Barfield would deny this, so far as notions like inspiration and intuition can be rationally discussed at all, Barfield discusses them far more clearly than Steiner does, and with far more relevance to the contemporary situation. I shall deal more closely with these ideas a little further on in connection with Barfield's essay "Imagination and Inspiration" and with his book *Unancestral Voice,* in which these ideas are dramatized, given a life of their own. Here I shall try to stay in touch with the argument of *Saving the Appearances* by presenting Barfield's main example of the trained imagination in the person of Goethe, though a few remarks that Barfield has made elsewhere about Coleridge and his relation to Goethe's thought will perhaps also serve to clarify the issue.

Let us return for a moment to the letter "U" analogy cited earlier. Man, on his ascent of the right-hand limb, will "pass" stages of his previous descent; he will in effect re-live them. But because the ascent is toward Spirit, toward ever fuller consciousness, he will re-live them consciously. Thus early man's unconscious participation in his phenomenal world will be re-lived not only as a conceptual notion but as a conscious experience. The very concept of the unconscious mind is one of the "premonitory signs" of this next level of consciousness. Goethe's scientific work was an attempt to perceive from this next level of consciousness, to participate consciously in the phenomenal world as early man had participated unconsciously in it. And since Barfield's whole epistemological argument supposes that as the mind participates in the phenomena, it "makes" the phenomena, gives meaning to the "represented," it follows that a *conscious* experiencing of the phenomena will reveal more meaning than an *unconscious* experiencing will. By analogy, the adult sees more meaning in phenomena than the child does. Goethe worked—in the phrase quoted earlier—in the no-man's-land, or every-man's-land "which lies between the net Given and the specious Given," in the realm of Susanne Langer's "formulation."[23] What he tried in a half-comprehending way to do is what future man will do easily and naturally. To use Coleridge's term, what Goethe did was to transfer "the esemplastic imagination from literature and art to science" (p. 34). What Goethe called the *Urphänomen,* or the prime phenomenon, the thing in itself, corresponds to Coleridge's term "Idea" when Coleridge speaks of a science " 'which in the Ideas that are present to the mind recognises the laws that govern in Nature if we may not say the laws that *are* Nature' " (p. 148). Barfield describes Goethe's study of natural phenomena in terms that recall not only Coleridge but other romantics such as Hazlitt and Keats and Shelley who talked of the power of the "sympathetic" imagination by which the poet could identify himself with objects.

> His method differs from the ordinary method of induction in that the observer, when he reaches a certain point (the "prime phenomenon"), stops there and endeavours rather to sink himself in contemplation *in* that phenomenon than to form further thoughts *about* it. It implies a certain—if one may use the word—*chastity* of thought, a willingness not to go beyond a certain point. The blue of the sky, said Goethe, *is* the theory. To go further and weave a web of abstract ideas remote from anything we can perceive with our senses in order to "explain" this blue—that is to darken counsel. (p. 34)

If we accept the premise that the phenomenal world is unconscious meaning, then Goethe's attempt makes some sense, since what it involved was "an actual participation in the Thinking that is present and active in the world of nature" (p. 235).

> It was by this method that Goethe discovered that morphological principle which is now laid down on almost the first page of many botanical text-books—the principle that all the parts of a plant can be regarded as metamorphoses of the leaf. It was by this method that he discovered—not only that there was, but that there *must* be (please note)—a bone in the human skeleton hitherto unknown to science—the *Os Intermaxillare*. (p. 34)

He could make these discoveries because "as imagination reaches the point of enhancing figuration itself, hitherto unperceived parts of the whole field of the phenomenon become perceptible."[24] Or, to say it differently, certain unconscious meanings of the phenomenon become conscious. Goethe's views were not accepted in his own time and are not now, because empirical science insists on treating the phenomena as "idols" in which the human mind has no part. But there is an attempt being made to study the phenomenon of cancer by a Steinerite group, the Society for Cancer

Research in Arlseheim, Switzerland. Their method—the Goethean method—"involves investigation of a part of the field of the whole phenomenon named *blood* which, for a non-participating consciousness, is excluded from it, not by empirical proof but rather . . . by definition" (p. 140). Goethe's method is decribed by a modern scientist, Sir Charles Sherrington (who rejects it completely), as follows:

> The phenomena of Nature, he tells us, are of two grades. The majority do not lend themselves well to analysis because in them the fundamental is obscured by the accessory. There are, however, certain natural phenomena which do lie open to human inquiry in their naked simplicity. This latter class are Urphänomenen. . . . It is something . . . self-explanatory. We comprehend it instinctively. Science cannot, and never will, resolve further an Urphänomenen. But by it a foundation is given on which to build. It allows insight into Nature.[25]

Barfield might add to this, it allows insight into Nature for the participating consciousness only.

However we regard Goethe's attempts, the fact is that he tried to practice final participation as a means of finding pattern and order in the universe. As we have seen, at the present time we are engaged in scouring all meaning from the universe by our insistence on the empirical method. We acknowledge our unconscious participation in our phenomena but insist nevertheless on treating the phenomena as if they have independent existence. But our consciousness is evolving, changing, expanding; and it follows from this that we shall be bringing new meanings to our phenomena—"seeing" them differently—as the conscious mind reveals more and more of the potential meaning latent in the unconscious mind. If evolution has become conscious of itself in the mind of man, if man stands in a "directionally creator" relation to the phenomenal world, then it is possible for man to "direct" evolution, to choose which way the phenomenal world of the future will be seen, and thus be. (If it is objected here that it is meaningless to speak of "directing" evolution, that by definition evolution simply goes on by itself, then I think the reader must determine whether he is thinking of Darwinian evolution, or Barfield's evolution of consciousness, or Steiner's mystical ascent to the One. If he is thinking of Darwin's or Barfield's evolution, then an answer to the objection is that in both cases the evolutionary process has no direct bearing on morality; expanded consciousness, in either version of the evolutionary process, implies merely an expanded field for moral choice; it does not imply moral goodness. Even a belief that mankind is evolving toward a more spiritual stage of being does not imply this, unless we assume some sort of Manichean point of view and argue that man's capacity for evil resides in his body. If the reader is thinking of Steiner's evolution, an automatic ascent of man toward God, then even that belief does not imply immediate moral goodness, only ultimate moral goodness. Barfield is talking about the *moral* future of mankind.)

But though man may direct the evolution of consciousness, he cannot stop it: that is where the note of inevitability comes in. We may choose a further evolution toward an even greater idolatry, choosing to cut ourselves off even more from the world outside us. If we do eliminate even the vestigial sense we have of original participation and do not substitute any other for it, we "will have done nothing less than to eliminate all meaning and all coherence from the cosmos," because "all the unity and coherence of nature depends on participation of one kind or the other." Such schools of philosophy as logical positivism, for example, have already tried to eliminate meaning from language, and meaning is "a valid relation to nature." And science in general shows the same signs of coming chaos:

> science, with the progressive disappearance of original participation, is losing its grip on any principle of unity pervading nature as a whole and the knowledge of nature. The hypothesis of chance has already crept from the theory of evolution into the theory of the physical foundation of the earth itself; but, more serious perhaps than that, is the rapidly increasing "fragmentation of science.". . . There is no "science of sciences"; no unity of knowledge. There is only an accelerating increase in that pigeon-holed knowledge by individuals of more and more about less and less, which, if persisted in indefinitely, can only lead mankind to a sort of "idiocy" . . . a state of affairs, in which fewer and fewer representations will be col-

> lective, and more and more will be private, with the result that there will in the end be no means of communication between one intelligence and another. (p. 145)

Or we may choose to direct evolution in the path suggested by Steiner and Goethe, the path toward final, conscious participation in our phenomena. But even this course involves dangers. "Imagination is not, as some poets have thought, simply synonymous with good. It may be either good or evil." Barfield cites the example of surrealistic painting: "so long as art remained primarily mimetic, the evil which imagination could do was limited by nature." But when the fact of the directionally creator relationship of man to his phenomena—and to his memory images of phenomena—becomes apparent to the artist, there is the possibility of "aberrations."

> In so far as they are genuine, they are genuine because the artist has in some way or other experienced the world he represents. And in so far as they are appreciated, they are appreciated by those who are themselves willing to make a move towards seeing the world in that way, and, ultimately, therefore, seeing that kind of world. We should remember this, when we see pictures of a dog with six legs emerging from a vegetable marrow or a woman with a motor-bicycle substituted for her left breast. (p. 146)

Such aberrations suggest the possibility that we "could very well move forward into . . . a fantastically hideous world," just as the choice to move in the direction of a further idolizing of the phenomena could move us into a world that is "chaotically empty."

The choice, then, is portentous. We must choose the way of the imagination, but we must use the imagination religiously. That involves our understanding that the imagination is a religious capacity, and in fact a divine one.

> The appearances will be "saved" only if, as men approach nearer and nearer to conscious figuration and realize that it is something which may be affected by their choices, the final participation which is thus being thrust upon them is exercised with the profoundest sense of responsibility, with the deepest thankfulness and piety towards the world as it was originally given to them in original participation, and with a full understanding of the momentous process of

> history, as it brings about the emergence of the one from the other. (p. 147)

Thus we must understand the nature of man and the nature of the world before the magnitude of our choice can be comprehended. Original participation began as "the unconscious identity of man with his Creator." But that this state of things was not to remain is clear from God's commandment to the Jews to forsake idolatry, the characteristic sign of original participation. We must understand that Christ (if we accept His own claims) "came to make possible in the course of time the transition of all men from original to final participation. . . ." The physical participation in the Eucharist may be regarded as preparation for and adumbration of this final end. We have been uttered by the Word and feel "the seed of the Word stirring within us, as imagination." The Incarnation has not been turned off like a tap; it continues, "for Christ *is* the cosmic wisdom on its way from original to final participation." And final participation, as the Jews learned, but forgot, is the state "whereby man's Creator speaks from within man himself. . . ." Thus is the Word continually made flesh. And thus men are not hollow idols, any more than their phenomena are; they are "the theatre on which participation has died to rise again . . ." (p. 185).

> If, in Christ, we participate finally the Spirit we once participated originally; if, in so doing, we participate one another—so that "men" once more become also "man"; if, in original participation, we were dreamers and unfree, and if Christ is a Being who can be participated only in vigilance and freedom, then what will chiefly be remembered about the scientific revolution will be the way in which it scoured the appearances clean of the last traces of spirit, freeing us *from* original, and *for* final, participation. And if what is produced thereby was, as I have suggested, a world of idols, yet, as of Augustine of old could contemplate the greatest of evils and exclaim *Felix peccatum!* so we, looking steadily on that world, and accepting the burden of existential responsibility which final participation lays upon us, may yet be moved to add:
>
> *Felix eidolon!*
>
> "Peor and Baalim forsake their temples dim" . . . the other name for original participation . . . is, after all, paganism. (p. 186)

For the reader acquainted with Barfield's earlier work, *Worlds Apart* (1963) is a delightful and surprising book, because all of Barfield's forty-year-old argument is repeated but in a form that the reader never expected to find Barfield using. Within a slight fictional framework, the book is really a symposium, a grouping together of characters who represent various intellectual points of view. (Perhaps the form suggested itself to Barfield as a result of the various seminars and symposia that he himself began to take part in from about 1960 on.) The characters include the narrator, Burgeon, "a solicitor with philological interests"; Hunter, "a professor of historical theology and ethics"; Ranger, "a young man employed at a rocket research station"; Brodie, "a professor of physical science"; Sanderson, "a retired schoolmaster" who taught for several years in a Rudolf Steiner school; Upwater, "a biologist engaged on research work"; Dunn, "a linguistic philosopher"; and Burrows, "a psychiatrist."[26] The narrator, who describes himself as a friend of Barfield's, is bothered by the fact that, as Barfield said in *Saving the Appearances,* there seems to be no unity in modern science, no science of sciences, that the various sciences work within "watertight compartments," with almost no communication among them. Accordingly, he arranges for the above-named people to meet over a week end, and the book consists of a series of arguments—including a full-dress Socratic dialogue between Burgeon and Brodie—that lasts from Friday night till Sunday afternoon. Ostensibly the book is an attempt to give every dog his day, but this is merely an illusion on Barfield's part. What he has done is to spread his own point of view around among several characters—primarily Burgeon and Sanderson—and set up his old enemies (Darwinian evolution, false theories of language, the crudities of some depth psychology) among some of the others, especially Dunn, Upwater, and Ranger. Thus the book is really a monologue—dizzying in its brilliance—but not essentially unlike the method to be found in Aquinas, for example, where an idea is advanced, argued for, controverted, finally proved false, and so on. There are some interesting sidelights to the book. Hunter, for example, will likely remind the reader a good deal of Lewis. And there is some humor. Some of the names obviously suggest their characters' professions: Ranger the rocket man, Burrows the psychiatrist, Upwater the evolutionist. Probably the best joke concerns Dunn, who takes the worst beating of all Barfield's opponents. A linguistic philosopher, and thus concerned only with the way that words "work" and not at all with "unverifiable" speculations in philosophy and theology, he drives a car with a "shabby body and perfectly tuned engine."

The form of the book prevents any summary which would give the real flavor of the symposium—the brilliant give and take of the arguments themselves, the occasional misunderstandings and quibblings, the way that one argument leads to another, and so on. Perhaps the best way to deal with the book in anything briefer than another book is to indicate where the real emphasis falls and to show why. Out of the welter of argument to be found on the first day and most of the second, and especially on the third, Sanderson's point of view, or a combination of Sanderson's and Burgeon's, emerges as the victor—if not for all the characters in the book, certainly for the reader. In short, Burgeon and Anthroposophy carry the day, as a dream by Hunter at the end of the book indicates.

Briefly, the major disputed questions in the first two parts of the book are as follows: (1) Darwinian evolution—whether or not it is true, and if it is, whether or not it is still continuing beyond the biological sphere, in the social and intellectual spheres as well; whether or not mind produced by this assumed evolutionary process can ever arrive at objective truth, or whether what Hunter calls Reason must exist outside this process, since arguments based on material and thus irrational grounds are always suspect (Lewis is surely echoed here). Sanderson's comment on this dilemma is that thinking may be a part of nature but not be *produced* by nature. (2) Modern science—whether it is justified in dealing with phenomena as things wholly distinct from the human mind (as idols); particularly, whether science is justified in treating the human psyche as such a "thing" when it is other "things" that are analyzing it; whether, in fact, there really is such a thing as a duality of matter and mind. In the course of discussing these questions Burgeon brings up the whole problem of epistemology and resolves it generally as Barfield resolved it in *Saving the Appearances:* the mind participates in the phenomenal world. There is no absolute distinction between phenomena and observer; as Whitehead said, though he found it impossible to believe it, " 'nature is man's configuration.' " Barfield's earlier "collective representations" and "specious Given" become now "familiar nature," while his "unrepresented" and "net Given" (the Kantian noumena) become "inferred nature." (3) The relationship between the conscious and unconscious mind—whether there is such a thing as unconscious thought (Burrows claims that seven-eighths of thought is unconscious); whether the symbolic forms in which the unconscious expresses itself can be said to be latent discursive thought. If it is the unconscious mind which is at work in perception of the phenomenal world, then the question is whether the unconscious mind not only "fills out" the percept by adding a concept but also constructs whole systems of percept-concept combinations. In any case, if the phenomenal world is at least in part a construct of the human mind, then there is no need to put Reason outside of Nature, as Hunter did, because Nature itself is not merely a material and irrational thing, but a thing at least partly mental. Finally, if the phenomenal world is the result of a combination of "inferred nature" and the human mind, then the whole Darwinian argument for a long pre-historic age in which there was a solid earth on which man later appeared is simply a hypothesis unsupported by evidence. For the solidity of the phenomenal world is impossible without the presence of the perceiving and thinking human entity.

Ranger, younger and more naive than the others, serves as a foil at this point, as at many others. He asks if the whole first day's dispute can be repeated the next day. All agree, and the repetition takes the form of the Socratic dialogue already mentioned, with Burgeon as Socrates and Brodie as his pupil. The whole epistemological argument is re-fashioned, with additional reference to earlier scientific views. The classical analysis of phenomena into primary and secondary qualities—as in Galileo and later in Locke—is brought up and disposed of. All the primary qualities which were once presumed to inhere in the phenomena themselves—such as solidity and extension—are now known to be secondary qualities which inhere in the observer, with the sole exception of number.

As Brodie is forced to admit to Burgeon's Socratic question, "We now know, beyond any doubt, that all the attributes of the earth which we call qualitative are subjective." In the course of the argument that follows the dialogue, Dunn remarks that he feels as if he has been "assisting at a veritable orgy of subjectivism." He follows this remark with a disquisition on linguistic analysis which implies very strongly that most of what has been said at the symposium is quite literally nonsense, because the speakers have been using "a type of language which is appropriate to one set of circumstances, when we are talking about another set." They have all confused particulars with universals, he asserts, and have talked about abstract nouns as if they were "things," whereas they are only words which take on their meaning from their usage. About the whole epistemological argument that has taken place, he comments:

> *when we are discussing how we know anything, or what we can be said to know,* it is a delusion to talk about meanings and dreams, and so forth, as if they were entities of which anything at all can be predicated. Any such statement is unverifiable, and I mean by that, not that it is untrue, but that it cannot be shown to be either true or false. Therefore it is meaningless. . . . you have all been trying to ask what knowledge itself is made of. Knowledge is not made of anything. The "made of" vocabulary applies to things like pies. It is meaningless to speak of perceptions as "made of" sensations, or of sensations and thoughts. (pp. 102–3)

Burgeon in reply mounts a blistering attack on logical positivism and linguistic analysis. It assumes the viewpoint of positivism in general—of the whole complex of scientific attitudes from Galileo on—but it denies what positivism takes for granted, that the acts of perception and cognition can be analyzed into their component elements. It assumes, as Darwinian evolution assumes, that "man is a tool-using animal and language is one of his tools." But then it argues in a circle. Dunn implies "that language is no more than one of the tools of a tool-using animal; and if I or anyone else tries to prove the contrary, he objects that we are not using language as a tool-using animal uses tools, and therefore cannot be listened to." Such an abridgement of knowledge is "an outbreak of linguicidal mania" (p. 106). Dunn has some things to say after this point, but it is significant that at the end of the symposium, when the participants discuss whether they should meet again, he is the only one to say categorically that he will not join them.

It is at about this point that the Burgeon-Sanderson-Barfield-Steiner argument begins to take over the symposium. It begins with Burgeon's objections to the rather crude Freudianism which Burrows advocates. Burrows, in a minor tour de force, reduces Burgeon's whole intellectual position to an infantile craving for a return to the security of the womb, and argues further that not only all intellectual positions but the great myths and great works of art in general can be so reduced:

> most, or perhaps all, of the symbols that appear in dreams can be reduced to infantile experience, which is predominantly physical, and . . . even the most grandiose imagery, whether it occurs in a dream or in a work of art or in one of the great myths, is usually a pictorial account of primitive bodily functions or their frustration or feared frustration. (p. 113)

Burgeon's retort to this is much like his rebuttal of Max Müller's linguistic thesis that there once existed a time when every word had a literal meaning and no more. In reducing all symbolism to infantile or early sexual experiences, Burrows is assuming the Darwinian notion that matter precedes mind, and that the child's earliest memories will necessarily be memories of his physical being. But as all words had at one time an old unindividuated meaning, so do the great symbols of myth and art. They will evoke early physical memories but others as well:

> Of course the liquid ocean is a symbol of our origin.
> It is a symbol of the one spirit, the matterless universe, from which we all sprang—for we certainly did not spring from a mindless one. Of course the physical womb from which we also emerge from unconscious into conscious existence is another symbol of it. And of course the paradise-imago is another symbol of it and one which focuses our nostalgia. (p. 123)

And after citing Eliade approvingly, he goes on:

> It seems to me that the paradise-imago—or myth, or story—is in a way *the* symbol *par excellence*. I imagine that is why it is so universal and why it has so many ramifying significances. It is the symbol of symbols; because it symbolizes, not so much any single, non-physical archetype, but non-physical existence in general. . . . You will never understand symbols until you have grasped that prehistoric man in his unconscious goes back, not to the animal kingdom, as the nineteenth century fondly imagined, but to a paradisal state when there was no death, because there was no matter. (p. 124)

And Sanderson adds immediately, "And which for the same reason could never have been fully realized on earth."

A little later on, when Sanderson is joshed about his debt to Steiner, he replies quite seriously for both himself and Barfield when he says that "Steiner is more like a natural phenomenon than an ordinary writer or lecturer" and that he himself divides Steiner's work into three categories: (1) the things Steiner has said that Sanderson has both understood and in some way tested, such as Steiner's "theory of knowledge, and a good deal of what he has said about the etheric world and about the etheric bodies of living organisms"; (2) the things which Sanderson at least partly understands but has never been able to test or experience, such as Steiner's "account of telluric and planetary evolution"; and (3) the things Steiner has said that Sanderson does not understand at all (p. 132). Sanderson makes it clear that he speaks only of things taken from the first two groups—particularly the first—and makes no claims to originality, though he finds it increasingly hard to distinguish his own thought from Steiner's.

The argument turns back at this point to space and space travel. Sanderson, having said earlier that "the 'contradiction' between spirit and matter is of the same kind as that between conscious and unconscious," suggests now that "it is not true to say that the human mind, and particularly its less conscious processes, are cut off from the processes of nature because the former go on inside our skins and the latter outside them." When Hunter asserts that this can only be speculation, Sanderson replies that "the actual relation between human thinking and the processes of nature can be investigated scientifically." The capacity for pure thought, "the geometrizing faculty," appears in children, according to Sanderson, at about the time they change their teeth; before that it was latent in the unconscious mind. This latency, or potential thought, can be studied, and when it is studied one finds that this potential thought has given the human entity its "whole shape and quality." Even T. H. Huxley, watching a newt's egg hatch, remarked that it was like watching the work of a " 'hidden artist,' " not simply a natural process. "The form," Sanderson says, "is built from without inwards," as if by an invisible artist. One may watch this hidden artist at work as Goethe did if one rids himself of the preconception that "thinking is an activity that stops short at the skin." If one sinks himself in the phenomenon one discovers that it is a case of mind meeting mind, not of mind observing matter. Further, the "homology" between ontogenesis and phylogenesis gives us a primary way of examining the evolutionary process, for the development of the individual at least roughly recapitulates the evolution of the race. Both processes "are instances of the way in which a physical organism emerges from a spiritual background and becomes in its turn capable of spiritual activity." Psychoanalysis has shown that there is a way of bringing the workings of the unconscious into the light of consciousness, but there is another way as well, and if we utilize it we can look back, or bring to consciousness, the early development of the individual human being and, by implication, the early development of the race. For the development is a qualitative and spiritual process, not simply an organic one. We can watch the "inside" of organic evolution, as Goethe did. This involves bringing one's "willing" systematically into his thinking. But this willing is not mere subjective feeling; it is "objective feeling, which can be used as a means to clearer thinking and deeper perception." Here Burgeon adds, "Any competent poet or painter knows that." By means of this willful thinking, "he begins to penetrate, with consciousness, into those other parts of his organism where the older relation between man and nature still persists"; he is able to gain "direct access to the past" (pp. 127–53).

And when one sees into the dim past, he does not see Darwinian evolution but a descent from an immaterial origin, like Barfield's (and Burgeon's) view of meaning as incarnating itself progressively in language. As to the question of when man as man first appeared in the world, Sanderson says,

> I say he was there, in his unconscious, from the beginning. And I say it is just that beginning to which those paradise myths . . . point back; that they are a dim recollection in tradition of the state of affairs that obtained before his more conscious life had developed. If your [Darwinian] picture is right, one would expect the recollection and the tradition to contain some trace of it. Why don't they? Why do none of the myths anywhere symbolize this ascent of man from animal, which you say covers all the facts? (p. 160)

On the third day, after a few preliminaries, Sanderson, pushed by the others to elaborate on the basis of his and Steiner's views, does so in what amounts to practically lecture form. By strengthening one's thinking, that is, by turning one's attention to the thinking process itself instead of theorizing about phenomena, one may become aware "of a conceptual area which was previously unconscious." And since thinking participates in the act of perception, one may begin to "perceive parts of the world of which you were previously unaware." It is a kind of "controlled clairvoyance." He cites Steiner's analogy of the eye and light which we have already seen: "How much of the light I make . . . my own, depends on how much looking I do. I do not create the thoughts I think any more than I create light. Thinking becomes conscious in me to the extent that I make it my act." This kind of thought, which Upwater calls "mystical," is thought that "expands from inside the brain to outside it." When Hunter asks incredulously, "Do you mean to imply that you yourself can exist outside your body?"—a notion loathsome to Hunter—Sanderson replies: "I did not say *I* could. I said it could be done." As Burgeon points out, the whole idea of privacy or solitude which we prize so highly is really fallacious, for their whole epistemological argument has been that the individual mind is literally in touch with the phenomenal world, that it forms it and is thus a part of it. In addition, the literature of "anguish"—Nietzsche, Kafka, Existentialism—has discovered that absolute subjectivity is a horror: man's terrible freedom comes only when God is dead (pp. 173–76).

But, as Upwater objects, if we suppose that there is such a thing as potential consciousness outside the individual body, and if we assume that part of this consciousness has localized itself in men as self-consciousness, then how can we talk of an evolution of self-consciousness? For self-consciousness implies individuality, and it dies with each individual human. Sanderson's answer is simple: reincarnation, "repeated earth-lives" (p. 184). The Oriental view of reincarnation—that it is a catastrophe—is wrong, but the fact is right. It may even be—as Upwater agrees—that evolution is on the verge of a new stage, something like Chardin's notion that man is "converging" toward an Omega point. If, by strengthened thinking, more and more men lose their sense of solitude, go out of themselves in thought into the thought outside them (doing this by repeated incarnations), then we may even say that men are evolving into Man. Sanderson sums it up by referring to what Burgeon has earlier said about "taking in" nature as we take in a symbol, not by theorizing about it but by letting it work on us:

> As to knowledge of nature and knowledge of God, if knowledge is the doing of a jig-saw puzzle with atomic events, there is no more to be said. But if it is really a participation through the symbol in the symbolized, it is a different matter. It is a different matter if the sequence of a divergent followed by a convergent evolution is a positive fact and not just a cleverly invented analogy; if humanity was originally one and indistinguishable in the unconscious and is now aiming to become both one and many in full consciousness. (p. 207)

The symposium ends, and a week later Burgeon receives a letter from Hunter, who had expressed some doubt about coming back to the next one. He has had a dream, he tells Burgeon. He was in front of two great closed doors made of some metal that seemed to be bronze. Music began, the doors opened, and three men-like figures came successively out. He paid no attention to their bodies, only to their heads. The first "had on his shoulders a kind of round box with two holes in it, rather like one of those turnips they say boys used to pierce and put a candle in, to make a bogy." And he thinks there may have been a candle in it, "for light was blazing out of its eye-holes in all directions." In some way or other he knows this figure to be Subjective Idealism. The second figure wears a lion's head—"an emblematic sort of lion with a very emphatic mane—spread out in rays—you know, the kind that suggests those old woodcuts of the sun." This figure is The Key of the Kingdom. The third figure is "a man with no head at all!" He is The Kingdom. The whole dream, he adds in Greek, was "Like a breeze blowing from excellent places, bearing health" (pp. 210–11). One need not be an analyst to see the progression Barfield intends: from the solitude of private thought, to the strengthened thought that rays out into the thought of the universe, to the absolute dissolution of private thought *in* the universe, or the Kingdom—or from subjective idealism to Anthroposophy to heaven. Sanderson and Burgeon have had their argument verified in Hunter's dream.

Though Barfield's "Imagination and Inspiration" was published two years after his *Unancestral Voice* (1965), it serves as a useful introduction to that book. The essay traces the decline of the belief in literal inspiration (a being outside the poet speaking to him or through him) to its modern sense of imagination. The concept has always implied the crossing of a threshold or boundary, the coming to be in the writer's mind of something which he has not consciously made. The evolution of self-consciousness has made it necessary to transfer that boundary from outside to inside the writer's subjective existence, from a "wholly other" outer being to the unconscious mind—whether that unconscious mind be regarded as personal or in some sense collective. The older notion implied some sort of possession or mania or ecstasy, so that (as Plato said) the poet did not know what he was saying; he merely repeated what was "told" him. The more modern concept still implies a kind of mystery, in the sense that the language of the imagination is the language of the unconscious; it is not a conceptual message which the poet finds in the unconscious but a message or meaning clothed in metaphor and symbol. And (as we recall from the discussion of the paradise-imago in *Worlds Apart*), it is the nature of the true symbol to be ambiguous, to carry many meanings. Thus the critic or philosopher seriously concerned with myth, symbol, and imagination finds himself in a dilemma:

> Either we strive to discuss metaphor, symbol, image, and meaning in the ordinary terms of logical discourse—in which case, because imagination almost by definition transcends logic, we become entangled in a more and more complicated mesh of thinner and thinner intellectual abstractions; *or* we cut through that Gordian snarl by proclaiming that meaning is something that cannot be talked about at all.[27]

For Barfield, the dilemma can only be resolved by moving away from the notion of the imagination as an end in itself, for this connection of imagination with poetic creation is "a vein that has been, or very soon will be, worked out."

In place of this Barfield turns to what Coleridge called the "philosophic imagination," which is a means to knowledge, a perception (as we have already seen) of Goethe's prime phenomena or the Ideas inherent in the universe itself. " 'Ideas,' as Coleridge said, 'correspond to substantial being, to objects the actual subsistence of which is implied in their idea. . . . they are spiritual realities that can only be spiritually discovered.' " It is the reason that intuits these Ideas, not the understanding, for (in Barfield's paraphrase) the understanding "is the isolated intellect of each one of us, but the reason that irradiates it is superindividual." Coleridge identified "the unconscious self with superindividual reason," and we know that matter, or the material world, is largely a construct of our unconscious minds in the act of perception. Thus to see Ideas in nature is to explore the unconscious mind, for the boundary between mind and matter is now within us, not without. The Ideas exist in both "nature" (outside) and the "unconscious" (inside) and are thus neither subjective nor objective. "What in its subjective aspect is idea, in the objective aspect may, for instance, be a law of nature."[28]

This philosophic imagination, Barfield believes, might better be termed inspiration, because though it does not imply possession or ecstasy, it still does imply "some communication with individual entities, individual beings beyond the threshold." Not Ideas, but "entities"—these will be the discoveries that inspiration will make. Using I. A. Richards's terminology for metaphor—the vehicle (image) and tenor (meaning), or, really, meanings—Barfield asserts that the future of this kind of imagination will involve the discovery of clearer meanings than are to be found in metaphor or myth. The tenor will no longer be "polysemous" as in metaphor but "monosemous" as in allegory. He concludes:

> I do not see us profitably returning to the rhetorical devices of personification and allegory as they were known in the past, but I do hazard the prophecy that, if imagination advances towards transformed inspiration, it will be accompanied by something like a transition from metaphor to transformed personification and from myth and symbol to transformed allegory. It will be a question of finding a kind of . . . language that is not merely polysemously suggestive, but of which the words convey reasonably identifiable and repeatable meanings—the kind of meanings that we can hold, so to speak, between our lips and taste and explore them with our tongues while we do so, though if we attempted to seize them with our teeth they would collapse into dust.[29]

Unancestral Voice is the chronicle of one man's encounter with an "entity" from beyond the threshold, an entity which (or who) reveals knowledge that is both monosemous and personified. The knowledge revealed is, more precisely than in any of the other major books, Anthroposophical "wisdom"—though, interestingly, Steiner's name is not mentioned. Burgeon is once again the central figure in a very slight fictional framework, and the "story" of the book is soon told. It begins with Burgeon and two friends arguing about the recent trial at which Lawrence's *Lady Chatterley's Lover* was declared not obscene. In Burgeon's view, Lawrence's arguments for "blood consciousness" and unintellectualized sexuality are hopelessly muddled because Lawrence knew nothing of the evolution of human consciousness. The next morning something happens to Burgeon as he is lying in bed. Something like a voice begins to speak within him, though he does not actually *hear* the voice. "And yet a train of thought began presenting itself to him in the same mode in which thoughts present themselves when we hear them from the lips of another. They included thoughts which he himself was not aware of having ever previously entertained."[30] (The reader will recall here Sanderson's description of objective thinking, of allowing Thought to manifest itself in the mind, and also Steiner's analogy between the eye and light and the mind and thought.) This is the first of many such "visits" by what Burgeon begins to refer to as "the Meggid," after he has read an account of a sixteenth century Jewish lawyer who claimed to have been visited by a being whom he called a Maggid—a being whom the author of the account variously describes as " 'identical with the divine Logos,' " or an angel, or a being capable of inducing " 'unreflecting intuitions' " (p. 21). In the course of the story, Burgeon comes into contact with the phenomenon of teen-age destructiveness and hatred of authority when he tries, first, to talk to the teen-aged son of a client, and, second, when he has to deal with another client who is closing up his club for teen-agers because they periodically destroy his property. He comes up against the problem of penal reform when he attends a lawyers' debate on the subject. He meets two men on a cruise who argue with him from the viewpoints of Roman Catholicism and Buddhism. And finally he encounters the "crisis" in modern physics when a young physicist friend of his gives a lecture on the subject to a group of fellow scientists. On all these subjects and many more, the Meggid has much to say within Burgeon and, on one occasion, within the consciousness of the young physicist, Flume.

In the beginning the Meggid's revelations are simply cryptic phrases—"interior is anterior" and "the transforming agent"—which Burgeon is left to meditate on. Later the Meggid's messages become much fuller, and he occasionally even answers direct questions, but at all times he stresses the necessity of Burgeon's thinking for himself, using in his own way the knowledge imparted to him. The most important revelation—given to Burgeon in many ways and on several different occasions—is the truth about evolution. It is the view we have already seen: that evolution is a descent from unindividualized spirit into individualized spirit and matter—man and phenomena—and then a continuing upward movement back toward spirit—a return to the One, but not a submerging of the individual spirits in the One, rather a convergence of the fully individuated and fully conscious Many in the One. The Meggid emphasizes that true evolution is a process of the continuing metamorphoses of a single "thing"—the transforming agent—not a process of substitution, not a sequence of many disparate things following each other in time. The single thing underlying all transformation is spirit. The turning point in the process—the point at which descent of spirit into matter stops and ascent of matter (and consciousness) into spirit begins—is the Incarnation. The Meggid speaks of two Jesuses, not one. The birth and genealogy of one is described by Matthew, those of the other by Luke. Jesus of Bethlehem—or his soul—was the product of many reincarnations, as all men's souls are. But the soul of Jesus of Nazareth had never known any previous earthly life; it was "an Eden-soul, unfallen, and given intact from the Father Spirit to be the persisting link between the old state of the human spirit and the new." The two Jesuses became one—but not physically, the Meggid says. Those two souls united

> to form, as it were, a chalice in which the Timeless . . . that both dies and dies not, could indeed enter into time—as it did when the man Jesus was baptized by John in the River Jordan, and the uncreated light, the untransformed transforming, entered his consciousness and became also the Christ of history. (p. 113)

Christ is "the transforming agent in nature" and also "the ultimate energy that stirs in the dark depths" of men's wills. He is the *energeia* of which St. Paul spoke—not me but God within me. And it is He, not men themselves, who thus confronts the "adversaries" (p. 114).

These adversaries are "personified entities," forces which are also beings. They are the enemies of true evolution, or transformation. Burgeon has seen them at work in the debate over penal reform. He has seen them even more clearly in the case of a young friend who turned to Communism from motives of compassion for the poor and oppressed. But, as a fellow-traveler whose function was to create discontent by any means, including lying and fraud, he has become completely cynical. The original compassion has disappeared; he has become "energized principally by hate." His experience seems to Burgeon to be "a sort of psychological progress from warm feeling, through thought, into bitterness and cold." And so it was, as in the penal reform debate, where those who argued for compassion for criminals at once turned vindictive as soon as their plan was challenged. What Burgeon has seen at work are the processes set in motion by the two beings whom the Meggid names Lucifer and Ahriman. Lucifer works in the realm of warmth and light, Ahriman in the realm of cold and darkness. Together, it is their aim to thwart true evolution. Ahriman works "principally in the field of mind, leaving the feelings for Lucifer to exploit." They attack evolution from opposite directions.

> Evolution is the process by which a past form, or a past condition, is transformed into a future one. Lucifer seeks to preserve the past from dissolution; Ahriman to destroy it utterly and substitute his own invention. . . . (p. 61)

Opposite to Lucifer and Ahriman are two other beings who also manifest themselves as forces in the world, and they are the shapers of true evolution. The first is Gabriel, whose work is incarnation: "the course of his impulse and activity" is the turning of spirit into matter; he alternates with Michael, whose "field is the thinking that has been set free from the flesh. He is in the light, but not the physical light. He seeks to descend on the wings of that light into the nest which Gabriel has built for him in the minds of individual men." The Meggid himself is "one of the least of Michael's servants." The Gabriel age has extended from about the time of the scientific revolution to the end of the nineteenth century; and since Gabriel's province is matter and the world of the senses, he has directed men's gaze to the physical world and to their own sense perceptions. At this point—which is the present—the combined work of Lucifer and Ahriman has interfered with evolution, has delayed what should be the start of the Michael age in which man will develop a higher kind of thinking, a thinking independent of their own bodies (Coleridge's "philosophic imagination" in short, the Reason which takes part in the superindividual Reason of the Logos).

Thus man stands at the moment between two phases of evolution, almost, in Arnold's phrase, between a dead world and one powerless to be born. The world of solid matter, of the distinction between the perceiver and the perceived, of the warm sense of subjectivity—in brief, the Gabriel world—is past, or at least is passing, though Lucifer seeks to retain it beyond its time. Ahriman, for his part, seeks to substitute something essentially different from what has gone before—as Darwinian evolution sought to make mind simply follow matter, not really proceed from it. His purpose is "to destroy everything in human thinking which depends on a certain warmth, to replace wonder by sophistication, courtesy by vulgarity, understanding by calculation, imagination by statistics" (p. 59). And as the race itself stands between these two phases of evolution, so do the teen-age Mods and Rockers, for, as the Meggid says, the phylogenesis-ontogenesis relation is a faint mirroring of the true interior process in the universe. The teenagers have just emerged, as the race has, from the relative security of instinct and sense impression, but, like the race, do not know where to go. They sense what is true: that their elders are as aimless as they themselves are but will not admit it—thus their hatred of authority and tradition, which are hypocritical.

The Meggid also reveals much to Burgeon about the traditional world views of East and West as they relate to true evolution. On a trip to South Africa Burgeon meets and argues with Grimwade, a Buddhist, and Chevalier, a Roman Catholic. They discuss Toynbee's theory of history, which Burgeon finds tainted by assumed notions of positivistic evolution. When Burgeon speaks of evolution as necessarily being transformation, and therefore requiring an "immaterial agent" of transformation, Grimwade agrees. The doctrine of "Mind-Only," he says, is good Buddhist doctrine. But they diverge on the question of time. For the Buddhist Grimwade, time is cyclic; for Burgeon, and for Western man in general, time is linear. In this matter of time, the Meggid says, the forces of Lucifer and Ahriman can again be seen at work. Lucifer is the particular enemy of the East, retaining the notion of the perpetually recurring past and thus preventing evolution, which involves a movement forward in time. Ahriman is the enemy from the West, allowing men to see time as linear and non-repetitive but attempting to distort their views of the past (Darwinian evolution) in order to prevent the next evolutionary stage. Man's view of his past is supremely important, for without an accurate view of the past man's notion of what he *is* is distorted; he cannot understand that the immaterial transforming agent of history works within himself so long as he sees himself as simply the product of organic or even inorganic causality. His understanding of true evolution is necessary in order to "fertilize" his future (p. 68). In the same way the Eastern notion of time and reincarnation prevents evolution, for though it implies repetition of individual life, it also implies that these individual lives are static—except for the few who "awaken" mystically to the fact that they are in or with Brahma. But, as Burgeon argues, if awakening is possible for the individual, why is it not possible for the race as a whole?

With Chevalier (who reminds the reader of Hunter in *Worlds Apart*) Burgeon's argument concerns the place of the Roman church in the evolutionary process. In general, it has ignored history, in the sense that it has never officially "studied" history in order to try to find a pattern. It has been content to remain at rest with its deposit of faith, with Revelation, and to assume that Revelation contains the only essential meaning of the world. It has been content to regard the Incarnation as what Charles Williams called " 'The flash and the prolongation' " (p. 93), rather than as an ongoing process in history. That is why, Burgeon says—speaking much like a Death of God theologian—the Church and Revelation are largely unintelligible and thus irrelevant to most of the world today. It has been so sure that history is a meaningless sequence of events that when someone like Chardin argues to the contrary he cannot even be published till after he is dead. And many of today's most depressing social phenomena—the destructive teen-agers, the plays of Pinter, indeed the whole notion of the Absurd—are directly traceable to the assumption that history has no meaning.

But the Church has more than this to answer for. The Meggid, speaking through Burgeon, asserts that it was precisely at the time of the Council of Constantinople in 869 that the Church destroyed the belief that man participates in the divine Spirit, the Logos. It claimed it was dealing with what it called the heresy of the two souls in man, but what it really did was to obliterate man's sense of the Spirit being somehow within him. It retained the word *spirit* itself, but it turned it into an empty abstraction. In so doing, it destroyed any possibility of man's recognizing that this Spirit is the immaterial agent present in the world-process of transformation. "The real point at issue was the Dionysian teaching of the Divine Hierarchies—whether it should continue to be studied and meditated, or should be lost sight of for four or five centuries." The Church thus proclaimed that the human soul did not participate in the Divine Spirit; it proclaimed that the human soul was simply something like "the ghost of a Roman citizen owing allegiance to the ghost of a Roman Caesar." In this way the Church "gradually scribbled over the sublime image of God the Father all those insipidities of God the Paterfamilias" (p. 102). In short, the Church interfered with the process of transformation by substituting something unconnected with the past, succumbed to the force of Ahriman.

The Meggid goes on to speak of the necessity of reincarnation in true evolution. Life and death are part of the "rhythmic alternation" of the process itself, and are echoed throughout nature itself and even in man in his movement from waking to sleeping, in "his breathing and even in the pulsation of his heart and blood" (p. 107). Death and rebirth are necessary, and this necessity is evident once man has abandoned his incomplete distinction between soul and body fostered by the Church. He will see, not only the necessity but the desirability of death, to be followed by rebirth. "But this can come about only as the crude duality of soul and body, or mind and body, comes to be superseded by a growing understanding of threefold human nature in body, soul and spirit" (p. 108). Every death is an embosoming in Divine Spirit (like Emerson's soul "embosomed for a season in Nature"), and every reincarnation is a step toward the final and endless life in that Spirit. But the step forward can only be possible by continuing deaths: death is the gradual movement of soul into Spirit. As men advance further into the Michael age, they will begin to investigate that gestation period—that "period purgatorial and celestial" (p. 108)—between death and birth. They will discover more about the transforming agent underlying all evolution—Spirit—and will see further into the significance of the fact that this Spirit is emerging more and more into the individual soul with every reincarnation. The Meggid concludes:

> I have tried to show you how that emergence is rhythmically accomplished, as is the incoming of a tide with its advancing, and yet continually withdrawing, waves. While he is dead—and then also during his life, while he is asleep—the slowly and painfully emerging individual spirit is again encapsuled for a time within the choir of the hierarchies who brought about its birth and who foster its growth into maturity; yet—more within them now, as more without them when he was awake in his earthly life—he himself becomes increasingly the co-agent of his own transformation. It was the knowledge, it was the very possibility of conceiving this contained identity of the individual spirit within the whole world of the spirit, which . . . was suppressed by the Western Church. (pp. 107–108)

The most difficult part of the book is that dealing with the "crisis" in modern physics. Burgeon's young friend, Flume, describes the crisis to a group of his peers, offers some suggestions about the direction future physics must take, is challenged by several members of the audience, and anwers them—or rather the Meggid answers through him. (In the essay "Imagination and Inspiration" Barfield describes a similar situation from real life. He refers to a lecture by a professor from the Department of Electrical Engineering at Brandeis University in which the professor suggested many of the same difficulties that Flume discusses). The crisis has occurred since research in sub-atomic physics began. The behavior of sub-microscopic particles in many cases does not accord with the laws of classical physics—Newton's laws of motion and Maxwell's laws of electro-magnetic radiation. The system of quantum mechanics was devised to overcome these difficulties, and it is a "brilliant achievement" (p. 120). But it has cost physicists the notion of causality and replaced it with the notion of probability. Moreover, a new version of an old problem has arisen, and quantum mechanics seems unlikely to be able to solve it. Flume describes this crisis:

> In the old days you took the atom as final; then you found that at certain energy-levels this atom of yours was unstable and subject to transformation. So you went deeper and discovered that the atom itself had components and an inner structure. Result: the Rutherford-Bohr planetary atom. But then again you found that, at certain energy-levels, the nucleus of the atom was itself unstable and the behaviour of the particles far from planetary. Your predictions had ceased to accord with your experiments. Result: quantum mechanics. And now? Now you were finding that at certain still higher energy-levels, and when extrapolated to very short distances . . . what? Not exactly that your last haven of refuge had become unstable—because the relation of quantum mechanics to actuality was such that there was nothing to become unstable. But you were again finding—and for a physicist it was the acid test—that in these circumstances your predictions ceased to accord with your experiments. (p. 121)

Experimentally, there is nowhere to go, for quantum mechanics is simply mathematics, dealing only with "pure abstractions" (p. 121). Whether radiation is best described as "waves" or "corpuscles," they are describable only mathematically. Once the statements of quantum mechanics have been formulated, it is "impossible to *reinterpret* them in any way that could render them descriptive of actual 'sub-quantum' events . . ." (p. 122). Quantum mechanics has so limited our perception that it has made it impossible for us to give "any *meaning*—in terms of physical observations—to statements *about* these supposed sub-quantum events" (p. 122). Quantum mechanics works by assuming that the "elementary particles" (p. 122) are purely mathematical points that do not occupy space. Then how can we speak of the *structure* of anything, when the very word seems to imply that the phenomenon being examined occupies space? Historically, physics has always advanced by suggesting a new hypothesis, a kind of model, and then attempting to verify it by experiment. There was advance even when the hypothesis or model was proved wrong. Now the problem is, "How could any new theory ever swim into our ken if we continued to have simply no way whatever of representing to our minds what actually goes on at the sub-microscopic level?" (p. 125).

Flume suggests one possibility. What is needed is a realm of mind that exists somewhere between absolute mathematics on the one end and the "picture" or "model" type of thinking on the other. Very tentatively, he advances the imagination as this realm. He has been told, he says, by those who have worked with the imagination, that it is "especially adapted for apprehending a relation between a whole and its parts different from that of aggregation. . . . It has been said that imagination directly apprehends the whole as 'contained' in the part, or as in some mode identical with it." Further, he has been told, the imagination "apprehends spatial form, and relations in space, as 'expressive' of non-spatial form and non-spatial relations." (That is, the imagination apprehends spatial forms as "symbolic.") Finally, it has been claimed that the imagination is anterior to normal perception and thought, that "it functions at a level where observed and observer, mind and object, are no longer—or are not yet—spatially divided from one another; so that the mind, as it were, becomes the object or the object becomes the mind" (p. 127). What, in fact, Flume has been told about the imagination—by Burgeon—is what Barfield has said about Coleridge's "philosophic imagination": that it is Reason working in the superindividual realm of the Logos. Flume, of course, does not say this to his fellow physicists. What he does say is that he believes they may have to abandon the concept of an "inner structure" which implies the existence of Newtonian space. They may have to conceive of an "external structure," some kind of "negative, or perhaps a potential, space, for which they had no model and therefore, as yet, no equations" (p. 130). One of the things that the Meggid has earlier revealed to Burgeon is that "Space is both interior and exterior" (p. 45). Sanderson, we recall, said the same thing. Flume concludes his lecture by suggesting that

> the elementary particle for which they sought might be conceivable, might some day be conceived, as the detectable moment of transition from structure, or potential structure, in negative space to ordinary "inner" structure in Newtonian, three-dimensional space—with the electric and magnetic fields affording perhaps some slight tantalizing evidence of the anterior process leading up to it. (p. 130)

His conclusion, in Coleridge's and Barfield's terms, then, is that the ultimate elementary particle, the ultimate stable element in a universe of perpetual flux, may be actualized by the interaction of the Idea in the mind with the corresponding Idea in the universe—for we recall that the same Idea has subjective existence in the mind and objective existence as a law of nature, or perhaps as an ultimate elementary particle. "External structure" will be applied by the human imagination.

In the question period that follows the lecture Flume is sharply attacked for his unscientific views, is asked where his equations are. He defends himself well, even pointing out that it is not absurd to say that the imagination may see the whole in the part, for it is an accepted principle of physics that "a single sharply defined wave must occupy the whole of space" (p. 143). In these later stages of his defense he is aided by the Meggid—as Burgeon realizes, though Flume does not. Thus it is really the Meggid who draws Flume's final conclusion.

> What *kind* of source can there be for the complex interacting rhythms of energy, of which we now find that the physical universe consists? What other can it be than a system of non-spatial relationships between hierarchies of energetic beings? And how can we obtain access to their realm, unless we learn somehow to think of them without the help of models . . . ?
>
> Perhaps that will necessarily involve ceasing to think *of* them, and beginning, instead, to think their activity itself. Perhaps it will involve so thinking that their energy, transformed, becomes our thought. Perhaps it is the same as saying unless we learn to hear them speaking directly to us—or through us. (pp. 143–44)

In the days that follow the lecture, Burgeon and Flume discuss the question of chance in physics. Flume does his best to make the law of probability clear to Burgeon, but Burgeon does not really understand it. Later, the Meggid speaks to him on the same subject. The earth, he tells Burgeon, is "the living body of mankind" (nature is man's unconscious being) and it includes "the new life that looks forward to the future" (p. 154). This new, or potential, life includes the future wills of men, now unconscious; and though the wills of the future are not capricious, as the wills of waking and living men are, neither are they regular, in the sense of being individually predictable. Burgeon immediately draws an inference from this about the law of probability:

> Chance in nature, then . . . irreducible chance, is the one token we have so far detected of that sleeping life of will—or rather lives? Technology must seek to calculate even the incalculable—and it can do so only by averaging out the effects of all those unconscious, incalculable wills. (p. 154)

To this the Meggid's reply is a rather cryptic comment that true transformation "can come only from a transforming agent that transforms itself," implying that the self-transforming agent will make its own "laws" by choice. This is indeed Existentialism, as Burgeon says, for it is clear that the Meggid means that man is being made one with the transforming agent. The Christian man of the western world, says the Meggid, has always looked backward to the Father for law in the sense of regularity. "The law of the Father is regular, but the law of the Son becomes only inevitable." To this hard saying he adds that when the Son does the will of the Father, "he will do it voluntarily" (p. 155). The problem of chance will only be solved when the will of the Son has been investigated. (If this last statement also seems cryptic, perhaps it may be paraphrased to read, "when, by successive reincarnations, we have been drawn further into the Divine Spirit and have in this way made our wills accord with that of the Son.")

In the final, apocalyptic chapter Burgeon and the Meggid have their last "conversation." The Meggid reminds Burgeon of the implications of all Burgeon has learned. The further man penetrates into both his own unconscious mind and nature, the more aware he becomes of the vast destructive powers latent in both—but not "both," for space is both exterior and interior, the mind and the object are one. Earlier, the Meggid, speaking of what Lawrence called "potency," has revealed that this sense of power has also been subject to an evolutionary process. In ancient days it was thought to reside in the head, in the courtly love of the Middle Ages it was held to reside in the heart, and in the present it is felt to reside in the loins. Man's present choice is either to take this potency "down into animalism or back into the 'logos' " (p. 33). The peculiar greatness of Lawrence was that he guessed a part of this great truth and was bewildered by it. Early in the book Burgeon has mused over two passages from Lawrence's *Apocalypse,* one dealing with man's physical being, the other with his mind. Of the physical Lawrence wrote: " 'Man wants his physical fulfilment first and foremost, since now, once and once only, he is in the flesh and potent.' " And of the mind he wrote: " 'There is nothing of me that is alone and absolute except my mind and we shall find that the mind has not existence by itself, it is only the glitter of the sun on the surface of the water' " (p. 15). Somehow Lawrence divined that man's sense of potency was no longer mental, had descended to the loins, and he could see no other option than following the descent further into animalism. But in his comment on the mind he also showed that he had divined the truth that man's reason is not personal but superindividual. Thus he had a partial and a puzzling view of the true nature of man. What he did not perceive was that this potency, which Lawrence (somewhat like Freud) often described as a kind of repressed explosiveness that warped man until it was set free, is capable of a kind of creativity in a sense beyond the obvious sexual one. Now, the Meggid tells Burgeon, man must "begin to inform nature, to inform the earth itself. This he can only do by pouring his morality into the heart and centre of destruction that he carries within himself." Lawrence's vision is a part of a great truth: "the truth that nature on the one hand and human morality on the other are not . . . divided by an impassable gulf, but, in the depths from which all transformation springs, are one" (pp. 160–61).

There remains for Burgeon one burning question: who is the Meggid? He is answered. Because the Meggid is a spirit he is all those who contain him—"I am all that speaks through me" (p. 163). Long ago he was called by many different names.

> Men have called me also *Sophia*. Once I was the ancestral voice of the Father-wisdom, the *theosophia* that spoke inarticulately through blood and instinct, but spoke articulately only in the mysteries and through the sibyls, the prophets, the masters. But at the turning-point of time, by that central death and rebirth which was the transformation of transformations, by the open mystery of Golgotha, I was myself transformed. I am that *anthroposophia* who . . . is the voice of each one's mind speaking from the depths within himself. (p. 163)

To Burgeon's nearly frantic question—when a man has heard that voice what shall he do?—the Meggid replies with the great paradox of the Incarnation: Burgeon can be told what to do only by

> the Master of my masters; who is also their humble servant, as each one of them also is mine; as you—if your "doing" should be only a writing—will strive to be your reader's, and as
>
> I am
> yours. (p. 163)

Barfield's most recent work, *Speaker's Meaning,* though published in 1967, perhaps serves best as what might be called a Barfield primer, a useful, introduction to his work that can be read along with the *Saturday Evening Post* article and a few other essays such as "Poetic Diction and Legal Fiction,"[31] "Greek Thought in English Words,"[32] and "The Meaning of the Word 'Literal.'"[33] Based on a series of lectures given while he was a visiting professor at Brandeis University in 1965, the book is mostly a return to the philological aspects of his larger argument. The reader who has followed this argument from *History in English Words* through *Unancestral Voice* will find the larger implications of the argument only in muted form in *Speaker's Meaning*. There is no explicit argument for poetry as a means to knowledge (as in *Poetic Diction*), no obvious advancing of the Sanderson-Burgeon-Steiner world view (as in *Worlds Apart*), no Meggid speaking revealed truths (as in *Unancestral Voice*). Like *Poetic Diction,* it is a study in meaning, but a much more sedate and simple one.

Barfield stresses the necessity of the historical approach to meaning. The work of the linguistic analysts must be supplemented by such historical studies as Lewis's *Studies in Words*. The linguistic analyst argues that words mean what the normal speaker wants them to mean in normal discourse, but without the historical supplement to this position we can never know *why* the normal speaker means what he does by his words. Barfield cites Lewis's distinction between the "lexical" or dictionary meaning of the word and the "speaker's meaning"—the way in which an individual speaker uses the word in a new way and thus expands the meaning of the word. This tension between the "settled" meaning of the word and the speaker's attempt to use it in a larger sense (Newton's use of the word *gravity*, for example, to mean more than the sub-lunary force which impels objects to seek the center of the earth) is what brings new meaning into the language. By implication, this capacity of the word for expansion is also what makes scientific advance possible, as in the case of Newton's law of gravity. What Barfield calls (in *Poetic Diction*) the poetic impulse versus the rational impulse in language, he now calls the "expressive" versus the "communicative." The expressive impulse is toward fullness and sincerity, the communicative impulse toward accuracy; but they are "sweet enemies"—they "conflict, but they also co-operate."[34] The individual speaker's battle with settled language and the poet's comparable battle to make metaphor are "virtually identical." "In both cases language is being employed in what I would call, in its widest sense, 'the poetic mode' " (p. 60). These "polar contraries"—the Do and Suffer of language and meaning—may be called "the principle of seminal identity" (p. 39). The concept of polarity itself is not merely a form of thought, like the principles of identity and contradiction; it is also "the form of life" and "the formal principle which underlies meaning itself and the expansion of meaning" (pp. 38–39).

Towards the end of the book, Barfield suggests briefly a portion of the argument that we have seen elsewhere on a larger scale. There is something, he says, that "the whole character and history of language" (p. 113) shows us. That is that language and myth arose in a pre-historic time, more precisely, in a pre-human time. Neither language nor myth has its origin in individual human intention but in Nature itself. What the study of language shows is

> that the prevailing assumption that matter preceded mind in the history of the universe is a historical fallacy. . . . It becomes clear to us that, both ontogenetically and phylogenetically, subjectivity is never something that was developed out of nothing at some point in space, but is a form of consciousness that has *contracted* from the periphery into individual centers. Phylogenetically, it becomes clear to us that the task of *Homo sapiens*, when he first appeared as a

> physical form on earth, was not to evolve a faculty of thought somehow out of nothing, but to transform the unfree wisdom, which he experienced through his organism as given meaning, into the free subjectivity that is correlative only to *active* thought, to the individual activity of thinking. (pp. 113–14)

So Barfield's great argument ends, at least for the moment. He has said that he is working on a full-length book on Coleridge, and when that appears it should be (to echo Johnson) not only worth seeing but worth going to see. In fact, my assumption throughout the preceding pages has been that Barfield's whole argument is worth going to see. But the nature of that argument is such that I have tried to let each work speak for itself, at the risk of tedium and repetition for better trained minds than my own and that of the general reader. I have assumed that Barfield's argument is like Plato's and Coleridge's and Emerson's: to redact them is to distort them. Transcendentalism, as Emerson once said, is Idealism in the nineteenth century. So we might say that Barfield's argument is neo-Platonism in the twentieth, but neither label suggests the plain fact that neither Idealism nor neo-Platonism is ever quite the same from century to century. They are "open-ended": they take on not only the tone and temper of the times but, more importantly, they utilize the newer evidence that the newer times provide. And since we live in the world of common sense which Idealism insists is a world of "idols," in a way we have to keep repeating the Idealistic argument because our common experience refutes it every day. We cannot *live* idealistically—or at least not yet; we can only *think* that way, and with some effort.

I have said that Barfield's work may be called Anthroposophy philologically considered. It is a clumsy phrase but an accurate one, and it suggests the main contention of this book: that in Barfield's work (as in that of the men yet to be considered) romanticism is really inseparable from religion, that religious beliefs are inherent in romantic doctrine. Romanticism for Barfield is what he himself calls Esoteric Christianity; it is an attempt to explain the world that St. John described as brought into being by the Word and sustained by the Word. In fact, it is hardly too much to say that Barfield's work is a gloss on St. John's later words—*in ipso vita erat, et vita erat lux hominum.* As the Cambridge Platonists said, Reason is the candle of the Lord, our participation in the Word; and the Word, as Barfield has said, is the cosmic process on its way from original (unconscious) to final (conscious) participation in God. The religious position, again, is not a new one—in fact, it may well be the oldest Christian one—but the point is that Barfield has arrived at it by romantic means and that he defends it by romantic means, the doctrine of the creative imagination.

What perhaps cannot be stressed too much is that Barfield's thought (as he says of Coleridge's) exists largely in sets of polarities, sweet enemies that both conflict and co-operate: forces that exist by virtue of the tension that they set up between them. In every case, what keeps them from being pure opposites is the imagination of man—"a repetition in the finite mind of the eternal act of creation in the infinite I AM"—or, more prosaically, man's relation with God or (ultimately) man's qualitative link with God which will occur as the last phase of evolution. We have seen all these sets of polarities in the preceding pages: unconscious-conscious; man-phenomena; poetic-rational; Do-Suffer; act-potency; mind-matter; Gabriel-Michael; Lucifer-Ahriman; speaker's meaning-lexical meaning; death-birth; finally, man-God. The cosmic process—what the Word is speaking—is a great dialectic, as is suggested by Barfield's equating God with Meaning and aboriginal Meaning with unconscious Nature. Meaning may be "given" in the beginning, but it changes only as a dialectic transformation of the unconscious to the conscious. So God may be "given" in the beginning, but He too transforms Himself—remains Himself but becomes something new in Christ—and is thus not only the paradigm of all earthly transformations but the universal constant that underlies all those earthly transformations. Man participates in God by means of the imagination—more and more consciously since the Incarnation—and it is by means of this participation that he resolves the apparent conflicts that the various polarities suggest. God is the universal transforming agent: but this is another way of saying that all the polarities exist within the Logos, for exterior is interior, as we have seen. Opposites may exist between disparate planes, but polarities can only exist on the same plane.

Thus all polarities are echoes of, or reverberations of, the archetypal polarity in the Logos; and that is the polarity of unconscious-conscious, or God-man. The seeming disparity of mind and matter, for example, is done away with once the function of the human imagination in perception is discovered. In the same way the seeming disparity of God and man is done away with once the imagination perceives itself as man's link with God. Once the function of the imagination is acknowledged, nowhere in the universe can there be absolute disparity between man and any other thing—only polarity of man and language, man and familiar phenomena, man and inferred phenomena, and man and God.

But the notion of a polar relationship between God and man is open to over-simplification. Polarities exist on the same plane, but they are not necessarily on that account equals. In fact, there is only one instance of a polar relationship existing among equals, and that is the polar relationships among the members of the Trinity. To the extent that man, through the interaction of grace and free will, unites himself with Christ, his relationship to Christ echoes that of Christ the Son's relationship with the Father and the Holy Ghost. But this relationship is not now and never will be a relationship between equals. (Charles Williams, we shall see, takes a similar position when he argues that the "co-inherence" of the members of the Trinity forms a pattern for all human existence). The involution of God's consciousness of Himself into the unconsciousness of man does not diminish God's consciousness. To say that God is ever more fully revealing Himself in man is not to say that God is becoming increasingly conscious. He has always been ineffably conscious of Himself within man. Man is growing in self-consciousness, being "enlarged" by the consciousness of God. From the purely temporal point of view, then, we may say that God is manifesting Himself in man; but He is not thereby diminishing Himself, nor is He evolving. He exists timelessly; it is rather our relationship to Him that is evolving. At any point in this evolution—that is, so long as man exists in time—the infinite light of God's consciousness must appear to man as the darkness of his own unconscious mind. As Milton's Son says to the Father, "Dark with excess of bright Thy skirts appear." And Henry Vaughan echoes the polarity of temporal man and eternal God in "The Night," when he speaks of man's longing for union with God:

> There is in God (some say)
> A deep, but dazzling darkness; as men here
> Say it is late and dusky, because they
> See not all clear;
> O for that night! where I in him
> Might live invisible and dim.

Thus polarity in time will always involve process; and it is this process in time that Barfield has dealt with. Anthroposophy, as Barfield has said, is "the concept of man's self-consciousness as a process in time."

But it is important to remember that man's relationship to God, even though a temporal one, really does echo the eternal polarity of the Trinity. Coleridge, says Walter Jackson Bate, speaks

> neither of an identity nor of an absolute distinction, but of a "consubstantiality." The ground of this consubstantiality he discovers in the second person of the Trinity, "Alterity." For the Son or Logos is of God, the same "substance" or "being," and yet also distinct from the Father, and, as Coleridge says, this distinction provides the ground of all other distinctiveness.[35]

Man's relationship to God, then, to be precise, is one of polarity in time, but it *is* one of polarity, not one of absolute difference. But such a statement, though a communicative one, is hardly an expressive one. When we are speaking of a qualitative relationship between God and man we seem to need something more: perhaps obvious metaphor, not dead metaphor, perhaps St. John's metaphor of kinship, with all the implications of warmth and intimacy and duty that go with it. *Quotquot autem receperunt eum, dedit eis postestatem filios Dei fieri:* sons of God if we *choose* to be. Yet even St. John's words do not convey the enormity of the fact that God is manifesting Himself in Christ, and thus in man, that His nature and His power are immanent in man's unconsciousness, within partial reach of the human will and imagination. For this fact implies not only that man's nature depends upon what God is, but also that our knowledge of man's increasing consciousness will reveal whatever we can know of God's nature. Thus the ancient oracular message "Know thyself" becomes in effect theology. The Meggid's last revelation to Burgeon puts it precisely: wisdom is no longer only Theosophia but Anthroposophia, not only the wisdom of God but also the wisdom of man.

Chapter Three

C. S. Lewis and the Baptism of the Imagination

A friend of mine, now in his middle fifties, once told me that when Chesterton died it was as if part of his own mind had died too. Whenever a puzzling question about literature or religion had come up, he had always tried to find out if Chesterton had said anything about it. You could always rely on him, my friend said; even when he was wrong, he was so solid. I believe many of us felt something like this when we heard of Lewis's death, and I think the comparison with Chesterton would have pleased him. *Light on C. S. Lewis,* a collection of essays and recollections by Lewis's colleagues, friends, and former students, bears out this feeling of having lost a solidity of mind, a mental and moral outlook that one had somehow always to deal with. I do not mean that the pieces in the book do not pay tribute to Lewis's character; many of them do, very specifically, and all do at least by implication. But it is the man's mind and work that they are mainly concerned with. None of the pieces is sentimental, much less maudlin. Some of them take issue with Lewis on any number of subjects, arguing with him as if he were still alive. Barfield, for example, after forty years of disputing with Lewis alive, is still arguing epistemology with Lewis dead.

The general praise of his work is judicious and discriminating.

J. A. W. Bennett recalls Lewis's comment on Spenser, that to read Spenser "is to grow in mental health," and turns the compliment to Lewis's own work. Probably none of the writers would dispute Coghill's comment on Lewis's critical work:

> he has illuminated a whole way of sexual feeling in *The Allegory of Love,* a whole age of poetry and prose in *The Sixteenth Century,* a major poet in *Preface to Paradise Lost,* and a forgotten universe in *The Discarded Image:* these are magistral books and I do not know of any critic of our times who can equal this achievement.[1]

There are in the collection many tributes to Lewis's style, certainly appropriate, since Lewis is for most people a delight to read, whether he is writing fiction, doctrinal work, or literary criticism. Coghill's praise is the most precise: "His sentences are in homely English, and yet there is something Roman in the easy handling of clauses, and something Greek in their ascent from analogy to idea." It may be added that Lewis's work in general is characterized by a feeling for the fine phrase and by quotation and allusion so appropriate that they seem to have grown naturally out of the sentence. Style, as Newman said, is a thinking out into language, and it is also the shadow of the man. And Lewis's work, like that of Johnson or Newman himself, often has a charm and attraction that derive from his style: partly from the process of the idea being actuated lucidly in language, but also partly from the shadow of the man himself, who is suggested in the clarity and forcefulness of the prose. It has been said that in conversation Lewis, like Johnson, sometimes argued for victory. Certainly it may be said that Lewis's style, like any good style, argues for victory. In literary or philosophical or theological matters he does not dispassionately present an idea or an attitude; he participates in his argument with the whole weight of his imagination and personality. Of course, this is only to say that he does what Johnson and Newman and Chesterton and the other fine stylists also do. It follows that it is "dangerous" to read Lewis in the sense that it is dangerous to read any stylist. With these people, one is not being given Descartes's clear and distinct ideas but the ideas as they have been apprehended and reacted to by the writers. We are relatively safe with

Aristotle and Aquinas and Dewey and other such colorless writers. But we are on different ground when we read Newman's description of the Fall as "some terrible aboriginal calamity"; or when we read Johnson's condemnation of *Measure for Measure* because in it a cynical villain is "dismissed to happiness"; or when we read Ishmael's remark about Queequeg's home island: "It is not to be found on a map; true places never are." DeQuincey's distinction seems as valid as ever, though practically it is no more helpful than ever: with Lewis (and, I should add, with Williams and Tolkien) we are not dealing with the literature of knowledge but with the literature of power.

I have called this chapter "The Baptism of the Imagination" (it is Lewis's metaphor) because I mean to show the progress of a certain sort of romantic imagination from irreligion into Christianity, and show further that the characteristic work produced by the baptized romantic imagination is baptized romance. It is not that the early imagination changes in the course of the progress; it is rather taken up into, subsumed by, religion. Lewis's metaphor puts it neatly: it is baptized; it remains essentially the same but, like the baptized soul, it begins to live in a new sphere in addition to the old. For my purpose the fictional work is of prime importance, since it shows most clearly the romantic attitude toward religion, in fact the romantic use of religion. But I hope also to show that this romanticized religion is also a part of Lewis's popularization of Christian doctrine.

The progress mentioned above began in Lewis's childhood. He is by his own admission a congenital romantic of a certain sort; from the moment that he could choose his own books he was listening for "the horns of elfland."[2] So far as he can recall, his early experiences of beauty were "already incurably romantic, not formal" (p. 14). The very Irish countryside contributed to the romanticism:

> And every day there were what we called "the Green Hills"; that is, the low line of the Castlereagh Hills which we saw from the nursery windows. They were not very far off but they were, to children, quite unobtainable. They taught me longing—*Sehnsucht;* made me for good or ill, and before I was six years old, a votary of the Blue Flower. (p. 14)

Looking back on his boyhood, he distinguishes three separate experiences in which the longing made itself known. The first was a "memory of a memory" (p. 22). He stood in the garden one summer morning and suddenly recalled an earlier summer morning when his brother had brought his toy garden into the nursery. An indescribable emotion came over him, a wave of desire for something which he could not even conceive. In a moment it was past, leaving behind it only a "longing for the longing" (p. 22). It was over in a moment, but "in a certain sense everything else that had happened to me was insignificant in comparison" (p. 22). The second experience occurred as a result of reading a children's book, Beatrix Potter's *Squirrel Nutkin*. "It troubled me with what I can only describe as the Idea of Autumn. It sounds fantastic to say that one can become enamoured of a season, but that is something like what happened; and, as before, the experience was one of intense desire" (p. 23). He returned to the book often, not because there was a possibility of gratifying the desire—he did not know what he desired—but to re-awaken the desire itself. The third experience came through poetry, from Longfellow's translation of *Tegner's Drapa*. He read the lines

> I heard a voice that cried,
> Balder the beautiful
> Is dead, is dead

and immediately the longing possessed him again:

> I knew nothing about Balder; but instantly I was uplifted into huge regions of northern sky, I desired with almost sickening intensity something never to be described (except that it is cold, spacious, severe, pale, and remote) and then, as in the other examples, found myself at the very same moment already falling out of that desire and wishing I were back in it. (p. 23)

Analyzing the three experiences, Lewis finds their common quality. It is an "unsatisfied desire which is itself more desirable than any other satisfaction" (pp. 23–24). This quality he calls Joy, which is not to be confused with either happiness or pleasure. It has only one characteristic in common with them: "the fact that anyone who has experienced it will want it again. . . . I doubt whether anyone who has tasted it would ever . . . exchange it for all the pleasures in the world" (p. 24). Nor is it to be confused with esthetic pleasure; it is *sui generis,* having what nothing else has, "the stab, the pang, the inconsolable longing" (p. 74). It cannot even be said to be really a possession; it is a reminder of what one does not have, "a desire for something longer ago or further away or still 'about to be' " (p. 79).

He found Joy again, in his later youth, in Wagner and in the Norse and Teutonic myths, discovering in these what he had found earlier in *Tegner's Drapa,* the "Northerness," the vision of spaciousness, severity, even bleakness. Compared to the Joy of Northerness, the religion which he professed seemed weak and pallid. His inherited Anglicanism was merely formal, while the Northerness offered him scope for "something very like adoration, some kind of quite disinterested self-abandonment to an object which securely claimed this by simply being the object it was" (p. 78). He found it again in William Morris, in *The Well at the World's End, Jason, The Earthly Paradise.* But it was becoming rarer as the years went on, and finally it began to take the form of a memory of the experience, "joy in memory yet." He had to be content with the memory of what had been even in the beginning only a reminder.

It was then, at the age of sixteen, that he first read George Macdonald. The night that he read *Phantastes* marked the beginning of his reconversion to real, in place of merely accepted, Christianity. What he found in the book was romance of the Morris and early Yeats sort combined with religion; never had "the wind of Joy" (p. 170) blown so strongly through a work before:

> I had already been waist deep in Romanticism; and likely enough . . . to flounder into its darker and more evil forms, slithering down the deep descent that leads from the love of strangeness to that of eccentricity and thence to that of perversity. Now *Phantastes* was romantic enough in all conscience; but there was a difference. Nothing was at that time further from my thoughts than Christianity and I therefore had no notion what this difference really was. I was only aware that if this new world was strange, it was also homely

> and humble; that if this was a dream, it was a dream in which one at least felt strangely vigilant; that the whole book had about it a sort of cool, morning innocence. . . . What it actually did to me was to convert, even to baptise . . . my imagination.[3]

At the time the baptism extended only to the imagination, not to the intellect or to the conscience. Later, when the final conversion to Christianity had been effected, he could return to Macdonald and see much that he had not seen the first time; but what he had seen the first time was a great deal. He had seen that romance and religion could be combined, and that when they were so combined the feeling of Joy was at its strongest. The later stages of his conversion enabled him to see more clearly the real character of Joy, this feeling that came to him most strongly on reading Christianized romance. "The form of the desired is in the desire. It is the object that makes the desire harsh or sweet, coarse or choice, 'high' or 'low.' It is the object that makes the desire itself desirable or hateful" (p. 208). He had not, he discovered, really desired Joy itself; he had desired the object of which Joy itself was the desire and which had given Joy the form it took. But the object had no connection with any state of his own mind or body; a process of elimination had shown him this. Therefore the object of Joy was something wholly other from himself; and this conclusion brought him "already into the region of awe" (p. 208). He was not yet a Christian, but the recognition of a wholly other had made him religious,

> for I thus understood that in deepest solitude there is a road right out of the self, a commerce with something which, by refusing to identify itself with any object of the senses, or anything whereof we have biological or social need, or anything imagined, or any state of our own minds, proclaims itself sheerly objective. Far more objective than bodies, for it is not, like them, clothed in our senses; the naked Other, imageless (though our imagination salutes it with a hundred images), unknown, undefined, desired. (pp. 208–209)

The baptism of the imagination had raised *Sehnsucht* to religious awe; it only remained to determine whether any present religion was the "true" religion. And here we may turn to *The Pilgrim's*

Regress, where the progress from romanticism to religion already described is shown to have a universal as well as a personal significance.

The book, which is "An Allegorical Apology for Christianity, Reason and Romanticism," tells the story of a boy, John, whose early religious training serves merely to frighten him by pressing upon him religious duties which he cannot perform. Occurring at the same time as his religious training, but wholly unconnected with it, are "fits of strange Desire, which haunt him from his earliest years, for something that cannot be named; something which he can describe only as 'Not this,' 'Far farther,' or 'Yonder.' "[4] As he grows into youth, the desire begins to assume the form of an image of an island which is "partly in the west, partly in the past."[5] He gives up his religion with relief, though he retains to some degree his moral ideals, and goes in search of the island. He is in the condition that Plato described:

> This every soul seeketh and for the sake of this doth all her actions, having an inkling *that* it is; but *what* it is she cannot sufficiently discern, and she knoweth not her way, and concerning this she hath no constant assurance as she hath of other things. (p. 11)

He travels westward, away from the eastern mountains and the dimly discernible spires of the Landlord's castle (the Church). He stays for a while in the shire of Aesthetica, where thrilling romantic poetry promises that it will show him the object of his desire. It fails to do so; he discovers in it "the disguised erotic element" (p. 31) which purports to be something more. "He piques himself on seeing through adolescent illusions (as he now calls them) and adopts cynical modernity" (p. 31).

He moves on to the shire of Zeitgeistheim, where he examines current literature and the Freudian rationale from which it often proceeds. He comes to think that the Desire he feels is merely "a mask for lust, and that all systems save materialism are wish-fulfillment dreams" (p. 51). But he is not content in Zeitgeistheim; it occurs to him that Christianity cannot be a wish-fulfillment dream, for who would wish a system involving the dreadful punishments which Christianity threatens? He leaves Zeitgeistheim, returns to the main road, and continues westward. He reaches the Grand Canyon and turns northward into the rarified intellectual climate of the Pale Men—Anglo-Catholicism (Eliot), Humanism (Babbitt), and Classicism (Santayana). These three are brothers, sons of old Mr. Enlightenment; they present a united front against a common enemy—the masses. But they are all intelligence; there is no room in their systems for the emotion which accompanies his desire—which *is* his desire. He leaves them and moves even further north, into the land of Fascism and Marxian Communism; he discovers that their glorious promises are only a "heroic façade," and that they really are "a genuine recrudescence of primeval cruelty and a rejection, along with the humane, of the human itself" (p. 115).

He moves southward along the canyon, through and out of the land of " 'broad-church' modernist Christianity" (p. 137), into the shire of Hegeliana (which is just north of the shire called Anthroposophia and a good deal north of the vast region called Palus Theosophica). Here he discovers room for his desire and also for his moral obligations. But he also discovers that idealism never stands alone in practice. "The Hegelians of the right draw their real strength from Christianity, those of the left from Communism" (p. 137). He tries to become a philosophical monist, but finds that he cannot maintain the theoretical distinction between the Hegelian Absolute and the Christian God. In spite of himself he begins to pray, and in this he is assisted by Divine Grace. As a result, he can no longer doubt "that his Desire, and his moral conscience, are both the voice of God" (p. 173).

So John, like Lewis himself, has been brought by his Desire to the ante-chamber of religion. To explain the next step in the journey, and to point out that the journey assumes an importance beyond the conversion of one man, it is necessary to turn for a moment to Barfield. For the next step—a very large one—is one which Lewis learned from Barfield's doctrine of the universe as the slow speaking out of the Divine Logos. (John did not object to Hegel; in fact he became a Hegelian Christian).

Until he met Barfield, Lewis had been a philosophical realist:

he had held that "rock-bottom reality" consisted of "the universe revealed by the senses." But at the same time he had "continued to make for certain phenomena of consciousness all the claims that really went with a theistic or idealistic view." He had held that the mind was capable of achieving logical, moral, and esthetic truth if it abided by certain rules of thought. Barfield convinced him that such a view was illogical.

> If thought were a completely subjective event, these claims for it would have to be abandoned. If one kept (as rock-bottom reality) the universe of the senses, aided by instruments and co-ordinated so as to form "science," then one would have to go much further . . . and adopt a Behaviouristic theory of logic, ethics, and aesthetics. But such a theory was . . . unbelievable to me. . . . I was therefore compelled to give up realism. . . . Unless I were to accept an unbelievable alternative, I must admit that mind was no late-come epiphenomenon; that the whole universe was, in the last resort, mental; that our logic was a participation in a cosmic Logos.[6]

Lewis felt forced to accept, then, the general world-view of Barfield which has been examined at length in the preceding chapter. Now Barfield's evolution of consciousness (or Revelation of God in man) throws a new and strange light on the subject of myth. We recall that current meanings of words are products of the active principle of division operating in human consciousness (as rational thought) and therefore operating in language itself. If we could trace the plurality of meanings (both literal and metaphorical) in a given word, we would, presumably, be moving back to a time when the word meant all its present meanings and more; we would be moving backwards toward that other great principle operating both in human consciousness and language which Barfield calls living unity.[7] Now what one finds in the classical myths, according to Barfield, are any number of these old single meanings before the divisive and analytical process has begun to work on them, meanings which are "delicately mummified" for our present inspection. They explain (or contain), often enough, what we have come to call the "natural" metaphors, the relation between sleep and death and winter or the reverse of these, waking, birth, summer. If we could trace back such a natural metaphor as the one just mentioned, we should find an ancient single meaning from which all later meanings have descended.

> in the beautiful myth of Demeter and Persephone we find precisely such a meaning. In the myth of Demeter the ideas of waking and sleeping, of summer and winter, of life and death, of mortality and immortality are all lost in one pervasive meaning. . . . Mythology is the ghost of concrete meaning.[8]

Now Lewis, as well as accepting Barfield's evolving spiritual universe, learned from him "a more respectful, if not more delighted, attitude toward Pagan myth."[9] It is not hard to see why his attitude should be respectful. For if myth is the ghost of concrete meaning, it follows that myth is, in a way, true. It is true so far as it is the correct embodiment of the consciousness which evolved it (or as Barfield would say, perceived it). Like everything else in the world which is in the last resort mental, it is something which has been uttered by the Logos, and which therefore has presumptive relevance to that world. The relevance is explainable if we assume that myth prefigures later truth, adumbrates later truths arrived at through conceptual thought or, in the case of Christianity, through revelation. The process might be compared (though Lewis does not so compare it) to what biblical scholars call "accommodation," the theory that God reveals His word to man in the way that man at that particular stage of civilization is best fitted to receive it. Accepting this view, then, Lewis asks, "Where has religion reached its true maturity? Where, if anywhere, have the hints of all Paganism been fulfilled?"[10]

Christianity is thus seen as the culmination of a long religious evolution; as the Old Testament prefigures the New, so all the dying gods that Frazer and others recorded, far from being proof that Christianity is only another such pagan myth, are really glad tidings of great joy, messages sent on beforehand to make straight the path of the real dying God. Regarded in this way, as Chesterton pointed out, pagan myths "make dust and nonsense of comparative religion."[11] This is the lesson that John learns from Father History; but what is more important for our present purposes is that he also learns the historical function of both his Desire and his author's Joy.

Father History explains to John that the Landlord has sent both "rules" and "pictures" to the tenants of his land, though he has not sent them together. The rules were sent to the Shepherd people (the Jews); the pictures have been sent to all the other tenants at various times.[12] At one time, presumably, there was no conflict between the rules and the pictures, but now, because of the machinations of the Enemy, there is. (At the risk of being tiresome I point out that the pictures symbolize the imagination, and the rules the moral injunctions of God or conscience.) The best thing, says Father History, is to live with Mother Kirk from infancy "with a third thing which is neither the Rules nor the pictures and which was brought into the country by the Landlord's Son" (p. 194). But this happens very rarely:

> Even where Mother Kirk is nominally the ruler men can grow old without knowing how to read the Rules. Her empire is always crumbling. But it never quite crumbles: for as often as men become Pagans again, the Landlord again sends them pictures and stirs up sweet desire and so leads them back to Mother Kirk even as he led the actual Pagans long ago. There is, indeed, no other way. (p. 194)

Contrary to the usual belief that the Landlord never spoke to the Pagans, he "succeeded in getting a lot of messages through" (p. 195), in spite of the enemy's attempts to hinder him by passing about any number of false stories about him. The messages he got through were mostly pictures; in fact, one of the pictures was John's picture of his island. The Pagans made copies of their pictures, tried to get satisfaction from what was meant only to arouse desire. They made up stories about their pictures and then pretended their stories were true; they tried to satisfy the desire in lechery or in magic. But the Landlord did not allow them to stray too far.

> Just when their own stories seemed to have completely overgrown the original messages and hidden them beyond recovery, suddenly the Landlord would send them a new message and all their stories would look stale. Or just when they seemed to be growing really

> contented with lust or mystery-mongering, a new message would arrive and the old desire, the real one, would sting them again, and they would say "Once more it has escaped us." (p. 195)

The Shepherds had the rules and the Pagans had the pictures; but neither was complete without the other, "nor could either be healed until the Landlord's Son came into the country" (p. 198). (The imagination is faulty till it is baptized.) John objects that many have said that the pictures were dangerous and could lead one to evil. Father History replies that this is true, but that for a pagan there is no other way. And most men, he adds, are pagans at heart; they will want to stop with the desire that the pictures awake in them (remain simply romantic). But though the pictures are dangerous, they contain the only possibility of conversion for those who receive them. It follows that "those who preach down the desire under whatever pretext—Stoic, Ascetic, Rigorist, Realist, Classicist—are on the Enemy's side whether they know it or not" (pp. 199–200).

Over the centuries the desire-arousing pictures have taken various forms; but always they have awakened in men the special desire for something above or beyond the world in which they live. In the early Middle Ages, for example, which began in the decadent lusts of dying paganism, the Landlord sent a picture, not of a woman, but of a Lady. Men thrilled to the picture and turned from her to the women around them and saw them too in the new light of Ladyhood. Of course, the Enemy managed to garble the message somewhat (presumably in the form of courtly love), but one of the tenants preserved the picture, the new form of the desire, carried it "right up to its natural conclusion and found what he had really been wanting. He wrote it all down in what he called a *Comedy*" (p. 200). Later, in the land of Mr. Enlightenment, when people were being forced into new cities and when Mammon was inventing the assembly line, the Landlord sent them a picture of the actual countryside. In this romantic revelation, men looked at the picture, then looked at the real countryside and saw it differently.

> And a new idea was born in their minds, and they saw something—the old something, the Island West of the world, the Lady, the heart's desire—as it were hiding, yet not quite hidden, like some-

> thing ever more about to be, in every wood and stream and under every field. And because they saw this, the land seemed to be coming to life, and all the old stories of the Pagans came back to their minds and meant more than the Pagans themselves ever knew: and because women were also in the landscape, the old Idea of the Lady came back too. For this is part of the Landlord's skill, that when one message has died he brings it to life again in the heart of the next. (pp. 201–202)

John's last fear is that his island may not have come from the Landlord, since it seems all at odds with the Rules which the Landlord has promulgated. Father History replies that John has proved that the picture came from the Landlord merely by living. Angular (Eliot, Anglo-Catholicism) would say that it did not; but Angular had not lived with it; he had only thought about it. But John's life has proved the origin because John has sought the object of desire in everything in this world and has found that "this desire is the perilous siege in which only One can sit" (p. 204).

I have said that *The Pilgrim's Regress* raised Joy to a universal level. In a later edition of the book Lewis added marginal comments to help the allegory along. One reads: "There was really a Divine Element in John's Romanticism" (3rd ed., p. 151); and another, "Even Pagan mythology contained a Divine call" (p. 153). We may now fairly expand this to read that many things, romantic longing and pagan myth among them, are sent by God to arouse in man that desire for the wholly other which is Himself. *Sehnsucht,* the mountains of the moon, *Das Ferne*—all this is God-directed, a pulley (to use Herbert's phrase) meant to haul man into Christian heaven. "Man's most persistent dream," the momentary and fleeting anguish of knowing somehow that something is *missing,* are but arts of the Almighty, devious means for accomplishing His ends, necessarily devious, since the Fall has made His ends different from ours. Hulme, Lewis notes, has defined romanticism as spilt religion. Lewis accepts the description. "And I agree that he who has religion ought not to spill it. But does it follow that he who finds it spilled should avert his eyes? How if there is a man to whom those bright drops on the floor are the beginning of a trail which . . . will lead him in the end to taste the cup itself?"[13]

We may now turn to the creative work which a baptized romantic imagination will produce, the work of a man who considers romanticism to be religion purposefully spilled by the Creator. Knowing as we do the influence on Lewis of both Macdonald and Barfield, we should not be surprised to find that the baptized imagination expresses itself most characteristically in the creation of myth, or, frequently, in giving traditional myth new depth and meaning. Romantic imagination baptized will remain romantic.

It is tempting here to make an easy association between myth and romanticism—tempting because such an association is partly true. Blake and Shelley and Keats surely use myth, or make myth, in a different way than Pope and Johnson do. If we could simply use the term "myth" to mean any story that is wonderful rather than probable (whether it is truly mythological in the sense of having come down from the past, or whether simply invented), then it would be easy enough to point out that Pope or Dryden or Swift use their myths or mythical allusions largely for illustrative purposes, whereas Shelley, in *Prometheus Unbound,* and Melville, in *Moby Dick* and *Pierre,* bury their meanings in their mythological structures. Charles Moorman believes that Yeats and Auden and Eliot use myth as a way of imposing order on a chaotic modern world, and seems to think this is the main use of myth in the Arthurian writings of Lewis, Williams, and Eliot. "Myth . . . functions as a whole symbol, already ordered and complete in itself, which the poet may use as a poetic referent in order to facilitate the ordering of his particular experience and point of view within the poem."[14] This use of myth, I think, does not differ essentially from what I have called the "illustrative" use. It goes a good way toward explaining *Gulliver's Travels,* and Joyce's *Ulysses,* and perhaps *The Waste Land.* But it does not seem to me to explain *Moby Dick,* or much of Faulkner. This notion of myth recalls Lewis's discussion of "magistral" metaphor in his essay "Bluspels and Flalansferes." One who understands X describes it in terms of Y for someone ignorant of the subject. But once both teacher and student understand X, then there is no further need of Y. Melville and Faulkner and Thoreau and Whitman, I think, talk of X in terms of Y because that is as close as they can come to X. Their metaphor, or myth, is not magistral or illustrative; it is final. The touchstone would almost seem to be clarity or lack of it. Myth as Moorman describes it will lead to a clear view, an ordered experience, even a closed experience. Non-magistral myth, or myth used as the closest approximation to something unsayable any other way, tends toward density and opaqueness, tends in fact to take on the characteristics of real myth, myth that has filtered down over centuries or even aeons. But I do not mean to be dogmatic on a subject that has occupied so many of the finest minds of our times and has been the field of study for so many disciplines: linguistics, anthropology, psychology, history, philosophy, comparative religion. To discuss myth seriously is to discuss the work of Jung, Freud, Cassirer, Eliade and a host of others. In any case, Moorman's distinction is very useful. His definition of myth, I think, applies to Lewis's trilogy but not to *Till We Have Faces,* to Williams's Arthurian poetry but not to Tolkien's trilogy.

Lewis has had much to say about myth. We have already seen that he considers Christianity to be the culmination of the fragmentary truths inherent in the pagan myths: that "the myth must have become fact: the Word, flesh; God, Man."[15] He has even created a "myth" to explain what happened to man at the Fall; it is, he says, "an account of what *may have been* the historical fact," and it is "not to be confused with 'myth' in Dr. Niebuhr's sense (i.e., a symbolical representation of non-historical truth)."[16] Elsewhere, he works out a kind of progressive scale of truth from mythical to historical, though the scale is "tentative and liable to any amount of correction."[17] According to this scale, "the truth first appears in *mythical* form [Here he presumably means mythical in the sense of 'a symbolical representation of non-historical truth.'] and then by a long process of condensing or focussing finally becomes incarnate as History" (p. 161). Thus there is a progress from pagan myth to the Old Testament and a further progress from the Old Testament to the New, the last parts of the Old being scarcely less historical than the events recorded in the New. Such a progress

> involves the belief that Myth in general is not merely misunderstood history (as Euhemerus thought) nor diabolical illusion (as

some of the Fathers thought) nor priestly lying (as the philosophers of the Enlightenment thought) but, at its best, a real though unfocussed gleam of divine truth falling on human imagination. (p. 161)

He adds that the Hebrews, like the pagans, had a mythology; but, because they were the chosen people, "so their mythology was the chosen mythology—the mythology chosen by God to be the vehicle of the earliest sacred truths . . ." (p. 161). Here again, though Lewis does not mention "accommodation," it looks very much as if what he is saying is that God grants man as much truth as man can at that moment assimilate, and that He grants this truth in the form most intelligible to man at that moment. The Hebrews were not yet able to comprehend the full truth about God, what we might call the final literal truth; thus they were given a mythical explanation. Here Lewis seems to be trying to look at Barfield's evolution of consciousness from the point of view of God, and this is really impossible; it requires the reading of God's mind. Barfield would say that the Meaning that the Logos was uttering had not yet arrived at the stage of conceptual thought in human consciousness, and so existed as myth. But Lewis, though he has accepted Barfield's "mental world," continues to stress God's transcendence rather than His immanence.[18]

I do not mean to impale Lewis on the horns of a dilemma which is, after all, one of the central problems of Christian theology. He does not address himself to the problem at this point, but years later, in *Letters to Malcolm,* he touches on it, again with reference to Barfield:

> You remember the two maxims Owen . . . lays down in *Saving the Appearances*? On the one hand, the man who does not regard God as other than himself cannot be said to have a religion at all. On the other hand, if I think God other than myself in the same way in which my fellowman, and objects in general, are other than myself, I am beginning to make Him an idol. I am daring to treat His existence as somehow *parallel* to my own. But He is the ground of our being. He is always both within us and over against us. Our reality is so much from His reality as He, moment by moment, projects into us. The deeper the level within ourselves from which

> our prayer, or any other act, wells up, the more it is His, but not at all the less ours. Rather, most ours when most His. Arnold speaks of us as "enisled" from one another in "the sea of life." But we can't be similarly "enisled" from God. To be discontinuous from God as I am discontinuous from you would be annihilation.[19]

Later in the same book he repeats, "I stick to Owen's view,"[20] and goes on to argue that among Pantheists we must emphasize our independence of God, while among Deists we must stress His divine presence.

At any rate, the view that truth evolves slowly from mythical (that is, symbolical) to historical is understandable. In this view, as we have seen, the Incarnation becomes myth made fact; Christianity becomes historical truth, and all pagan fables and philosophies are seen to be more or less true guesses of the shape of things to come—anonymous revelation—a view quite close to Newman's. Virgil's "Messianic Eclogue" becomes a true guess; the Manichean and Platonic guess about the evil of matter, a false guess. "Plato might have despised the flesh," Chesterton observed, "but God had not despised it."[21] And Yeats echoes the change:

> Odor of blood when Christ was slain
> Makes all Platonic tolerance vain,
> And vain all Doric discipline.[22]

But Lewis sometimes seems to depart from this view, perhaps because it assigns to myth a function which is now past and assumes therefore that myth can be dispensed with, like a magistral metaphor. It is difficult to maintain a "respectful attitude" toward pagan myth if it amounts to little more than a fine primer, useful for the boy but superseded for the man. Thus Lewis remarks that "our mythology may be much nearer to literal truth than we suppose."[23] (In a later story called "Forms of Things Unknown," Lewis decribes three space travelers who land on the moon and are turned into stone when they look behind them and see the head of Medusa.[24]) And John, having on the advice of Mother Kirk taken a headlong dive into the pool and come up beyond the land of *Peccatum Adae,* is taught "many mysteries in the earth," and he passes "through many elements, dying many deaths."[25] According to the scale discussed above he should be dealing now (in the Church) with fact, not myth. But this does not seem to be so. Wisdom tells him that what he is experiencing must be figurative; and the marginal note in the later edition reads: "He comes where Philosophy said no man could come."[26] But a voice behind him says:

> Child, if you will, it *is* mythology. It is but truth, not fact: an image, not the very real. But then it is My mythology. The words of Wisdom are also myth and metaphor: but since they do not know themselves for what they are, in them the hidden myth is master, where it should be servant: and it is but of man's inventing. But this is My inventing, this is the veil under which I have chosen to appear even from the first until now. For this end I made your senses and for this end your imagination, that you might see My face and live. What would you have? Have you not heard among the Pagans the story of Semele? Or was there any age in any land when men did not know that corn and wine were the blood and body of a dying and yet living God?[27]

It is easy enough, of course, to speak loosely of Christianity as the "true" myth, the real story as distinct from all the pagan rumors. But if truth (like Tennyson's freedom) slowly broadens down from precedent to precedent and becomes in the end historical fact, then to call Christianity myth may seem merely to muddle matters. The above passage may be taken to mean that Christianity (for John hears this after he has returned to the Church) is a further and higher "accommodation"; or, to put it differently, it may be taken to mean that Christianity is not Truth but only relative truth, more accurate than pagan myth and Old Testament prefiguration, but still mythical, still metaphorical. But the issue is only confusing if we assume that Lewis's scale of movement toward Truth implies that Christ, because He is the end and fulfillment of all previous symbols and prefigurations, abolishes myth and begins the era of historical truth (fact). But fact and myth do not necessarily exclude each other; pre-Christian myth (as in Lewis's scale) may be largely non-factual, but post-Christian history will be not only factual but still mythic as well. What was recorded in the gospels, as Charles Williams was fond of saying, is still happening. To have known the historical Christ, as the apostles did, was still but to know only half the metaphor. They knew only the factual part of an infinitely larger whole, knew Christ as man, but could not know Him as God. In this sense Christ was not only historical but symbolic as well; for symbols, as Coleridge said, are a part of what they symbolize.[28] Thus Lewis advances the notion in his trilogy that all myth may exist as fact somewhere in the universe, as Medusa existed on the moon in the story cited earlier. The notion is not simply fanciful, nor simply an *ad hoc* argument for the reality of his interplanetary story. In a world which is in the last resort mental, all fact, as Emerson said, will be a manifestation of spiritual truth; a fact (including the historical Christ) will be the phenomenal representation of a noumenal reality.

In this very basic sense, then, Lewis's religious novels, like all other depictions of religion, must be symbolic. In addition, however, they are symbolic or mythic in a much more obvious way. They may be best described as he himself described Macdonald's work: "fantasy that hovers between the allegorical and the mythopoeic." And this kind of fantasy has an impressive effect on the reader. "It gets under our skin, hits us at a level deeper than our thoughts or even our passions, troubles oldest certainties till all questions are re-opened, and in general shocks us more fully awake than we are for most of our lives."[29] In the novels, then, we see a professed Christian turning to romantic fantasy and myth with a serious purpose, uniting the religion with the myth so that the eternal good news of Christianity comes to the reader with an imaginative shock, comes to him, in fact, as romance. Lewis's remark on Christian literature is here appropriate, though he would be the last to claim such praise for his own work.

> When Christian work is done on a serious subject there is no gravity and no sublimity it cannot attain. But they will belong to the theme. That is why they will be real and lasting—mighty nouns with which literature, an adjectival thing, is here united, far over-topping the fussy and ridiculous claims of literature that tries to be important simply as literature.[30]

We may begin with *Till We Have Faces,* which is last in the order of publication but first in the sense that it deals with the end of paganism and is in fact a kind of preamble to Lewis's mythical version of Christianity. The book is "A Myth Retold," that of Cupid and Psyche. The only extant source of the original myth is the second century *Transformations of Lucius Apuleius of Madaura,* or, as it has come to be known, *The Golden Ass of Apuleius.* In Apuleius's book the story is told by an old woman to a young girl being held prisoner in a cave by a band of brigands. It is often taken as an "allegory of the progress of the rational soul towards intellectual love,"[31] though in *The Golden Ass* it seems to have only a tenuous connection with Apuleius's conversion to a mystery religion. Listening to it in his asinine form, he remarks merely that it is a "beautiful story."[32]

Briefly, the story of the myth as it appears in Apuleius is as follows. Cupid has the west wind carry off Psyche, the youngest of a certain king's three daughters, to a secluded place. There he visits her bed only by darkness so that she never sees his face. Under the urging of her jealous sisters, she lights a lamp one night as he sleeps, a drop of hot oil splashes on his shoulder, and he vanishes. Venus, vexed that her son should marry a human, apprehends Psyche, flogs her, and sets her various tasks to do. She must sort out a huge quantity of different kinds of seeds; in this an army of ants helps her. She must then fetch Venus a hank of wool from the sides of the golden sheep of the gods. She contemplates suicide but is dissuaded by a reed, which also tells her to wait till the sheep are asleep and then pluck the wool; she succeeds. Venus then orders her to climb the mountain Aroanius and bring back a jar of water from a stream at the place where the stream begins from the rock. She cannot cross the River Styx and pass the dragons to reach the stream, but an eagle takes her jar and fills it for her. Enraged, Venus orders her to descend into the underworld of Tartarus, go to the palace of Pluto, and bring back a box containing a small bit of the beauty of Queen Proserpine. A tower dissuades her again from suicide and tells her to go to the city of Taenarus, where she will find an entrance to the underworld. She must carry with her two pieces of barley bread soaked in honey water and two coins in her mouth. She is to pass by a lame ass and its lame driver when the driver asks for her help. When she reaches the river of the dead, she is to let Charon take a coin from her mouth as his fee. On the ferry she will look into the water and see the corpse of an old man which will raise its hand imploringly, but she must feel no pity for him. Again ashore, she will meet three women weaving cloth who will ask for help, but she is forbidden to touch the cloth. All of these apparitions, says the tower, are traps set by Venus to make her relinquish her barley bread, the loss of which will keep her forever in the underworld. The bread she must feed to Cerberus, one piece as she enters Pluto's palace and one as she leaves. While she is there she will be offered sumptuous fare, but she must decline it, sit on the ground, and eat only bread. On the way back she must give her second coin to Charon; and she must not open the box containing divine beauty. All this is fulfilled; but when she returns to the upper world she cannot resist opening the box, whereupon she falls into a deep sleep. She is rescued by Cupid, who pleads their marital cause before Jupiter. They are married with all godly ceremony, and Psyche bears Cupid a daughter named Pleasure (Voluptas).

Now Lewis's retelling of this myth is anything but simple, and as a result the book has been much misunderstood. Lewis has remarked that he "felt quite free to go behind Apuleius,"[33] because he considers Apuleius to be the transmitter of the story and not its inventor. Apuleius's story "in relation to my work . . . is a 'source,' not an 'influence' or a 'model'" (p. 313). Of course, what is "behind" Apuleius is not a version of the myth at all but only the material (what Barfield would call the "undifferentiated meaning") out of which Apuleius's late version has been fashioned. What Lewis is trying to do in the book is to recreate the ancient consciousness which saw a part of reality in terms of the myth; and such a consciousness is a good deal older and more naive than the consciousness of the man who wrote it down in the second century after Christ. Or, to revert to Barfield once more, the mind perceiving reality in terms of myth is not nearly so conscious of itself. What we have in the novel is a picture of man just beginning the last phase of Steiner's "flight from nature," attaining to self-consciousness and thereby acquiring the corollary of self-consciousness, the conceptual intellect. When once it is recalled that primitive man did not, for centuries, see himself as distinct from nature, and therefore was not rational, and therefore was not Man in the usual sense of the word, then much of what seems puzzling about the story becomes clear.

The story is told in the form of a complaint to the gods by Psyche's oldest sister, Orual. She has written down her version of the Psyche story as a vindication of herself and an accusation against the gods. The three daughters of the king of Glome (which is vaguely to the east and north of Greece and, in time, somewhere between Aristotle and the historical Incarnation) are tutored by a captured Greek rationalist named the Fox. The kingdom worships a goddess called Ungit under the appearance of a great shapeless mass of stone in a misshapen stone temple. But the Fox has taught Orual and Psyche (the third sister, Redival, is too stupid to care) to treat Ungit in the new Greek rationalist fashion—in effect, to debunk her. The Fox equates Ungit with the Greek Aphrodite: both are merely lies of poets. The land of the kingdom becomes barren, and the high priest of Ungit tells the king that a sacrifice is required. Because of Psyche's beauty and goodness, rumor has gone about that she can cure ills by touch, can impart beauty to others, can, in short, dispense favors like a goddess. The priest fixes on Psyche for her supposed blasphemy and demands that she be given to the god of the Grey Mountain, who is also called the Shadowbrute.

All the Fox's rational admonishment cannot persuade the king to save Psyche, for the king believes the priest when the priest tells him that "the Brute is, in a mystery, Ungit herself or Ungit's son, the god of the mountain; or both" (p. 48). The victim must be tied to a tree atop the mountain and left for the Brute. To the Fox's assertion that the priest is calling Psyche the best and the worst of the land at the same time, and so contradicting himself, the priest replies that he has dealt with the gods for three generations and knows that

> they dazzle our eyes and flow in and out of one another like eddies on a river, and nothing that is said clearly can be said truly about them. Holy places are dark places. It is life and strength, not knowledge and words, that we get in them. Holy wisdom is not clear and

> thin like water, but thick and dark like blood. Why should the Accursed not be both the best and the worst? (p. 49)

Psyche herself partly believes the Fox, partly the priest. She concludes finally that the Fox does not have all the truth, that there is much in what the priest says. She then reveals to Orual that, as long as she can remember, she has had a longing for death. In fact, what she felt was something very close to the *Sehnsucht,* the vision of the island, already discussed. She would look across the valley at the mountain.

> And because it was so beautiful, it set me longing, always longing. Somewhere else there must be more of it. Everything seemed to be saying, Psyche come! But I couldn't (not yet) come and I didn't know where I was to come to. It almost hurt me. I felt like a bird in a cage when the other birds are flying home. (p. 74)

Ultimately she convinces herself that she has always longed for the god of the mountain, and goes happily to the sacrifice.

Weeks later Orual and Bardia (the commander of the palace guard) journey up the Grey Mountain to see if there are any remains to be buried. They are dismayed to find Psyche alive and looking like a goddess. She tells Orual her story. She was lifted out of her chains by West-wind—not an *it, he.* Looking on him, she was ashamed of being a mortal. He carried her to his palace, where spirits bathed and fed her. Later he came to her in the darkness. As she tells Orual this, she leads her into the palace. But Orual cannot see the palace, only trees; she cannot taste the wine Psyche gives her, only water. She thinks Psyche either hoaxed by some lecherous monster or simply mad. Psyche in turn is heartbroken that Orual cannot see what she herself sees; there is "a rasping together of two worlds, like the two bits of a broken bone" (p. 120).

Camped across the stream from Psyche's palace, Orual sees (or thinks she sees) the palace for a moment, but it fades into swirls of fog. Bardia voices what would be the belief of all Glome when she asks him what he thinks has happened:

> The god and the Shadowbrute were all one. She had been given to it. We had got our rain and water. . . . The gods, for their share,

> had got her away to their secret places where something, so foul it would not show itself, some holy and sickening thing, ghostly or demonlike or bestial—or all three (there's no telling, with gods)—enjoyed her at its will. (p. 137)

Orual goes back to Glome and hears the whole thing explained away by the Fox. She prays to the gods *de profundis,* but receives no answer. She returns to the mountain and threatens to commit suicide unless Psyche will light the lamp and look on her lover. Psyche sadly agrees, asserting that Orual's love differs little from hatred.

Orual crouches beside the stream that night, looking into the blackness. A light glints; there is a shout of god-like sound, then the noise of Psyche's sobs. Amid thunder and lightning the bright man-like figure of the god stands before Orual, and she feels that she has always known that Psyche's lover was a god, that she has been wilfully and hatefully blind. The god speaks to her:

> Now Psyche goes out in exile. Now she must hunger and thirst and tread hard roads. Those against whom I cannot fight must do their will upon her. You, woman, shall know yourself and your work. You also shall be Psyche. (pp. 173–74)

In time, Orual becomes queen of Glome. Ten or fifteen years later she takes a trip to neighboring Essuria, where she comes upon a little roadside temple. The priest tells her that it is a temple of the new goddess Istra (Psyche). When she questions him about Istra, he tells her the whole story of Cupid and Psyche much as it appears in Apuleius: both sisters went to the palace, both saw it, both were jealous. It is then that Orual determines to write her book, her accusation against the gods; for she of all people knows that the story the gods have implanted in human imagination is false.

> I say the gods deal very unrightly with us. For they will neither . . . go away and leave us to live our own short days to ourselves, nor will they show themselves openly and tell us what they would have us do. For that too would be endurable. But to hint and hover, to draw near us in dreams and oracles, or in a waking vision that vanishes

> as soon as seen, to be dead silent when we question them and then glide back and whisper (words we cannot understand) in our ears when we most wish to be free of them, and to show to one what they hide from another; what is all this but cat-and-mouse play . . . ? Why must holy places be dark places? (p. 249)

In spite of her hatred of the gods, Orual cannot fail to perceive that the simple people of Glome derive comfort from Ungit. Soon both her waking and sleeping mind becomes obsessed with Ungit: in what seems to be a dream she replies to her dead father's question, "I am Ungit" (p. 276). After that she can no longer tell dream from reality, and in fact is half convinced that there is no essential difference. She goes to a river bank, intending to drown herself, but a god's voice tells her that she cannot escape Ungit by going to the deadlands; Ungit is there also. "Die before you die," he tells her; "there is no chance after" (p. 279). She concludes that the god means something like the Eleusinian mysteries in which an initiate is said to die in evil in order to live in good. And then she remembers her Socrates, his saying "that true wisdom is the skill and practice of death" (p. 281). She sets out to lead the true Socratic, examined life, but fails miserably.

Then in another dream she sees the golden-fleeced sheep of the gods. As she goes forward to pluck their wool they turn and trample her. When she recovers, she sees another woman calmly picking the shreds of wool from the thickets which the rams have rushed through in their onslaught on Orual. Orual now despairs "of ever ceasing to be Ungit" (p. 284). She comforts herself with the thought that at least she has loved Psyche truly; but then, in a vision, she finds herself walking over desert sands, carrying an empty bowl. In this vision she is Ungit's prisoner and must bring back the water of death from the spring that rises in the deadlands. An eagle from the gods comes to her, but on finding that she is Orual refuses to help her. She discovers that the bowl has become her book, her complaint against the gods. She is taken to a vast cave and placed on a promontory before the endless masses of the dead. Her complaint is to be heard.

She is stripped naked. "The old crone with her Ungit face stood naked before those countless gazers. No thread to cover me, no bowl in my hand to hold the water of death; only my book" (p. 289).

Orual reads out her harangue: the gods have stolen Psyche from her, have made Psyche different from what Orual wanted her to be. "We want to be our own," she tells them (p. 291). As she reads she becomes aware that she is confessing her real selfishness and cruel love, that she is at last speaking in her real voice. The judge asks if she has been answered. She replies that she has been: "The complaint was the answer" (p. 294). She has said what has been buried in her soul for years but which she has never been able to say, the word that has revealed her to herself as a responsible being. "I saw well why the gods do not speak to us openly, nor let us answer. Till that word can be dug out of us, why should they hear the babble that we think we mean? How can they meet us face to face till we have faces?" (p. 294).

The shade of the Fox reveals that his easy Greek rationalism is too shallow to hold the truth about the gods. He has taught her to think of the gods as lies of poets and as false images; he should have taught her that they are "too true and image of the demon within" (p. 295). He has learned since death that the way to the gods is not through rationalism but through something much more like the Ungit worship. "The priest knew at least that there must be sacrifices. They will have sacrifice—will have man" (p. 295). The Fox takes Orual to a chamber where the walls are covered with paintings that come alive and move. She sees Psyche at the river bank, contemplating suicide; she sees Psyche, helped by ants, sorting out the seeds; she sees Psyche taking the rams' wool at her leisure as the rams trample down an intruder. She sees Psyche in the desert with herself as Psyche's shadow; the eagle comes and fills Psyche's bowl for her with the water of death. The Fox tells her that much of Psyche's anguish she has herself borne. "We're all limbs and parts of one Whole," says the Fox. "Hence, of each other. Men, and gods, flow in and out and mingle" (pp. 300–301). Orual bore the anguish, but Psyche achieved the tasks.

They look at the last picture. It is of Psyche descending to the deadlands to perform the last of Ungit's tasks. Orual asks if there is a real Ungit. The Fox replies:

> All, even Psyche, are born into the house of Ungit. All must get free from her. Or say that Ungit in each must bear Ungit's son and

> die in childbed—or change. And now Psyche must go down into the deadlands to get beauty in a casket from the Queen of the Deadlands, from death herself; and bring it back to give to Ungit so that Ungit will become beautiful. (p. 301)

But Psyche must speak to no one on her journey or all is lost. First she meets a crowd of people from Glome who ask her to be their princess and oracle; she continues on without speaking. She meets the Fox, who tries to rationalize her out of her task; she ignores him. Finally she meets Orual, who tries to persuade her to come back to their old world; Psyche is much moved but goes on, unspeaking. All things in these pictures are true, the Fox tells Orual; she and the Fox really have done these things.

> She had no more dangerous enemies than us. And in that far distant day when the gods become wholly beautiful, or we at last are shown how beautiful they always were, this will happen more and more. For mortals . . . will become more and more jealous. And mother and wife and child and friend will all be in league to keep a soul from being united with the Divine Nature. (p. 304)

When Orual asks how the gods will become beautiful, the Fox replies that he knows little of it, even though he is dead; but he does know that the age in which they live "will one day be the distant past. And the Divine Nature can change the past. Nothing is yet in its true form" (p. 305).

Psyche returns with the casket and gives it to Orual, to make Ungit beautiful. Orual sees that Psyche is radiant, like a goddess; but then she concludes that she has simply never seen a real woman before. The god comes to judge Orual; she stands hand in hand with Psyche beside the pool in a pillared court.

> I was being unmade. I was no one . . . rather, Psyche herself was, in a manner, no one. I loved her as I would once have thought it impossible to love, would have died any death for her. And yet, it was not, not now, she that really counted. Or if she counted . . . it was for another's sake. The earth and stars and sun, all that was or will be, existed for his sake. And he was coming. The most dreadful, the most beautiful, the only dread and beauty there is, was coming. (p. 307)

She looks down into the water at her feet; she cannot tell which reflection is hers and which Psyche's: both are beautiful. The voice of the god says again, "You also are Psyche" (p. 308). Orual awakes from her vision to find herself in her garden, her book open before her. Her book concludes with her death:

> I know now, Lord, why you utter no answer. You are yourself the answer. Before your face questions die away. What other answer would suffice? Only words, words; to be led out to battle against other words. Long did I hate you, long did I fear you. I might— (p. 308)

The book, as I have said, has been often misunderstood. One critic has called it religious allegory which is "plain to read," religious allegory "in which the great gulf between faith and skepticism yawns wide, in which rationalism is shown to be blind when it stands on the threshold of revelation. . . ."[34] And another critic comments, "This is not allegory; call it symbolism and forsake quibbling."[35] The truth is, I think, that the book is exactly what the title says it is, a myth retold; and a myth retold remains a myth, not an allegory, not symbolism; it remains the kind of truth "which must be grasped with the imagination, not with the intellect."[36] Lewis has, as he says, gone behind the story as Apuleius recorded it; he has gone behind Apuleius's neat allegory (if it *is* an allegory), which is a late and rational redaction of the myth, to deal with Barfield's concrete meaning, of which the myth itself is merely the ghost. The story is a myth retold, but it is not the Apuleius story retold; we may say, in fact, in terms of the origin of the Cupid-Psyche myth, that Lewis's version comes first and is a source for Apuleius's version. For Lewis's version is an attempt to present the almost unindividuated meaning itself out of which myth, allegory and symbol may later be extracted. It is an attempt to present pure aboriginal meaning in which, as potency, all later meanings reside. If this is the case, it follows that the Lewis story ought to have the density and opacity of Barfield's ancient unity of meaning. And in fact it has these qualities: they comprise the critics' difficulties of interpretation.

The major obstacle that the reader encounters in the book is the temptation to accept the characters of the book as "real" characters, people who have a life of their own on the story level although they may "stand for" something else on another level. In short, the temptation is to read the book as an allegory of the sort to be found in *The Faerie Queene,* in which Archimago, for example, has a story life and a symbolic meaning as well. But Psyche and Orual become one, or are discovered to have been one all along: this is incomprehensible on the story level unless we assume that Psyche was literally taken up by West-wind and that Orual, in the end, is simply suffering from anile hallucinations. The truth is that Orual and Psyche are not "real" persons but rather adumbrations of real persons. They have a modicum of individuality and objectivity, but they have not become fixed and permanent. They hover between symbolic existence and fictional reality because the world they live in hovers between potential and actual existence. It is a dream and nightmare world, an early phase of a world which is in the last resort mental. Men and gods mingle and flow in and out of each other, as the Fox says. Nothing is fixed yet, nothing has assumed its final form. The matter of the myth is the last fluctuation of a world which has been in a state of flux since the beginning and is only to assume its final shape at some time soon after the story itself takes place.

None of the people in the story, then, has received the stamp of finality; none may truly be said to be Men. As Barfield said of the ancients who practiced original participation, they are all of them dreamers and unfree. They are (and also stand for) the penultimate stage in the evolution of man. "We're all limbs and parts of one Whole," says the Fox; in Barfield's terms, what the Fox means is that all are aspects of the Idea of Man being progressively thought out by the Logos. All the characters in the book are subject to a revision of the pattern; they are malleable, they have not hardened yet; they are, as the title suggests, without individuality, without faces, the molten lead not yet poured into the mould. All the elements have been collected but are not as yet fused by the final creative act of the Word. In this sense, Psyche stands for, or is, the last creative touch of *digitus Dei,* the last ingredient necessary in the makeup of Man. All else has been present for centuries: rationality (the Greek rationalism of the Fox transferred to the passionate and naturally loving nature of Orual); the capacity to apprehend the numinous (shown in the priest and people of Glome); the very felt need of religion. The only thing lacking is what Psyche has always felt: the longing, the desire for what she can only call death, the wanting to be both with God and in another world. It is no accident that the closer toward union that Psyche and Orual come, the more dissatisfied Orual is with pagan polytheism and the more she feels that her faults lie not in her stars but in herself. Her complaint is against the gods; when she mingles with Psyche, Ungit becomes beautiful—the nightmare gods become "you" and "Lord." Man is finally created when human consciousness is capable of not only human love, rationality, apprehension of the numinous, and need of religious solace, but when it is capable of an intense otherworldly religious desire which can only be comforted in monotheism.

There is in the book what Barfield calls the "pervasive meaning" of myth. The meaning is one which fuses death and birth and life, the twilight of the gods and the birth of God: Orual, the level of consciousness which perceives the fragmentary truth of God as Ungit, and perceives that man makes his own gods, must die so that the Ungit in man's consciousness may die and so become beautiful in the concept of One God. We might say that the pervasive meaning is *growth:* continuous life sloughing off old forms and attaining to new ones (Barfield's "true evolution" or "transformation"). The process of growth is occurring in the consciousness of western man, and the process culminates in the union of ancient religious feeling with the concept of a single, transcendent and loving god.

Now if my imagination has grasped the myth rightly, or approximately so, certain interesting implications follow. I have said that the time of the story is roughly between Aristotle (whose *Metaphysics* Orual studies with the Fox) and the historical Incarnation. If this is the case, and if the myth suggests (as I think it does) that man is not really man until a certain religious consciousness has been reached, then man arrived at his final stage of evolution (and really became man) only at about the time of Christ. Or if that is too sweeping, then at least *western* man arrived at manhood at about that historical period. Before that time what we think of as western man was really what we should call western pre-man, or, as the myth suggests, a shadow and dream of western Man-to-come (in Barfield terms, the slow clarification of the Idea *Man* in the Logos). From this point of view, the ancients are relegated to a Limbo, are indeed little more than the shades in Homer's Hades, little bats' voices twittering and squeaking in the shadows of the underworld, potency in the mind of the world on its way to becoming act. Their existence is one of seed or sapling, an existence not so much extinguished as fused with the later, and final, stage of growth. Further, from this point of view, the Incarnation (and consequent return of the possibility of salvation) occurred as soon as it could, as soon as man was created, or re-created, after the Fall. There is no necessity of making the effects of the Incarnation retroactive to include the ancient pagans (which is Barfield's objection to Williams's theology), for the ancient pagans of a mental world are Man's youth subsumed in the grown Man. Lewis's myth of the Fall is relevant here. According to the myth (in the sense of what may have been historical fact), man, as a result of the Fall, lost "status as a *species*. What man lost by the Fall was his original specific nature." He had been originally "all consciousness"; all of his physical functions were under the direction of his will, as were his appetites. With the Fall, "rational consciousness became what it now is—a fitful spotlight resting on a small part of the cerebral motions."[37] If I read the myth of the later book rightly, and if I may presume to stretch Lewis's tentative theories of mythology, then what may have happened at the Fall was that man lost *all* consciousness, so became no longer man, and then was (so to say) re-created over aeons as consciousness returned slowly by stages of evolution. This view postulates a hiatus between the Fall and the Incarnation if we regard both events as historical occurrences, as Lewis presumably does: there must have been an indeterminate time when man, morally speaking, did not exist, the time coming to an end at the Incarnation. But a lapse of mere "profane time"[38] is of relatively little importance in an ultimately mental world. And the necessity and the effects of the Incarnation remain the same;

as soon as man is re-created he is in the state of original sin and needs redemption. Orual stumbles onto her own responsibility, the fact that she has sinned—and immediately arrives at the awareness of a single, redemptive God.

In any case, the myth is the preamble to Lewis's mythopoeic Christianity. I have said that the pervasive meaning that informs the myth is growth, which means both decay and birth. An air of *Die Götterdammerung* pervades the story. The rising rationalism, the coming of the conceptual intellect of which the Fox is symbolic (or which the Fox is a part of) is driving the gods into the limbo of abstractions where they will have their only existence for the Roman Empire to come. And parallel with the death of the gods is the changing concept of religious sacrifice: both the death and the change point toward something new, something about to be. The gods, says the Fox, will have sacrifice, will have man—in the wisdom of death perceiving that even pagan polytheism is closer to the truth than mere rationalism. Psyche and Orual share the burden of arriving at the new stage of humanity; they are phantoms who sacrifice (or as Williams would say, substitute) for each other. The consciousness of man is shaping itself toward, becoming capable of perceiving, the great and unique sacrifice that is to come to it, the Incarnation. In this sense the myth is a rumor; it is "a symbolical representation of non-historical truth." It is truth on its way from symbolic to historical: truth that will soon become fact at Bethlehem in "the uncontrollable mystery on the bestial floor."

From the preamble we may turn to the current stage of Christianity as it appears to the mythopoeic imagination, to what Lewis refers to as his "planetary romances." They owe much to the science fiction of Wells and his followers; they also owe much to the urbane and allusive school of thrillers or "entertainments" headed by Michael Innes. But they may most profitably be seen as attempts to do what Macdonald had done, to Christianize romance. They are attempts to throw over esoteric landscapes the holy light of Joy. The overall "conceit" of the trilogy is of battle; the books present a crucial moment in the life of humanity, part of a scene from the cosmic play that Aquinas called a purposeful drama.

Ransom, the philologist hero of the trilogy,[39] shares Lewis's views and clearly speaks for Lewis. The "anti-scientism" arguments of Lewis's *The Abolition of Man* (discussed later) are clearest in the first book, in which Ransom is kidnapped by the scientist Weston and taken to Mars, and in the third, in which Ransom, with the help of Merlin, defeats the nearly inhuman scientists of the National Institute of Co-Ordinated Experiments. The second book, in which Ransom travels to Venus and helps to prevent a new Fall by a new species, is perhaps the most purely imaginative book of the trilogy, although, oddly enough, it is the book which deals most directly with theology.

That the trilogy has its faults no one will deny. All in all, perhaps the first book is the most satisfactory of the three, the second the most beautiful. Most of the faults of the trilogy occur in the second and third books, and they occur for the very reason which it is the purpose of this chapter to point out. The trilogy seems to have grown under Lewis's hand, as is illustrated by certain minor defects. At the end of the first book the hero has been given the name "Ransom" as a fictional device, just as "Weston" is a pseudonym for a supposedly real scientist who would sue if his real name were used. But in *Perelandra* it is revealed to the hero that he has been picked for all eternity to do battle with the evil one on Venus; that is why his name is Ransom, which is also Maleldil's name, i.e., Christ. What seems to have happened is that the second and third books are attempts to continue the original story but to continue it in a new way. The first book presents a humanistic philologist fighting a misguided, amoral scientist; it presents a struggle between the old Christian-humanist values and those of godless modern scientism. In the first book the notion that myth may be fact is merely toyed with; in the second it is advanced seriously; in the third, it becomes the basis of the whole work, with various attempts to make it also the retroactive basis of the first two as well. In the third book, Ransom becomes in a way the focal point of all myth; he is the fisher king, the Pendragon, the return of the king. And the whole Arthurian legend is projected backwards into the second book by having Arthur reside in the Avalon of Perelandra and having Merlin confirm that this has always been so. What began as an ideological battle is continued as a battle between sheer good and evil; the transition from science fiction to cosmic mythological warfare is not quite smooth; some ragged edges of juncture show.

But I am not concerned so much with the defects of the attempt as with the attempt itself. As has been noted, Lewis has his hero meditate often on what he calls the "purely terrestrial distinction" between truth, fact, and myth; and Ransom finally concludes that what is myth on earth is fact somewhere else in the universe. What this conclusion allows Lewis to do, of course, is to use the grand improbabilities of myth as literal plot and detail; it makes the wonderful probable. Thus ancient and medieval astronomy and astrology, which most would regard as myth, present the reader with real truths of other worlds: the planets all have their guiding "intelligences" (the Oyeresu) as Plato and Averroes thought; the planets ray down influences on earth, as medieval astrologists thought. Venus is supremely warm and feminine, Mars supremely cold, male and martial. The heavens (Deep Heaven) are alive with intelligence in the form of eldila (angels) as in a medieval painting. Arthur is really carried off to Avalon and, in a way, is still not only *rex quondam* but *rex futurus,* since there has been an unbroken line of Pendragons since his time. Ransom is the fisher king, wounded, "with the arid plain behind me," who must be healed before the wasteland of the earth can become fertile. His wound will be stanched in the world where it was received, in Perelandra, and when Perelandra has made ten thousand turns around the Field of Arbol, the dark eldil of earth will be defeated and the world will become as it was in the time of Numinor, the true west, which was indeed a green and pleasant land.

Further, the use of myth as fact allows Lewis to use the great natural metaphors which run through the myths as cosmic facts. The moon's shadow and the dark veil around Venus are evil because they are dark (or are dark *and* evil) and will one day be dispersed by the good light of the Deep Heaven. The eldila are perceivable only as glints of light, and are explained in terms of light as well as motion. Ransom's vision of eternal beatitude at the end of *Perelandra* is described as a vast cosmic dance of bands and cords and patterns of light. Behind all this is a philological-metaphysical theory derived, in part at least, from Barfield's theory of ancient concrete meaning:

> if those original equations, between good and light, or evil and dark, between breath and soul and all the others, were from the beginning arbitrary and fanciful—if there is not, in fact, a kind of psychophysical parallelism (or more) in the universe—then all our thinking is nonsensical. But we cannot, without contradiction, believe it to be nonsensical. And so . . . the view I have taken has metaphysical implications.[40]

The use of natural metaphor as fact allows Lewis to use the "original equations" as the structure of planetary reality, a hierarchy in which the greatest good is light and the greatest evil, dark.

But it remains to ask the effect of mythologizing religion, to ask in short the point and purpose of the four novels. The answer, so far as Lewis himself is concerned, is simple enough: his purpose was to combine an old love with a newer, to combine the romance of the far off and faerie with the religion of his maturity, to unite what the imagination loved with what the intellect was convinced to be true. In short, his purpose was, as I have said in more general terms, to romanticize religion.

Now, it is often said by anti-romantics that the romantic throws up a screen between himself and reality, that he idealizes or dignifies a reality which he would otherwise find unendurable. As one such critic has it, he tries to "maintain an illusioned view of the universe"[41] in the face of broad scientific evidence that the real nature of the world is other than he wants it to be. He tries to see reality as wonderful when it is only probable and even predictable. Or, again, it is a criticism of the romantic that he inhabits (by choice) a dream world, simply abandoning the real world for that of faerie, the land of heart's desire. There is a substratum of agreement between the two criticisms: both hold that the romantic prefers, even demands, the wonderful—one party holding that the romantic romanticizes this world (witchery by daylight), the other holding that the romantic abdicates this world for another of his own making and closer to his heart's desire. The romantic can reply, alternatively, that this world is more wonderful than the anti-romantic supposes; he can, like Chesterton, romanticize even the very notion of being as the Aristotelian scholastics conceived it. Or he can reply, like Shelley, that his dream world has more reality and validity than our own, that his creations are "more real than living men, Nurslings of immortality." (We have already seen that Barfield praises this second school *because* their esemplastic images did not reproduce reality as we know it but instead created their own.)

Everyone will agree that the romantic will have the wonderful, one way or another. So it is too with a romantic religionist of Lewis's sort. He will have his religion because he believes it true; but he will also have it wonderful because he is romantic. Lewis sometimes dramatizes the romance of being, though never to the extent that Chesterton did in *Manalive* (perhaps because, in spite of Lewis's admiration for Chesterton, the fact remains that Chesterton was a Thomistic, "moderate" realist or "conceptualist" and Lewis is not). But what he does in his fiction is rather to take religion out of the normal world and translate it into the fairy land of myth. Thus the beginnings of Christianity (or the end of paganism) are seen against a backdrop of shadows and semi-darkness in *Till We Have Faces;* Christianity indeed is imaged as a bright dream following on aeons of dark and fearsome ones. All the dimness and opacity of the far mythical past are conjured up in order that they may enhance the birth of Christ; Homer, Sappho, Plato become dreams in order that Christ may seem more real. All the bright hard world of Aristotle is made pliable, is made to retreat into a swirling world of flux where Psyche and Orual are neither real nor symbolic but merely ingredients. The whole of the ancient world is made potency so that the Incarnation may be seen as act. It is the world of Cornford and Edwin Hatch, but it has been manipulated out of reality and into dream.

In the trilogy, Christianity—the very story of Christianity as well as many of its dogmas—is translated into mythology in order that Christianity may seem more wonderful (not more wonderful than it is, perhaps, but more wonderful than we ordinarily conceive it). Romance, beginning as a means to Christianity, is now used as a servant to Christianity. The whole trilogy is full of the old Chestertonian device of making something marvelous by describing it in terms that we never use for it, of making us see something as if for the first time. The drama of the Incarnation takes on a strange new light in being told by a naked green woman on a floating island on Venus, as the Fall assumes new grandeur by being almost repeated. Maleldil, so truly in motion that He is still (a psycho-physical parallel of God's infinite act?); Maleldil the Young locked in battle with the Dark Eldil of Thulcandra, setting an impassable frontier against him across the face of the moon; Maleldil reviving Merlin after fifteen hundred years so that he may join the Pendragon and the planetary Oyeresu in the fight against the Bent One—what could be more wonderful, what could be less like not only what Newman called "the dreary, hopeless irreligion" of the time but less like the very religion itself of the time? Lewis's religion seems hardly to belong to the same century, or the same world, as Eliot's *Thoughts after Lambeth,* or Jaspers's and Bultmann's discussion of myth and religion, or the work of Camus.

Nor is it improper to compare Lewis's mythology with the religious writings of the time, for none of the four books is simply donnish fooling with religion. There runs through all the books what has come to be called (since Otto) the feeling of the numinous; there is, in fact, the element which Lewis found in Macdonald and was forced to call holiness. But the feeling of the numinous is never directly attached to the Christian God or to Christ, but to Maleldil or Maleldil the Young; awe is not felt in the presence of the seraphim or powers but in the presence of the planetary Oyeresu. Orual feels that she is being unmade at the approach of an undefined and pre-Christian divine presence. When Ransom first sees Meldilorn, the island palace of the Oyarsa of Mars, Lewis describes it as "virginal," "still," and "secret" and adds, purposely, that its tree tops were taller than the cathedral spires on earth. When the Oyarsa of Mars comes before Ransom, Ransom's "heart and body seemed to be made of water." When he hears the funeral hymn of the hrossa, his spirit bows down "as if the gate of heaven had opened before him." In the closing pages of *That Hideous Strength,* Ransom, soon to be assumed to Perelandra, says goodby to the company of faithful and, prelate-like, blesses them in Old Solar: *"Urendi Maleldil"* (presumably *Dominus vobiscum*). In short, holiness or awe of the divine presence runs through the books, but it is always directed at the mythical counterparts of the Christian trinity or angelology. Given the framework of the books, of course, this is what is to be expected. But it is with the purpose and the desired effect that I am concerned here. And the purpose is to romanticize this-worldly Christianity by seeing it as something else or as a part of something else, the something else being other-worldly and wonderful.

The extent to which Lewis has romanticized Christianity in his fiction may be emphasized by a contrast with Christianity as it is presented sympathetically but "realistically" by such writers as Greene or Waugh or Mauriac. The best of Greene's characters have a touch of brightness about them that is due largely to their religion, but for the most part their lives are bleak and mundane. Often enough in his work the religion is accepted in a hopeless, desperate way, as in the case of Scobie in *The Heart of the Matter*, who says his Christian prayer as he commits suicide. Sometime it is accepted as a dreary answer to the dreary question of the world, as in the case of the police chief in *The Quiet American* who reads the "sad arguments" of Pascal while he waits for the next footpad or mugger to be brought in. And in Waugh, Christianity becomes a kind of passionless intellectual achievement at best, at worst a kind of social snobbery. For Richard Crouchback Christianity presents a system of abstract rules; it is a legalistic game which mortals play with God in which a man may try to make love to his divorced wife because he is still theologically married to her. Waugh's Christianity is much like Mr. Angular's: it knows all the answers, it is all intellect. When a mild theological controversy occurred concerning Scobie's ultimate destination (though a suicide, he had acted out of motives of sheer love for both his wife and mistress), Waugh displayed no indecision, no disposition to dwell on either *eros* or *agape;* Scobie, he said, was in hell, where he richly deserved to be. Now to "realistic" Christianity Lewis opposes mythopoeic Christianity, made wonderful by being shown to be a part of a vast web of cosmic romance, a religion grown out of a dim and flickering and unreal past into a present heightened by an interplanetary war between good and evil in which Arthur unites with the twelfth-century Platonists, a religion which will ultimately bring man to the pinnacle from which he can watch the Great Dance.

The romanticism of the trilogy is perhaps made more clear by setting it over against other attempts to do roughly the same sort of thing, that is, to show the battle of Christianity against the forces of evil. One of the clearest distinctions between classical and romantic may be drawn from a comparison of Milton's battle and Lewis's. Milton's is traditional and epic: the battle is between, not equals, of course, but between beings who are far above human capacity; Adam and Eve are, as it were, local pawns in the cosmic battle between forces of good and evil beyond their comprehension. All the grandeur and sublimity of the battle scenes, of the temptation, of the angelic fall from peace, derive from the fact that the beings involved are supernatural, with infinite capacities for good and evil, for suffering and joy. The angelic battle is described as a battle of the Titans because, for artistic purposes, it is simply that; it is heroic, the primal battle of the earliest age of the heroes. In Lewis the battle has descended to the human level: a middle-aged philologist counseled by the Almighty fights a middle-aged scientist possessed by the devil; the fight is no longer on the plains of heaven, nor even on the ringing plains of windy Troy, but in a glade, in the shallows of a lake, in an underwater cave. The whole thing has become localized and intimate, like part of a Wordsworthian landscape. And yet the issues are, if not the same, at least equally important. As much depends on Ransom as on Milton's Christ. But the sense of cosmic objectivity has gone, perhaps because the tradition itself has gone; Milton is retelling an old and "true" story, but Lewis is making one up. Intimations of the divine come flooding into Ransom from Maleldil much as intimations come flooding into Wordsworth from Nature, while in Milton any divine communication is simply formal, as when Michael lectures Adam on the future.

Again, Bunyan's Christian takes on a stature and nobility that Ransom or John (in *The Pilgrim's Regress*) never achieve because Christian is everyman, or at least every Christian. Bunyan's images, meant to convey the truths of Christianity, fail to be romantic by being clearly allegorical; the Slough of Despond and the Delectable Mountains (like Milton's darkness visible) have no local habitation, nor are they dwelt on for their own sake; they exist just so far as they are allegorical, as they are representations of the state of the soul.

But the romanticism of the trilogy is most distinguishable in the very romanticizing of reality itself, so far as the religious battle is concerned. The image of battle has always suggested itself as the appropriate one to convey the human religious situation. But battles in general, and particularly religious battles, are hardly ever exciting, or at least the excitement is hardly ever of any appreciable duration. Any soldier knows that, just as any religious man knows it. For every pitched battle, or even faintly exciting skirmish, there are long and bleak periods of entrenchment, or troop movement, or even of activity having nothing at all to do with the war. Every war is ninety percent sheer boredom or unwarlike occupations. As Auden says, "The Time Being is, in a sense, the most trying time of all." Ransom is always in the midst of battle; at every moment the outcome of the world is in doubt. But Auden suggests the real flatness of the great part of the struggle:

> In the meantime
> There are bills to be paid, machines to keep in repair,
> Irregular verbs to learn, the Time Being to redeem
> From insignificance. The happy morning is over,
> The night of agony still to come; the time is noon:
> When the Spirit must practise his scales of rejoicing
> Without even a hostile audience, and the Soul endure
> A silence that is neither for nor against her faith
> That God's Will will be done, that, in spite of her prayers
> God will cheat no one, not even the world of its triumph.[42]

For most Christians, the time is noon, but never for Lewis's characters.

It may be objected at this point that a writer like Lewis, who is not after all primarily a theologian, may choose to deal romantically with religion in his fiction without its following necessarily that his religion itself is romantic. But a brief examination of his doctrinal works and the general source from which they largely derive will show that this is not the case, that in fact (as I said in Chapter 1) his romanticism is not distinguishable from his religion. First of all, as an introduction to the doctrinal works, I must make one last point about the fiction. It will not have escaped notice that the fiction, the trilogy especially, manages to argue for Christianity without at any time going at all deeply into the real dogmas of Christianity. On the eve of Ransom's fight with the devil, for example, Ransom is in communion with the Almighty (Maleldil); and it is made perfectly clear that Ransom is to perform a heroic deed in order that a new Redemption will not be necessary on Perelandra. But in what exactly the earthly Redemption consists, what it was that Christ did, these questions of theology never occur. The only point of theology that is dealt with in the trilogy is the paradox of the fortunate fall (in *Perelandra*), and that takes on the aspect of a tour de force, with the devil admitting defeat in a mournful howl. Now I do not mean to suggest that fiction is the appropriate place for theological discussion; I do not mean to suggest even that the fiction suffers from the lack of it (the reverse is probably true). What I do suggest is that the presence of Christianity and the near absence of dogma may be at least as much an extension of a religious attitude as it is an artistic necessity.

Let us turn for a moment to Lewis's *Mere Christianity,* a book in which Lewis tries to sketch out for the unbeliever the body of belief which "has been common to nearly all Christians at all times."[43] In an effort not to scandalize the pagan reader, Lewis makes the section called "What Christians Believe" utterly undenominational (to the extent that various sects are mentioned only in alphabetical order). He attempts, as he does in the trilogy and other apologetical works such as *The Screwtape Letters* and *The Great Divorce,* to distinguish Christianity as a homogeneous body of belief which may be set over against paganism (old or new), modern materialism, and "scientism," which may be described as the emancipated modern belief that science holds the answers to questions about the human situation, questions that it has traditionally been within the province of religion to answer. Thus the whole historical aspect of Christianity—the religious wars, the doctrinal disputes, the Inquisition, the Reformation itself—all this is ignored on the ground that "Our divisions should never be discussed except in the presence of those who have already come to believe that there is one God and that Jesus Christ is His only Son" (p. vi). Throughout, an attempt is made to see Christianity, as it were, empirically; not to teach theology but to stress the fact that Christianity "works," is operative. Thus of the Atonement, Lewis comments that it has given us "a fresh start," but that "theories as to how it did this are another matter." And the Eucharist he calls "a mysterious action which different Christians call by different names." In the matter of dogma, in short, the conclusion is that "the thing itself is infinitely more important than any explanations that theologians have produced," and that "no explanation will ever be quite adequate to the reality" (p. 43).

Now an unfriendly or zealously rationalistic critic might see in such an attitude evidence of anti-rationalism or even fideism. But such a view is short-sighted and too simple. No one familiar with Lewis's university sermons (to mention only one source) could accuse Lewis either of irrationalism or lack of interest in theology. It is rather that, as a layman, he feels that he has to "walk *in mirabilibus supra me* and submit all to the verdict of real theologians."[44] But such admirable humility is yet only half the story. For the informing spirit of Lewis's Christianity, and for the position that theology occupies in his religion, we must turn elsewhere. I have already indicated Lewis's many debts to Barfield and have indeed spoken of Barfield as "the man behind" Lewis. But examination of Lewis's doctrinal work shows that the real man behind Lewis is, not unexpectedly, the same as the one behind Barfield: Coleridge. Examination shows that Lewis's Christianity is not merely "Pauline" (as Miss Nott[45] calls it) but rather transcendental in the sense in which that word is applicable to the beliefs of Coleridge and Kant. Once the kinship is seen, Lewis's doctrinal works fall easily and truly into place as complements to the mythopoeic Christianity of the fiction.

The clearest evidence of the religious kinship is to be found in Lewis's *The Abolition of Man,* a book which makes the same point as *That Hideous Strength*—that the real and crucial battle of our time is between Christianity and scientism. In the course of the argument Lewis refers to the "Tao," the combined wisdom of the world, which the Chinese had defined as "the reality beyond all predicates, the abyss that was before the Creator Himself. It is Nature, it is the Way, the Road. It is the Way in which the universe goes on, the Way in which things everlastingly emerge, stilly and tranquilly, into space and time."[46] It is this Way or "law of nature" that all must assent to, must affirm. It is the necessary premise to any argument; it is undemonstrable but obligatory. But how affirm an undemonstrable premise? By an act of the practical reason, for the premise is in fact a "platitude" of the practical reason, and "we must accept the ultimate platitudes of practical reason as having absolute validity. . . ."[47] Against the "understanding" of science in the realm of morality, Lewis opposes, in Coleridge's words, the "practical reason of Man, comprehending the will, the conscience, the moral being with its inseparable interests and affections—that reason . . . which is the organ of wisdom, and (as far as man is concerned) the source of living and actual truths."[48] In a word, the assent to the Tao is a non-conceptual assent, a moral affirmation.

Now such an affirmation supposes the whole of the Kant-Coleridge distinction between, respectively, the understanding and the reason, and the pure or speculative reason and the practical. The understanding, as Coleridge defined it, is an adaptive faculty common to both men and beasts; it is, in man, a higher and more subtle form of the instinct that leads the ant and the bee to build roads, walls, hives in order to obtain a certain goal of ease or security. It is discursive, it makes syllogisms, it abstracts and compares and generalizes. It is limited in its operation in the sense that the materials it works with are phenomena, that is, reality perceived according to the Kantian categories of space and time and organized according to the Kantian forms of perception (substance, quantity, cause, effect, and so on). It does not work with the noumenal reality because it does not perceive the noumenal reality; it can see noumena only in terms of phenomena (Barfield's collective representations). If it tries to go beyond this sphere, if it tries to deal discursively with noumenal reality, it becomes "the meddling intellect," murdering to dissect a transcendental reality perceptible only to the reason. The reason (either speculative or practical) is a single power of knowing in which all men share, while there are as many understandings as there are men and beasts. Reason is the Word, the Logos; it perceives things of the spirit as the senses perceive material things; it is "reasoning from infinite to infinite," while understanding is "reasoning from finite to finite" (p. 209). It is not inference (the Logos has no need to infer); it is spiritual perception.

It is this reason considered under its practical (or moral) aspect which Lewis utilizes in the assent to the existence of Natural Law, or to the reality and validity of conscience. We recall that he agrees with Barfield that our logic is a participation in the cosmic Logos, which is an echo of Coleridge's belief that reason is "part of the image of God in us" (p. 200). And it is reason considered under its pure or speculative aspect which is the basis of much of Lewis's doctrinal work such as *The Problem of Pain, Miracles,* and the university sermons. Coleridge had assigned a particular function to speculative reason in matters of theology. It is to be used to buttress the truths of faith which have been apprehended by the assent of the practical reason, truths which have been presented for acceptance by Revelation. "It is its office and rightful privilege to determine on the negative truth of whatever we are required to believe. The doctrine must not contradict any universal principle: for this would be a doctrine that contradicted itself" (p. 222). The distinction here is nice: it is not to establish the truth of dogma (that has been established by practical reason, or moral assent); it is rather to show that the dogma is not contrary to reason. In other words, the function of pure reason is to work at hypotheses, not in the hope of arriving at truth of dogma but rather in the hope of showing that it is not absurd to believe the dogma. So, in *The Problem of Pain,* Lewis's concern is to establish reasonable hypotheses about the existence of mental and physical anguish in the world; the fact that pain should exist must be shown to be not irreconcilable with the established truths of Christianity. Pain thus becomes "God's megaphone," a means by which God tries to make unrepentant man turn to Him. "It gives the only opportunity the bad man can have for amendment. It removes the veil; it plants the flag of truth within the fortress of a rebel soul."[49]

In *Miracles*, Lewis attempts to show that miracles are amenable to reason by hazarding that what seems miraculous in our nature is perhaps merely natural in another; what we perceive when we see a "miracle" is not really a miracle at all but a bringing together of two different and perhaps opposite natures. God, for reasons known only to Him, allows two such natures to come into contact, and for a moment one nature operates according to the laws of the other; the result seems to us miraculous (i.e., inexplicable). In any case, once the miraculous phenomenon has occurred, it is received into the nature we know, and begins to abide by the natural laws of our own earth. The Virgin Birth is a miracle, but Christ went through the nine months of gestation. Nature absorbs the miraculous into itself.

But the negative function of Pure Reason in theological matters is most evident in Lewis's university sermons, particularly in the two entitled "The Weight of Glory" and "Transposition." In the first, Lewis deals with the Christian concept of glory, the state we will assume in beatitude. If it means fame or good reputation, it seems to contradict the Christian notion of humility. But when it is suggested that it does not mean fame among men but rather praise by God, it is seen to be not contradictory to reason. And if it means "brightness, splendour, luminosity," it seems at first rather silly: "who wishes to become a kind of living electric light bulb?" But again speculation shows the doctrine not to be absurd, but in fact to be founded on one of the deepest and most common of human desires, the desire for beauty. Here and now we can only perceive beauty; but we want more.

> We want something else which can hardly be put into words—to be united with the beauty we see, to pass into it, to receive it into ourselves, to bathe in it, to become part of it. That is why we have peopled air and earth and water with gods and goddesses and nymphs and elves—that, though we cannot, yet these projections can, enjoy in themselves that beauty, grace, and power of which Nature is the image.[50]

In the state of beatitude, this deep desire will be somehow fulfilled, and though we do not know how, yet it is enough that the doctrine has been shown to be reasonable.

"Transposition" is an attempt to show the reasonableness of the phenomenon of "glossolalia," or "speaking with tongues." We believe that the apostles spoke with tongues, yet we have evidence from revival meetings that something much like that same phenomenon sometimes occurs and produces a torrent of gibberish. We are forced into the position of holding that "the very same phenomenon which is sometimes not only natural but even pathological is at other times (or at least one other time) the organ of the Holy Ghost." Lewis attempts to remove the apparent absurdity by pointing out that when the Almighty acts in our Nature, he acts within the limitations of that Nature; analogously, we have the case of lust and love, which both culminate in the sexual act but which are different things. The human body has limitations; its organs must be used for many purposes, and the same organs must be used to gratify lust in a waste of shame and to consummate the noblest kind of sexual love. Pepys, says Lewis, was ravished by hearing the music of *The Virgin Martyr,* and reported that it pleased him so much that it made him physically sick. Thus both aesthetic pleasure and sea-sickness (for example) bring about the same physical phenomenon, simply because the body is limited in its physical reactions to psychological and spiritual stimuli. And thus glossolalia and religious hysteria appear to be the same because what is rich and complex is being expressed in a poorer medium, translated into a cruder language, and using what comes to hand, the limited reactions of the body. Further, what is unpleasant in one case (the sickness) becomes pleasant in another. The sickness of the stomach common to both sea-sickness and aesthetic rapture is hated in one case and wanted in the other. The physical reactions themselves can be transformed according to the stimulus that effects them. There is perhaps an analogy, Lewis thinks, between this transposition and the theology of the Incarnation. As the sensation of sickness is subsumed by esthetic joy and made, as it were, a part of that joy, so in the Incarnation, which works "not by conversion of the Godhead into flesh, but by taking of the Manhood into God," man may be "veritably drawn into" God. But Lewis advances this only as a hypothesis, walking *in mirabilibus supra me.* The real truth (as distinct from its lack of logical absurdity), the way that glossolalia differs from hysteria, can be known only as St. Paul himself knew it: by Practical Reason, by spiritual perception. "Spiritual things are spiritually discerned."[51]

What might be called this distrust of "assertive" or positive theology is also evident in Lewis's approach to scripture itself. His *Reflections on the Psalms* may be fairly described as an attempt to remove the obstacles that the Psalms seem to present to the contemporary Christian. In the book he has "avoided controversial questions as much as possible"; he is merely " 'comparing notes,' not presuming to instruct." After commenting on such seeming difficulties to the modern reader as the "cursing" Psalms and the "second meanings" of many of the Psalms, he remarks that we find in scripture the Word of God, but only "by steeping ourselves in its tone or temper and so learning its overall message." Particularly the teaching of Christ Himself "cannot be grasped by the intellect alone, cannot be 'got up' as if it were a 'subject.' . . . He will not be, in the way we want, 'pinned down.' " We must take in His teaching in a way that transcends the intellect; we must make a moral affirmation:

> It may be indispensable that Our Lord's teaching, by that elusiveness (to our systematising intellect), should demand a response from the whole man, should make it so clear that there is no question of learning a subject but of steeping ourselves in a Personality, acquiring a new outlook and temper, breathing a new atmosphere, suffering Him, in His own way, to rebuild in us the defaced image of Himself.[52]

So too, in *The Four Loves,* after his discussion of Affection, Friendship, Eros, and Charity, Lewis comes to the final question of what it is for a man to love God. Here is a question, not of theology, but of subjective religious experience. But even here Lewis is not willing to assert anything definitive, though the subject is his own religious affections. Nor is this reservation due simply to his characteristic modesty in talking about his own religious life; it is rather a sense that, if God is not really the Wholly Other, He is at least the "Unimaginably and Insupportably Other."[53] I believe that *Sehnsucht* may be called (in the terminology Lewis uses in *The Four Loves*) "need love," a movement of the will toward God. But it is not necessarily "gift love": it does not necessarily imply proximity to God; it is not necessarily "a supernatural Appreciative love." Thus Lewis's conclusion:

> God knows, not I, whether I have ever tasted this love. Perhaps I have only imagined the tasting. . . . Perhaps, for many of us, all experience merely defines . . . the shape of that gap where our love of God ought to be. It is not enough. It is something. If we cannot "practice the presence of God," it is something to practice the absence of God, to become increasingly aware of our unawareness till we feel like men who should stand beside a great cataract and hear no noise, or like a man in a story who looks in a mirror and finds no face there, or a man in a dream who stretches out his hand to visible objects and gets no sensation of touch. To know that one is dreaming is to be no longer perfectly asleep. But for news of the fully waking world you must go to my betters.[54]

Mr. Austin Farrer perhaps puts the point too strongly when he says in this connection that Lewis "does not feel sure of his theology," and goes on to ask, "Is romantic yearning an appetite for heaven, or is it the ultimate refinement of covetousness?" But he adds, "One cannot but respect his sense of responsibility in voicing his doubt about what so deeply moved him."[55] I believe it might be more fairly said that Lewis's pure reason, or speculative intellect, had taken him as far as it could. The rest was up to the practical intellect, or the will. And about the movements of the will it is impossible to be definitive; affections, religious or otherwise, are hardly intellectually verifiable.

Finally, in *Letters to Malcolm,* the warning against the intellectual aspect of theology and the call for an imaginative reading of scripture echo both Barfield and Lewis's earlier remarks on meaning in "Bluspels and Flalansferes." He suggests two rules for exegetics:

> *(1)* Never take the images literally. *(2)* When the *purport* of the images—what they say to our fear and hope and will and affections

> —seems to conflict with the theological abstractions, trust the purport of the images every time. For our abstract thinking is itself a tissue of analogies: a continual modelling of spiritual reality in legal or chemical or mechanical terms. Are these likely to be more adequate than the sensuous, organic, and personal images of Scripture—light and darkness, river and well, seed and harvest, master and servant, hen and chickens, father and child? The foot-prints of the Divine are more visible in that rich soil than across rocks or slag-heaps. Hence what they now call "demythologising" Christianity can easily be "remythologising" it—and substituting a poorer mythology for a richer.

As in *Mere Christianity* and in the trilogy, we find in *Letters to Malcolm* the reluctance to define dogma, the wish simply to accept the phenomena of the Eucharist or the Incarnation. The last thing Lewis wants to do is "unsettle" any Christian by defining the Eucharist, for example, when that Christian "finds it profitable to represent to himself what is happening when he receives the bread and wine. I could wish that no definitions had ever been felt to be necessary. . . ." The Eucharist remains for Lewis simply a mystery; no theory explains it; nor can he even imagine what "the disciples understood Our Lord to mean when, His body still unbroken and His blood unshed, He handed them the bread and wine, saying *they* were His body and blood." Echoing Coleridge, he simply says to the theorists, " 'Your explanation leaves the mystery for me still a mystery.' " About the resurrection of the body he has "only speculations to offer." And about the hereafter, "Guesses, of course, only guesses. If they are not true, something better will be."[56]

Now what I have been saying of Lewis's doctrinal works, that they are basically products of the pure reason and thus really adjuncts to the practical reason or the will, is in some degree true, if not of Anglicanism as a whole, at least of some part or school of Anglicanism. Historical examination shows that Coleridge played no small part in nineteenth-century broad-church Anglicanism before the advent of Modernism.[57] Further such examination, which is beyond the scope of this work, might reveal why it is a "typically Anglican conviction that truth is larger and more beautiful than our imperfect minds are able to apprehend or conceive," and why Anglicanism, more than some other communions, should strive always "not to define too exactly those mysteries which God has hidden in His own knowledge."[58] I do not suggest that Lewis's romantic Christianity is identical with Anglicanism as such, any more than the romantic religion of Macdonald or Chesterton was identical with their formal religions. I do suggest that Lewis has come to terms with dogma in a typically romantic way learned from Coleridge, that he has done this in order to go beyond dogma to experience, the romantic experience of longing which he can now see as of religious significance. Lewis's transcendental Christianity preserves the value of both dogma and experience by explaining both as attempts to reach the same end, by showing that *Sehnsucht* approximates the Practical Reason or the will. Romantic longing is for what never was on sea or land, for the beyond "partly in the west, partly in the past"; Lewis's transcendental Christianity provides an ultimate reality that is opaque, unapproachable and unknowable except through the will. As Coleridge said, "*Omnia exeunt in mysterium.* . . . There is nothing, the absolute ground of which is not a Mystery. The contrary were indeed a contradiction in terms: for how can that, which is to explain all things, be susceptible of an explanation?"[59] And Lewis, speaking of the Eucharist, repeats this sense of a mysterious realm that the speculative intellect cannot really enter. Christ's death and the Eucharist are a kind of "magic": they have " 'objective efficacy which cannot be further analysed.' "[60] Christianity itself, in Lewis's transcendental terms, may be thought of as a myth or accommodation, so far as it is understood rather than perceived spiritually by moral means. Just so far as Christianity is formal and dogmatic, it is a limitation of the transcendent God, a form of perception like quantity or substance by which we mutilate and distort the I AM WHO AM. In order to know God we must love Him; there is no discursive way. Lewis's transcendental Christianity, like romantic longing, puts its good in "the High Countries,"[61] where the heart is.

Chapter Four

Charles Williams and Romantic Theology

The most extensive and perceptive criticisms of the work of Charles Williams to date are mostly those of his friends and close acquaintances. In fact, as John Heath-Stubbs has remarked, "His official public reputation is almost non-existent. . . ." Lewis has written a long and valuable commentary on Williams's Arthurian poetry, Anne Ridler (a friend and former student of his) has edited a good deal of his work, and Alice Hadfield, who for some years worked with him at Amen House, has written a full-length biographical and critical study. The most notable exception to this generalization about "friendly" criticism is the study by Mary M. Shideler. Mrs. Shideler is an American who did not know Williams but who was drawn to his work, as she says, because she found that Williams " 'speaks to my condition.' " No one can doubt that, other things being equal, to have known the man whose work you deal with is almost surely to possess insights into the work that other critics will not have. Yet there are dangers in such intimate knowledge. Coleridge was a better critic of Wordsworth after their estrangement, and no one turns to Boswell for a critical evaluation of Johnson's *Irene*. One might even argue that the more magnetic the personality of the writer, the less objective the criticism of his friends will be. Thus the tone of Mrs. Hadfield's book, for example, sometimes approaches that of hagiography rather than biography, while Mrs. Shideler's book is probably the most balanced and best commentary on Williams to date.[1]

It is necessary to point out this danger in the case of Williams, for he seems to have impressed his friends in a way not really susceptible of analysis by someone who did not know him. Lewis has said that when he tried to combine the idea of death with the idea of Charles Williams he found that it was "the idea of death that was changed." And, speaking of Williams's death, he records the testimony of two of Williams's friends:

> A lady, writing to me after his death, used the word *stupor* (in its Latin sense) to describe the feeling which Williams had produced on a certain circle in London; it would almost describe the feeling he produced on us after he died. There is, I dare say, no empirical proof that such an experience is more than subjective. But for those who accept on other grounds the Christian faith, I suggest that it is best understood in the light of some words that one of his friends said to me as we sat in Addison's Walk just after the funeral. "Our Lord told the disciples it was expedient for them that He should go away, otherwise the Comforter would not come to them. I do not think it blasphemous to suppose that what was true archetypally, and in eminence, of His death may, in the appropriate degree, be true of the deaths of all of His followers."[2]

Eliot, commenting on the unity of Williams's life and work, adds, "To have known the man would have been enough; to know his books is enough; but no one who has known both the man and his works would have willingly foregone either experience." Auden has said that his meetings with Williams were "among my most unforgettable and precious experiences." And Anne Ridler mentions that when he was lecturing—as he did both in London and at Oxford during World War II—he always found time to talk with his students, even the dullest. "His friends, to tease him, would call him promiscuous, and perhaps would wish him to be more selective, but would then recall that the saints were not selective."[3]

Now these testimonies to Williams's sanctity must be taken into account in any discussion of his work. The major theme of his theological work is what he calls "substitution," "co-inherence," and "exchange." In the following pages I shall discuss these principles as theological beliefs inducing, in Williams, certain attitudes, but I cannot discuss them as a practical way of life, even though, as Auden says, exchange and substitution may have been for Williams "a way of life by which . . . he himself lived." As a practical way of life, substitution and exchange become a kind of physical communion of the saints by which one man may literally bear the burden of another's pain and anguish. By an act of the will one may assume another's suffering, and by an act of the will one may yield up his suffering to another. Such a notion probably strikes the common reader as either grotesque (like something out of Williams's occult novels, where exchanges of this kind occur), or as a matter bordering on the miraculous—and either alternative makes the reader uneasy. But Williams's friends were not uneasy: knowing the man, they accepted the second alternative. Lewis said that he believed Williams "spoke from experimental knowledge" of these things, and some years later, according to Nevill Coghill, Lewis actually practiced this substitution-exchange when his wife was dying of cancer. Coghill asked him directly, " 'You mean that her pain left her, and that you felt it for her in your body?' " and Lewis replied, " 'Yes, in my legs. It was crippling. But it relieved hers.' "[4]

Eliot has also spoken of "states of consciousness of a mystical kind" that Williams "knew, and could put into words."[5] Certainly Williams often enough speaks of mystical experience, and one has the undeniable impression that he knows whereof he speaks, that he speaks, as it were, from the inside about Dame Julian of Norwich or Evelyn Underhill or the Pseudo-Dionysius. It may be that what looks from the outside like transcendental theology, which sees the world as various images of God, may be, from the inside, religious experience, knowledge arrived at by means of spiritual communion. If this were so, then we could say (recalling Professor Wilson's remarks on the verification of religious statements) that Williams's experiences verified his theology. And so they may have done, but it is impossible to demonstrate this. It may be that Williams, like Dame Julian, *saw* the essential unity of the world, but his work cannot show this. What it does show is that he seems to have been a man (as Wordsworth said of Coleridge) to whom the unity of things had been revealed—but revealed by natural means, exciting moments of imaginative insight. Nowhere in his work (so far as I am aware) does he lay claim to more than that—with one exception. I believe that the one experience that was for him more than simply an experience was the one he tried to "theologize"—the "falling in love" experience which in his theological system becomes the "Beatrician vision." It is this part of his theology that I want to examine most closely in the following pages.

Here I must say a word about the limitations I have imposed upon myself in my approach to Williams's work. There is at present no general agreement about whether Williams should be regarded primarily as a novelist, a poet, a dramatist, a critic, or a theologian. Unfortunately for the literary historian, Williams's talent splashes untidily into all these areas. Lewis regarded his poetry as his most important work and looked forward to the time when "Williams criticism" will sweep away what Lewis thought of as his own tentative and preliminary remarks on the Arthurian poetry. Another critic regards Williams as "a Miltonic poet" who in the Arthurian poems has "produced a new kind of poetic mythology." But many critics have found his poetry "repugnant," according to Heath-Stubbs, even though it has undeniably influenced the work of Eliot, Auden, and Dylan Thomas. His dramas have been largely neglected, but his novels have been much discussed, perhaps more than any other part of his work. And for one writer at least, Williams "is one of the major English critics. The essay on Milton [the introduction to the World's Classics edition of Milton] is, perhaps, the best vindication of Milton's genius ever written. . . ."[6]

Thus, from the literary point of view, Williams may be approached from many directions. But the shoemaker must stick to his last. I have sketched out problems for others that I intend to ignore myself. My intention, as I have said, is not literary evaluation as such but the examination of a religio-literary phenomenon, and therefore I have drawn no line among the several categories of his work. His religious ideas and attitudes are fundamental to all his major work, whether critical or creative or theological, and so I have tried to trace out these ideas and attitudes in whatever form they occur, using as criteria only the clarity or forcefulness with which they are expressed.

I shall begin with a term I have already used in connection with Barfield and Lewis—transcendentalism. Williams, one of his critics says, belongs "to the tradition of Christian transcendentalism in English poetry—the great tradition of Spenser, Vaughan, the later Wordsworth and Coleridge. . . ."[7] Yet it is not really helpful to call Williams transcendental in the sense that I have used the term of Barfield and Lewis. Within the rather vague confines of transcendental Christianity there are all sorts of emphasis possible; and though it may be true to say that Spenser and Coleridge belong in the same tradition, such cataloging is of little real help in establishing what it was that each man particularly believed and practiced. I have used the term transcendental of Barfield to refer especially to his use of the creative imagination as the concept comes from Coleridge and Steiner and, ultimately, from German romantic philosophy and neo-Platonism. I have also called Lewis's work transcendental, not only because he created mythic worlds in his fiction but because he revived Coleridge's distinction between rational and religious knowledge, between inference and spiritual perception. Williams, too, stresses the faculty of the creative imagination, but not in the same way as Barfield and Lewis do. There is more of Wordsworth than Coleridge in Williams's work. He is more the poetic romantic than the analytical romantic, more concerned with Wordsworth's vision than with Coleridge's glossing of the workings of the human mind. What we find in Williams's work is emphasis on the union of the intellect and the imagination as the highest means of reaching religious truth. We find him time and again insisting on this union in terms for which he has to resort to Wordsworth: this union results in "the feeling intellect," or "absolute power," or "reason in her most exalted mood." Thus Merlin in *Taliessen through Logres* magically sends his imagination into the "third sphere" in order to perceive Pelles the Wounded King and Lancelot outside the King's gate, reduced to wolf-shape after his enchanted begetting of Galahad on Helayne:

he sent his hearing into the third sphere—
once by a northern poet beyond Snowden
seen at the rising of the moon, the *mens sensitiva,*
the feeling intellect, the prime and vital principle,
the pattern in heaven of Nimue, time's mother on earth,
Broceliande.[8]

This union of intellect and imagination as a way to religious experience is argued most clearly in what Williams calls "the theology of romantic love," which is a part of a larger theological framework that I shall now try briefly to describe.

To begin with, Williams follows "one arrangement of doctrine rather than what is perhaps the more usual" but one "that . . . is no less orthodox."[9] This arrangement of doctrine holds that God (to speak in time) desired to become incarnate.[10] He could have done so without creating man and the universe, but He chose the latter course:

> He willed . . . that this union with matter in flesh should be by a mode which precisely involved creatures to experience joy. He determined to be incarnate by being born; that is, he determined to have a mother. His mother was to have companions of her own kind; and the mother and her companions were to exist in an order of their own degree, in time and place, in a world. They were to be related to him and to each other by a state of joyous knowledge; they were to derive from him and from each other; and he was to deign to derive his flesh from them. All this sprang, superfluous, out of his original intention—superfluous to himself and to his direct purpose, not superfluous to his indirect purpose of love. It was to be a web of simultaneous interchange of good. "In the sight of God," said Lady Julian, "all man is one man and one man is all man."[11]

From this description of the creation and Incarnation, we may proceed to the rest of the root ideas to be found in Williams's work; in fact, the above description makes clear another aspect of his transcendental vision. The universe, including the unity Man, is to be seen as a vast interlocking web of glory; all things manifest God in their degree; the hills skip for joy and the sons of God shout His praises. All things, man included, are glints of God; He is not in all things but, as it were, behind all things; the creation is an array of masks or images of God. It is thus that Taliessen envisions the Empire (the world); it is the unity of Byzantium (heaven) translated into multiplicity in order to be perceived phenomenally:

> The organic body sang together;
> dialects of the world sprang in Byzantium;
> back they rang to sing in Byzantium;
> the streets repeat the sound of the Throne.
>
> The Acts issue from the Throne.
> Under it, translating the Greek minuscula
> to minds of the tribes, the identities of creation
> phenomenally abating to kinds and kindreds,
> the household inscribes the Acts of the Emperor;
> the logothetes run down the porphyry stair
> bearing the missives through the area of empire.[12]

Thus there are, as Emerson and Swedenborg said, correspondences among things. This, for Williams, is particularly so in respect to man and God. The whole of this relationship between man and God, and between man and man, is describable by three of Williams's favorite terms: co-inherence, substitution, and exchange.

The three terms all refer to single aspects of the same thing, and this thing may be called the universal principle of existence. The principle may be stated negatively by saying that nothing, not even God, exists alone and without reference to anything else. The pattern of all existence is to be found in the Trinity: this is the supreme example of co-inherence and exchange. And the universe, as in the neo-Platonic tradition, mirrors or adumbrates the existence of God. All things co-inhere in each other and in God because, literally, that is the way existence is, that is the nature of existence, whether sacred or profane. And substitution, the model of which is the Redemption-Atonement, is a further application of this same principle. As all things co-inhere and practice exchange with each other, so all things substitute for each other. More accurately, in the case of man, who is a unity, all men substitute for each other and thereby serve themselves. Augustine, says Williams, stressed the existence and importance of this web of humanity:

> "*Fuimus ille unus*" he said; "we were in the one when we were the one." Whatever ages of time lay between us and Adam, yet we were

> in him and his guilt is in us. And indeed if all mankind is held together by its web of existence, then ages cannot separate one from another. Exchange, substitution, co-inherence are a natural fact as well as a supernatural truth. "Another is in me," said Felicitas; "we were in another," said Augustine. The co-inherence reaches back to the beginning as it stretches on to the end, and the *anthropos* is present everywhere. "As in Adam all die, even so in Christ shall all be made alive"; co-inherence did not begin with Christianity; all that happened then was that co-inherence itself was redeemed and revealed by that very redemption as a supernatural principle as well as a natural.[13]

But the nature of substitution and exchange, principles of existence as they are, does not permit them to be practiced only at the whim or will of the persons involved. Christ's substitution was a willing one, and man may imitate Him in sacrifice and desired suffering. But this is only a part of existence. Frequently Williams uses the image of a city as a symbol of the continual exchange that constitutes existence; the city exists only as a vast "exchange between citizens." And the exchange is not necessarily between lovers or even acquaintances; it may be, and often is, between enemies, people who despise each other.

> Hostility begins to exist . . . whenever and wherever we forget that we are nourished by, that we live from—whomever; when we think that we can *choose* by whom we shall be nourished. If *anthropos* has any meaning, if the web of humanity is in any sense one, if the City exists in our blood as well as in our desires, then we precisely must live from, and be nourished by, those whom we most wholly dislike and disapprove.[14]

Thus the very nature of existence, for Williams, may be nearly paraphrased by the Scholastic definition of *accident* as that to whose nature it belongs to exist by virtue of another. All things, it may be said, are accidents existing by virtue of each other and by virtue of the substance (the only substance) of the co-inhering trinity of God.

This is the way the world was before the Fall, but to speak in terms of time is inaccurate. Though Williams rarely mentions Kant, he seems to hold the Kantian notion that time is a mode of perception; we reduce the timeless to temporality and sequence because otherwise we could perceive nothing. Strictly speaking, past, present, and future are relative and provisional terms. Existence operates in timelessness: the past and the future are happening. The practices of substitution and interchange can and do operate in the past as well as in the present and future. Thus Taliessen envisions all Christian poets indebted to Virgil rushing out of the future at the hour of his death to substitute for him:

> Virgil was fathered of his friends.
> He lived in their ends.
> He was set on the marble of exchange.[15]

Thus we may warily hope that Herod does not slaughter the innocents, nor Salome demand the Baptist's head. Examples of this timelessness in the novels are numerous and have often been noted. The most spectacular occurs in *Descent into Hell:* the heroine, haunted by a döppelganger, allows another to bear her burden of fear; she in turn takes on the sufferings of her ancestor, a Protestant martyr who died at the stake under Bloody Mary, thereby providing him with the courage to go to his death singing the praises of God. Anne Ridler, who accepts Williams's doctrine of substitution, remarks on the advantages of substitution operating outside time:

> one of its great rewards is the liberation which it brings from the tyranny of time as well as space, so that the sense of guilt at any temporary forgetfulness is abolished: there is no such word as *too late:* all times, like all fortune, must be good. This is also surely the justification for those efforts to share imaginatively in the sufferings of Christ, which to some have seemed a masochistic practice: if the doctrine is true, even there the Creator may accept help from His creature—a help that speeds from any point in time.[16]

The nature of the transcendental, interlocking universe is good, as it is a divine façade. If we ask why man does not normally perceive the world as this way, why it is a vision reserved for saints and mystics, the answer lies in the nature of evil and of the Fall. Williams explains the nature of the Fall by what he calls "the myth of the alteration in knowledge." Before the Fall occurred (or occurs) man knew (or knows) the good as good; he existed "in a state of knowledge of good and nothing but good." But the Adam

(Williams stresses the human unity described by Lady Julian) also knew there was "some kind of alternative" to the good, and that God knew this alternative, knew evil at least as an intellectual possibility. The Fall consisted of their failure to be "lowly wise." "It was merely to wish to know an antagonism in the good, to find out what the good would be like if a contradiction were introduced into it. Man desired to know schism in the universe."[17] The Adam wished to be as God, knowing both good and evil. They received their wish, and knew at once "good lost and evil got."

> Unfortunately to be as gods meant, for the Adam, to die, for to know evil, for them, was to know it not by pure intelligence but by experience. It was, precisely, to experience the opposite of good, that is the deprivation of the good, the slow destruction of the good, and of themselves with the good.[18]

They wished to see "the principles at war" as God does; but what God sees as mere possibility they had to live:

> The Adam in the hollow of Jerusalem respired:
> softly their thought twined to its end,
> crying: *O parent, O forked friend,*
> *am I not too long meanly retired*
> *in the poor space of joy's single dimension?*
> *Does not God vision the principles at war?*
> *Let us grow to the height of God and the Emperor:*
> *Let us gaze, son of man, on the Acts in contention.*
>
> The Adam climbed the tree; the boughs
> rustled, withered, behind them; they saw
> the secluded vision of battle in the law;
> they found the terror in the Emperor's house.
>
> The tree about them died undying,
> the good lusted against the good,
> the Acts in conflict envenomed the blood,
> on the twisted tree hung their body wrying.
> . . . .
> they had their will; they saw; they were torn in the terror.[19]

Evil, for Williams as for other thinkers as different as Aquinas and Emerson, has no positive existence; it is good warped or bent or, more accurately, good misperceived.

> They knew good; they wished to know good and evil. Since there was not—since there never has been and never will be—anything else than the good to know, they knew good as antagonism. All difference consists in the mode of knowledge.[20]

The nature of the Fall, then, may be described as man's loss of vision. With the Fall he loses his clarity and accuracy of moral and metaphysical sight. "Hell," Williams observes, "is inaccurate." Man sees good as evil, awarding to evil the tenuous existence of a mode of perception, a *way* rather than a phenomenal existence. It follows, then, that the Redemption must consist of some way or ways of restoring the original accuracy of knowledge. And, according to Williams, the Redemption consists of two such ways: the Negative Way and the Affirmative Way. The Negative Way is the way of asceticism and denial, the rejection of all the images of God which make up creation in favor of the single image of God Himself. This is the way of what we usually call mysticism: the original clarity of vision, the true God-man relationship, are restored to the follower of the Way of Rejection by means of a direct communion with God. This is the way of the anchoress, the hermit, of St. John of the Cross and St. Theresa of Avila. In *Taliessen through Logres* Dindrane, whose religious name is Blanchefleur, follows the Way of Rejection, as Taliessen himself follows the Way of Affirmation. She rejects the good and pleasant life of the court for that of the nunnery where she will devote her life to bringing up Galahad. She

> professed at Almesbury
> to the nuns of infinite adoration, veiled
> passions, sororal intellects, earth's lambs,
> wolves of the heavens, heat's pallor's secret
> within and beyond cold's pallor, fires
> lit at Almesbury. . . .[21]

The pseudo-Dionysius, says Williams, is "the great intellectual teacher of that Way. . . ."[22]

The other Way is the Way of the Affirmation of Images, the determination to restore the original vision by affirming in some way that the images of God of which creation consists are still good;

this way consists not in ignoring or rejecting the world but in accepting it for what it is, but what it no longer seems to be—good. Now these images to be affirmed are not subjective; they are, as Williams said of them in respect to Dante, "the subjective recollection within him of something objectively outside him" (Barfield's collective representations); they are images "of an exterior fact and not of an interior desire." Thus, as Antony Borrow says, "Potentially . . . any and every thing known or perceived by man, including man, is an object from which such an image may be formed." Thus death, madness, bereavement, loss are images to be affirmed. "The Way of the Affirmation is . . . an acceptance of the world, including an acceptance of what we happen to see as evil, and at the same time continually striving to see it as one aspect of God."[23]

The mystic, the follower of the Way of the Rejection of Images, has his original vision restored, at least briefly, by direct communion with the Godhead; he has seen what Plato called the Idea of the Good, though when he returns to the mundane cave in which the rest of us live he can only speak to us of his vision in metaphors and dark conceits, can only tell us, like St. John of the Cross, of the light in the dark night of the soul, or, like St. Theresa, of the bright nuptial hymns she has heard. But a vision need not be intelligible; for a moment the mystic has seen the light turned on behind the universe, has seen the great wheels rolling, like Ezekiel. But how does the Affirmative Way restore the accuracy of prelapsarian vision? The answer to this, which is the burden of this chapter, is the essence of Williams's religious romanticism.

William's romanticism is what might be called "corrected" romanticism. It is theologized romanticism, the romantic experience seen *sub specie aeternitatis*. Williams, says Lewis, was a "romantic theologian."

> A romantic theologian does not mean one who is romantic about theology but one who is theological about romance, one who considers the theological implications of those experiences which are called romantic. The belief that the most serious and ecstatic experiences either of human love or of imaginative literature have such theological implications, and that they can be healthy and fruitful

> only if the implications are diligently thought out and severely lived, is the root principle of all his work. His relation to the modern literary current was thus thoroughly "ambivalent." He could be grouped with the counter-romantics in so far as he believed untheologized romanticism . . . to be sterile and mythological. On the other hand, he could be treated as the head of the resistance against the moderns in so far as he believed the romanticism they were rejecting as senile to be really immature. . . .[24]

It is the "uncorrected" romanticism, or what Williams calls pseudo-romanticism, which Williams dislikes. Uncorrected romanticism may be defined as the romantic experience unreflected upon, the romantic experience seen only as itself and not through the spectacles of eternity. If Wordsworth had been content to revel in the experience of Nature which haunted him like a passion instead of looking for its meaning, he would have been an "uncorrected" romantic. If the man in love does not try to see the significance of being in love, he, too, is an uncorrected romantic. The experience itself is not enough; it must be related to the rest of the web of existence. True romanticism must consist of the union of the intellect and the imagination; it must be passionate thought, analyzed passion. Wordsworth and Blake, says Williams, were true romantics.

> The true Romantic, maintaining the importance of what Blake calls "the visionary Fancy or Imagination," admits and believes that the holy intellect is part of it. . . . Both of these noble poets have been said to repudiate "the meddling intellect"; in so far as they did, it was precisely the *meddling* intellect which they discarded. The power which they felt and believed was defined by Wordsworth in the grand climax of the *Prelude*—"the *feeling* intellect."[25]

Williams's "true" romanticism, characterized as it is by the "feeling intellect," is a good deal like the current notion of metaphysical poetry which stems from Grierson and Eliot. If we may borrow Eliot's phrases, we may say that Williams's true romantic is one in whom there can be no "dissociation of sensibility," one who feels a thought as immediately as the odor of a rose, one whose thoughts are experiences which modify his sensibility. In Eliot, however, the unified sensibility serves largely as a faculty for the writing of poetry. In Williams, the union of thought and feeling serves, as I have indicated, as a means of arriving at religious truth.

Now theologized romanticism is one of the modes of the Affirmative Way, and thus one of the ways of restoring the prelapsarian vision. The romantic experience theologized, like Lewis's *sehnsucht,* is one of the potential benefits to man brought about by the Redemption. There are various kinds, or modes, of the romantic experience which, when joined with the intellect, may lead man back to the original vision. Williams nowhere in his writing develops them, but he apparently used them as talking points in his wartime lectures to Oxford undergraduates. John Heath-Stubbs catalogues them from this source:

> In a lecture which I heard him deliver at Oxford in 1943, Charles Williams distinguished five principal modes of the Romantic experience, or great images, which occur in poetry. They are:
> (*a*) The Religious experience itself. Having posited this, Williams proposed to say nothing further about it. Obviously, in a sense, it is in a category apart, and includes the others.
> (*b*) The Image of woman. Dante's *Divine Comedy* is the fullest expression of this mode, and its potential development.
> (*c*) The Image of Nature. Of this Wordsworth in *The Prelude* . . . was the great exponent.
> (*d*) The Image of the City. Had Williams not been addressing an audience composed of English Literature students, I have no doubt that he would have cited Virgil, in the *Aeneid,* as the great exponent. . . .
> (*e*) The experience of great art. Of this, Keats's *Ode on a Grecian Urn* was a partial expression.[26]

The only one of these five modes of the romantic experience which Williams ever fully developed is the image of woman, out of which subheading comes his theology of romantic love. Of the others there are only scattered hints throughout his work. The experience of great art, for example, he touches on briefly in the novel *Many Dimensions.* The plot centers about a certain stone by the use of which a man may travel through space and time. One of the persons in the novel, having experienced this travel, meditates its possibilities and causes:

> the past might, even materially, exist; only man was not aware of it, time being, whatever else it was, a necessity of his consciousness. "But because I can only be sequentially conscious," he argued, "must I hold that what is not communicated to consciousness does not exist? I think in a line—but there is the potentiality of the plane." This perhaps was what great art was—a momentary apprehension of the plane at a point in the line. The Demeter of Cnidos, the Praying Hands of Durer, the *Ode to a Nightingale,* the Ninth Symphony—the sense of vastness in those small things was the vastness of all that had been felt in the present.[27]

Before we turn to the theology of romantic love as Williams's most fully developed mode of the Affirmation of Images, there is one last general theological point which we must consider, for it plays a basic part in that mode: the point is Williams's beliefs concerning the body, its place and function in the religious life.

Anne Ridler believes that Williams's notions about the body came originally out of what we should call occult sources. Shortly after the first World War, Williams became friendly with A. E. Waite, who introduced him to the Order of the Golden Dawn, the theosophical society of which Yeats had earlier been a member. Though Williams's connection with the order was brief, he read with great interest Waite's book *The Secret Doctrine in Israel,* which is a study of the Jewish mystical work called the *Zohar.* Waite's book makes much of the body as symbolic:

> The frontispiece shows a diagram of the Sephirotic Tree laid out upon the figure of a man, with the different properties related to different parts of the body—e.g., *Chesed,* Mercy, is at the right hand, *Geburah,* Severity, at the left. In this book, I believe, are the foundations of Williams's thought about the symbolism of the body, and of his life-long attempt to develop an adequate theology of marriage. . . .[28]

There is also much of the Arthurian imagery of Waite's *The Hidden Church of the Holy Grail* in Williams's Arthurian poetry. There is an end-paper design in the English edition of *Taliessen through Logres* which indicates in Blakean fashion the symbolic geography of the poems.

> Here the Empire is represented as a human figure. The head is in Logres (Britain) for it is in Britain that the myth is to be enacted. . . . The breasts are in Gaul (where Christendom is nourished by the milk of learning and culture). The hands, at Rome, symbolize the manual acts of the Pope, which are the acts of the Church (blessing, laying on of hands, etc.). Byzantium, the seat of the Emperor . . . is the navel—traditionally the seat of the soul. Jerusalem is the genital organs—the place both of Crucifixion and Redemption. At the furthest remove from Logres (but nearest to Byzantium) is Caucasia, the buttocks—this represents the natural, but still essentially good, human functions.[29]

It is with such body symbolism in mind that one must read

> The milk rises in the breast of Gaul,
> Trigonometrical milk of doctrine.
> Man sucks it; his joints harden,
> sucking logic, learning, law,
> drawing on the breasts of *intelligo* and *credo.*[30]

Certainly much of the occultism of the novels concerns the body, not in a specially erotic way, but as a vehicle formed (according to both neo-Platonic and kabbalistic traditions) out of "prime matter." It has been suggested that Milton was also familiar with the teachings of the *Zohar* and kabbalistic lore;[31] in any case an acquaintance with the neo-Platonic and possibly kabbalistic traditions as they appear in Milton clarifies a great deal of the rather muddy background of many of Williams's novels. (Williams, as I have said, was a great admirer of Milton and so the comparison is relevant.) We recall Raphael's lecture to Adam on the properties of angelic bodies: they both eat and practice some form of intercourse. Matter (of which the angels are composed) is able to endure nearly endless "refinement" or attenuation, but it remains matter. It is out of prime matter, Chaos, that the Miltonic universe is created in *Paradise Lost;* Adam and all else have originally come from the swirling, indeterminate mass of hot, cold, moist, and dry which lies amorphously "beneath" heaven.

The magic stone of *Many Dimensions* is somehow a bit of prime matter on which have been engraved the letters of the Tetragrammaton. Its magical qualities derive from the fact that it is what an Aristotelian might call pure potency: it can, by an act of its user's will, become anything its user desires. Now the bodies of the characters in a Williams novel of course derive from this same substance; what is less obvious is that their souls do too, their souls being as much material as the "bodies" of Milton's angels. This is not often stressed in the novels, but when it does occur it leads to the same rather grotesque conclusion that we find in *Paradise Lost* as soon as we take Raphael's speech at all literally (as Milton gives us every chance to do). In *All Hallows' Eve* a dead woman returns to the scene of her active life, and still feels love for, and attraction to, her live husband. Because both she (though dead) and he (though alive) are of the same substance, some sort of semi-physical relationship is possible. And one critic has found "a suggestion of Swedenborgianism, perhaps, in the idea of a posthumous sexuality that more than one passage of this novel evokes."[32]

Other instances of this occult vision of the body and of matter are numerous in the novels. In the case of substitution that I have already cited from *Descent into Hell,* Williams makes it clear that the body as well as the mind accepts the sufferings of others: "The body of his flesh received her alien terror, his mind carried the burden of her world." In *The Greater Trumps* the heroine of the novel stands in her library with her lover, holding in her hands the greater trumps of the Tarot pack which are the archetypes of power and energy, keys to the prime matter out of which all things come. And by a union of her will with the primal energy of the cards, she creates:

> nor was it mere fancy that some substance was slipping between her fingers. Below her hands and the cards she saw the table, and some vague unusualness in it attracted her. It was black . . . and down to it from her hands a kind of cloud was floating. It was from there that the first sound came, it was something falling—it was earth, a curtain, a rain of earth falling, falling, covering the part of the table immediately below, making little sliding sounds—earth, real black earth.[33]

Now how far this occultism is to be taken seriously is problematical. Eliot assures us that he has "never known a healthier-minded man than Williams," that the occultism and magic are an "apparatus," that Williams merely "borrowed from the literature of the occult . . . for the sake of telling a good story." Others, however, are not so sure of this. The same critic who was bothered by the hint of Swedenborgianism in *All Hallows' Eve* finds that "a certain illuminism is apparent in the novels; moreover, the goetic element is clearly not intended to be symbolical only; one has the impression that Williams considered the magical events he described as possibilities that could be actually realized." And he agrees with another critic that Williams was "under the sway of erotic spiritualism."[34]

But however much or little Williams believed the occult views of matter and the body to be found in the novels, we must set over against such views his beliefs about the body and matter as they are related to the Incarnation. We recall that Williams chose to follow "one arrangement of doctrine" rather than another, and that the arrangement he chose involves the belief that God would have become incarnate even had there been no Fall. Such an arrangement of doctrine makes one point very clear: it is not possible to regard matter as in any sense evil. If the Fall necessitated the Incarnation, then one may be Platonist enough to hold that Christ's love for man enabled Him to take on "even" matter to save him; it is possible to retain the Platonic view of matter as evil and the body as punishment. One need only look at the great Augustinian tradition in Christianity to confirm this possibility. But if the Incarnation would have occurred even without the Fall, then this possibility no longer exists. We can no longer be pained that God had to assume the indignity of matter in order to save us; He *wanted* to assume matter; and therefore any indignity we see either in His assumption of matter or in matter itself must derive not from the object, matter itself, but from our misconception of it. In fact, it seems to follow that the usual view of matter as somehow less than spirit is simply a result of the Fall, part of our postlapsarian blindness.

Williams's views of the goodness of matter are somewhat tenuous, and I shall not make them any more explicit than he himself did. Certain things, though, are, in his view, clear enough. So far as we can understand the Fall itself, for example, we can see that whatever prohibition was violated by the Adam was violated by the spiritual side of the Adam, not by the physical. The sin of the Fall consisted in an act of the will, not the body.

> The body was holily created, is holily redeemed, and is to be holily raised from the dead. It is, in fact, for all our difficulties with it, less fallen . . . than the soul in which the quality of the will is held to reside; for it was a sin of the will which degraded us. "The evidence of things not seen" is in the body seen as this epigram; nay, in some sense, even "the substance of things hoped for," for what part it has in that substance remains to it unspoiled.[35]

It is perhaps worth remarking here on the eclectic quality of Williams's thought. So far as he is a transcendentalist, he is within the great stream of neo-Platonism; so far as he is an occultist, he is a part of a minor eddy of the same stream. But his evaluation of the body and of matter, his insistence on the goodness of matter, place him closer to the tradition of medieval Aristotelianism. Yet such a remark as the one we have just noted, that it is the soul rather than the body that has fallen, has little meaning in terms of Aristotelianism; it belongs rather to the neo-Platonic tradition which in the Middle Ages produced the endless debates between the body and the soul. Aquinas echoed Aristotle in holding that the union between body and soul is "substantial," that it is inaccurate to say that the eye sees or the ear hears or the will sins, but rather that the *man* sees with the eye, hears with the ear, sins with the will. Thus it was *man* that was involved in the Fall, and it was on *man* that the consequences devolved.

The objection is minor, however. Williams's main thesis is that the Church has, if not preached, at least tolerated and encouraged a kind of unofficial Manicheism. This is particularly so as regards marriage. "The hungry sheep look up for metaphysics, the profound metaphysics of the awful and redeeming body, and are given morals."[36] But the body, as we have seen, cannot be evil. It cannot be evil because of the nature of the Incarnation:

> it is clear that the Sacred Body was itself virtue. The same qualities that made His adorable soul made His adorable flesh. If the devotion

> to the Sacred Heart does not, in itself, imply something of the sort, I do not know what it does imply. The virtues are both spiritual and physical—or rather they are expressed in those two categories. This is recognized in what are regarded as the more "noble" members in the body—the heart, the eyes. But it is not so often recognized as a truth underlying all the members—the stomach, the buttocks.[37]

God operates, manifests Himself, in the two modes of matter and spirit; it follows that the two cannot be compared in terms of value —they are simply different. Yet the Church has allowed it to be assumed that the two modes could be so evaluated. Thus the word *sacramental,* Williams comments, "has perhaps served us a little less than well; it has, in popular usage, suggested rather the spiritual *using* the physical than a common—say, a single—operation."[38]

The Incarnation, for Williams, is the supreme example of God manifesting Himself in the two modes (the Eucharist is an echo of this manifestation). We say that God became man, assumed the body and soul of man in the person of Christ—"the Word was made flesh." But we may also say, with the author of the Athanasian Creed, that God became man "not by conversion of the Godhead into flesh, but by taking of the manhood into God . . . not by confusion of substance, but by unity of person." And "Not me," said St. Paul, "but the God in me." All men are literal members of the "Mystical Body of Christ." The virtues exist in the body as truly as in the soul, though differently.

> The Sacred Body is the plan upon which physical human creation was built, for it is the centre of physical human creation. The great dreams of the human form as including the whole universe are in this less than the truth. As His, so ours; the body . . . is also a pattern. We carry about with us an operative synthesis of the Virtues . . . the Sacred Body [is] . . . the Archtype of all bodies. In this sense the Eucharist also exposes its value. The "index" of our bodies, the incarnate qualities of the moral universe, receive the Archtype of all moralities truly incarnated; and not only the pattern in the soul and will but the pattern in the body is renewed. . . . We experience, physically, in its proper mode, the Kingdom of God: the imperial structure of the body carries its own high doctrines—of vision, of digestion of mysteries, of balance, of movement, of operation.[39]

Thus, for Williams, there can be no talk of the soul as "the divine element" in man; there are two divine elements in man—both the soul and the body. Taliessen meditates on the fact that women cannot be priests because they share, by menstruation, in the "victimization of the blood," and thus in a sense are part of the sacrifice itself. And he continues:

> Flesh knows what spirit knows,
> but spirit knows it knows—categories of identity:
> women's flesh lives the quest of the Grail
> in the change from Camelot to Carbonek and from Carbonek to Sarras,
> puberty to Carbonek, and the stanching, and Carbonek to death.
> Blessed is she who gives herself to the journey.
>
> Flesh tells what spirit tells
> (but spirit knows it tells). Women's travel
> holds in the natural, the image of the supernatural. . . .[40]

Man, at the Incarnation (whether in time or out of time), became "ingodded," became a "son of God" in body as well as in spirit. And thus the theology of romantic love, to which we may now turn, has much to say about the body as well as the spirit, for romantic love does not deal with the marriage of true minds but with total beings in whom God has manifested Himself in the two modes of spirit and matter.

Let us begin by recalling that romantic love, for Williams, is, or can be, one of the ways of practicing the Affirmation of Images, of following the Affirmative Way. If practiced rightly it leads to the restoration of the original vision of all things as good, to the removal of the scales from the eyes, to prelapsarian accuracy of knowledge. And, to move to the other end of the spectrum, it can lead out of the fallen world and to beatitude.

According to Anne Ridler, Williams wrote a complete book on romantic theology, but the authorities to whom he showed it objected to it, or to part of it, and it was never published. Thus his fullest treatments of the subject are to be found in a pamphlet called *Religion and Love in Dante,* and the books *The Figure of Beatrice* and *He Came Down from Heaven.* As two of the titles indicate, it is difficult to separate Williams's romantic theology from his views of Dante, for it was in Dante's work that he found the only real example of the particular mode of the Affirmative Way that is romantic love. It is in Dante, Williams thinks, that we find the first and greatest "true" romanticism: the union of thought and feeling leading to beatitude, the theologizing of the romantic experience as it came to Dante from the troubadours' treatment of courtly love. What Wordsworth is later to call Imagination is in Dante "the union of the mind and heart with a particular vision."[41]

Now the word "romantic" as Williams uses it to qualify "theology" is used "in some such defining sense as the words Pastoral, Dogmatic, or Mystical; it means theology as applied to a particular state—that of romantic love."[42] The first thing that the romantic theologian must decide is what romantic love is, what the experience of being in love consists of; and obviously it is not an easy thing to determine, though it is easy enough to lampoon. "It is neither sex appetite pure and simple; nor . . . is it necessarily related to marriage. It is something like a state of adoration, and it has been expressed . . . by the poets better than by anyone else." Thus Williams turns for a description of the state, not to one of the "more extreme Romantics,"[43] who might prejudice his case, but to Milton. Adam's explanation to Raphael of the state of mind that Eve produces in him, Williams thinks, serves as a useful introductory sketch (he neglects to mention that Raphael's reaction to the description is immediate apprehension and concern, and that Raphael warns Adam that such a state is a danger to prelapsarian bliss):

> when I approach
> Her loveliness, so absolute she seems
> And in herself complete, so well to know
> Her own, that what she wills to do or may
> Seems wisest, virtuousest, discreetest, best.
> All higher knowledge in her presence falls
> Degraded: Wisdom in discourse with her
> Loses, discount'nanced, and like Folly shows:
> Authority and Reason on her wait,
> As one intended first, not after made
> Occasionally: and, to consummate all,

> Greatness of mind and nobleness their seat
> Build in her loveliest, and create an awe
> About her, as a guard angelic placed . (*PL,* VIII, 546–59)

What has to be established about the experience so described is, "is it serious? is it capable of intellectual treatment? is it capable of belief, labour, fruition? is it . . . true?" These are the questions which romantic theology must answer. It is the work of romantic theology to discover if this experience can yield "the first matter of a great experiment." The end of such an experiment is the end of all the Ways to God. "The end . . . is known by definition of the kingdom: it is the establishment of a state of *caritas,* of pure love, the mode of expansion of one moment into eternity."[44]

Williams then proceeds to an analysis of the experience of falling in love, its potentialities and its consequences. His discussion, as I have said, largely consists of a gloss on Dante's *Vita Nuova, Comedy,* and *Convivio.* Dante himself analyzed his reaction to the sight of Beatrice quite accurately, says Williams, allowing for the differences between medieval and modern physiological terminology:

> The heart, where (to him) "the spirit of life" dwelled, exclaimed to him . . . "Behold a god stronger than I, who is come to rule over me." The brain declared: "Now your beatitude has appeared to you." And the liver (where natural emotions, such as sex, inhabited) said: "O misery! how I shall be disturbed henceforward."[45]

Dante sees her as "the youngest of the angels," as "the destroyer of all evil and the queen of all good" (p. 8). When she salutes him in the street he is cast into a state of such exaltation that he would have forgiven any injury done him and "if anyone had asked me a question I should have been able to answer only 'Love' " (p. 9). He is, says Williams, "in a state of complete good will, complete *caritas* towards everyone" (p. 9). He is, as we say, in love. "And therefore he calls her salutation 'blessed,' because it is beatitude which it inspires. In fact, he becomes for one moment in his soul that Perfection which he has observed in Beatrice" (p. 9).

But though the vision of Beatrice fills Dante's being with *caritas,* says Williams, Dante does not suggest that that state is in any way permanent. It comes upon him gratuitously, but it does not remain so. His being is acting according to a kind of natural law; having been granted the vision, "Love, charity, *agape,* was for the moment inevitable" (p. 10). But the vision would fade, as Wordworth's youthful vision of Nature faded; and like Wordsworth's vision it would have to be replaced by something which the vision had made possible. The problem for Dante, as for all romantic lovers, is to discover the Way to God that the vision has pointed him towards and made him aware of: "could he indeed become the Glory which he saw and by which for a moment he had been transfused?" (p. 10). The rest of Dante's work, says Williams, including especially the *Comedy,* is "a pattern of the Way" (p. 10).

Later in the *Vita Nuova* Dante sees coming towards him a girl named Joan, the beloved of his friend Cavalcanti; she is so beautiful that she is called "Primavera," Spring. She is followed by Beatrice; and the thought occurs to Dante that Joan goes before Beatrice as John the Baptist went before Christ. This is not, according to Williams, a conceit derived by adding theological or religious concepts to the tradition of courtly love. It is probably seriously meant, and if it is so meant,

> it is the beginning of a very high mystical identity. Beatrice is not our Lord. But Beatrice has been throughout precisely the vehicle of Love, of sexual love and of the vision in sexual love. She has awakened in Dante a celestial reverie; she has appeared to him the very carriage of beauty and goodness; she has, unknowingly, communicated to him an experience of *caritas.* These are the properties of Almighty Love. What Dante is now doing is to identify the power which reposed in Beatrice with the nature of our Lord. Love had been . . . a quality; now . . . he is on the point of seeing it as precisely the Person of Love. (p. 11)

The nature of the experience of falling in love is now fairly clear. The lover is given the experience gratuitously (like grace; in fact, such experience *is* grace); the lover is in a state of *caritas* because what he perceives in the person (the vehicle, the carriage) of the beloved in Love, is Christ. He sees, not only her, but Christ in her; and *caritas* is at once the condition of his seeing and the object of his vision. This mystical identity which Dante propounds in the *Vita Nuova* is carried to its great conclusion in the Purgatorio. Here Beatrice is a part of the procession of Angels, Virtues, Prophets and Evangelists led by the two-natured Gryphon who is Christ.

> She gazes into the eyes of the Gryphon . . . and it back into hers. There it is mirrored now as one, now as the other, "immutable in itself, mutable in its image." The Godhead and the Manhood are, as it were, deeply seen in those eyes whence Love began to shoot his arrows at Dante, by the Glory and the femininity. The moment in the *New Life* when the girl was seen as the vehicle of Love, preceded by Joan as Christ was preceded by John, is here multiplied and prolonged—one might say, infinitely. The supernatural validity of that "falling-in-love" experience is again asserted. . . . In the full Earthly Paradise, she is seen mirroring the Incarnate Splendour, as in Florence its light had been about her. (p. 30)

In a word, what the lover in the actual state of being in love perceives is the timeless fact of the Incarnation; he perceives the fact that the loved one is "ingodded," that human nature is taken up into Godhead, as the Athanasian Creed says. Dante himself could only symbolize this; he saw, he says, "the circle which is Christ painted with the image of man" (p. 35). It is the circle of which the apparition of Love had spoken in the *Vita Nuova,* the circle by which St Bonaventura had symbolized God when he said that God is a circle whose center is everywhere and whose circumference is nowhere. What the lover perceives, through this temporary return to prelapsarian vision, is the true nature of things; he sees accurately that Christ is *agape,* is Love, and that man, by the Incarnation, is ingodded in Him.

The lover, then, experiences a time of clear vision, which may be defined as the true knowledge and experience of the God-man relationship. But he experiences it only briefly. It may lead to the final Paradisal and permanent vision as Dante described it, but only if it is acted upon. Falling in love, being granted the Beatrician vision, is a mode of the romantic experience; if it is allowed to lie fallow, if it is untheologized, of itself it comes to nothing good. If it is theologized, it leads to power in this life and beatitude in the next. It is an invitation to follow a certain mode of the Affirmative Way; it is not in itself the Affirmative Way, for of its nature it is not lasting.

> The effort after the pattern marks the difference. The superstitions make heaven and earth in the form of the beloved; the theology declares that the beloved is the first preparatory form of heaven and earth. Its controlling maxim is that these things are first seen through Beatrice as a means; the corollary is that they are found through Beatrice as a first means only. The preposition refers not only to sight but to progress.[46]

The vision brought about by romantic love, like the vision brought about by Nature, is not beatitude; it is a return to prelapsarian vision in which all the images of God are seen as preparatory to the final experience of God. Nature, for Wordsworth, is not an end, but a way of arriving at; so, for Dante, "Beatrice is his Knowing."[47]

"Hell," says Williams, "has made three principal attacks on the Way of Romantic Love." The first is the assumption that the Beatrician vision is everlasting. As we have seen, this is not so. It is the false romantic who tries to retain the bliss of the vision by multiplying the number of his sexual love affairs. The vision "is eternal but is not everlastingly visible, any more than the earthly life of Christ." It is a momentary perception of God's glory in the love which is Christ. "The appearance of the glory is temporary; the authority of the glory towards pure love is everlasting; the quality of the glory is eternal, such as the heavens have in Christ."[48]

In *Taliessen through Logres* Williams gives an example not only of the transience of the vision but of the vision untheologized (and thus dangerous) in the experience of Palomides, the Saracen knight, when he visits the court of King Mark and there sees the Queen Iseult sitting between her husband Mark and her lover Tristram. He falls in love with the queen and experiences the Beatrician vision. But he cannot take the normal course of the Way of romantic love; he cannot marry the queen, who already has both husband and lover. And, as Lewis says, he is unwilling to take "the long pilgrimage of Dante to 'intellectual nuptials.' "[49] For a moment he sees the queen as holy flesh and holy spirit ingodded in Christ; but then the vision fades (because his will has failed to act upon it), and he is overcome with sexual jealousy, symbolized in the poem by the image of the Questing Beast. In the first flush of the vision he sees the queen's arm as it lies gracefully on the table; he sees it, as I have said, as Christ under the mode of matter, as a vision which begins the Affirmative Way: his heart and his thought flame in union, his mind moves

> by the stress
> of the queen's arm's blissful nakedness,
> to unions metaphysical. . . .

But the vision vanishes almost at once:

> Down the arm of the queen Iseult
> quivered and darkened an angry bolt;
> and, as it passed, away and through
> and above her hand the sign withdrew.
> . . . .
> division stretched between
> the queen's identity and the queen.
> Relation vanished, though beauty stayed;
> too long my dangerous eyes delayed
> at the shape on the board, but voice was mute;
> the queen's arm lay there destitute,
> empty of glory. . . .

And immediately he is overcome with jealousy:

> and aloof in the roof, beyond the feast,
> I heard the squeak of the questing beast,
> where it scratched itself in the blank between
> the queen's substance and the queen.[50]

The second assumption of Hell is that the love experience is a personal possession of the lovers. But love does not belong to the lovers; rather they belong to it. They cannot own love any more than they can own Nature or art or any other mode of the romantic experience. The experience is God-sent; they are meant for love, not love for them. The essence, Williams is fond of saying (echoing Dante), is meant for the function, not the function for the essence. Thus in Williams's play *Seed of Adam,* Mary, after the archangel has announced to her that she is to be the mother of Christ, enters the state of *caritas* as surely as any romantic lover, but realizes that the state is not a personal possession. Joseph asks her whom she is in love with, and she replies,

> Dearest, you did not hear: we said *in love.*
> Why must, how can, one be in love with someone?

To Joseph's objection that to be in love *with* someone is the nature of love, she answers,

> Dearest, to be in love is to be in love,
> no more, no less. Love is only itself,
> everywhere, at all times, and to all objects.[51]

To be in love is to be able to see accurately again; the sight is not limited to any one thing, but extends to all the images of God which constitute reality.

The third assumption of Hell is that "it is sufficient to have known that state of love."[52] This occurs when the experience is held to be thrilling and unique but only natural, when its transience is taken as proof that the experience is illusory and when, as a result, the experience is not related to the rest of life. The person who has been in love but has passed out of it without theologizing it is perhaps a good person, naturally speaking. But St. Paul allows him no place on the Way to God: he may have faith enough to move mountains, but if he has not *caritas* it avails him nothing.

This third assumption of Hell enables us to see what Williams means by theologizing the romantic experience. The lover must do what Palomides did not do. "To be in love must be followed by the will to *be* love; to be love to the beloved, to be love to all, to be in fact (as the Divine Thing said) perfect."[53] Thus a slave girl in *Taliessen through Logres* falls in love with Taliessen and experiences the Beatrician vision. There can be no hope of marriage, for Taliessen is the poet, the unicorn, not made for women. But she can do what Palomides did not do; she can direct her experience to holiness. And, with Taliessen's help, she does this. The vision, he tells her, is more than he is, more than his song is, though he and the song have effected the vision in the experience.

> The king's poet leaned, catching the outspread hands:
> *More than the voice is the vision, the kingdom than the king:*
> the cords of their arms were bands of glory; the harp
> sang her to her feet, sharply, sweetly she rose.
>
> The soul of a serving-maid stood by the king's gate,
> her face flushed with the mere speed of adoration.
> The Archbishop stayed, coming through the morning to the Mass,
> *Hast thou seen so soon, bright lass, the light of Christ's glory?*[54]

There are, in short, duties to be performed, Christian duties to be done in and through love. The Beatrician vision is a "way of return to blissful knowledge of all things. But this was not sufficient; there had to be a new self to go on the new way."[55] The lover for a moment sees the world as it is; it then becomes his duty to go on acting as if the vision remained with him, even though it does not. Having seen the Incarnation, the ingodding of man, and having thus perceived that all mankind is one, all men co-inhering in each other and all in turn co-inhering in Christ; having briefly seen and to a degree experienced all this, it becomes his duty to make the Beatrician vision modify his life. It is, in brief, his duty to become and remain a good Christian by means of the special grace which has been awarded him. All the things and the activities of the world are the matter to which *caritas* should be the form. After the vision come the duties; but the duties are only made possible by the vision.

The way of romantic love is only one mode of the Affirmative Way; the other modes also provide the particular stopping place at which a man may say, like Dante, *Incipit vita nova.* The other modes also provide the original infusion of *caritas,* the return through love to the true vision of the world; and the other modes equally demand the living of the life in *caritas,* the seeing of all things in *caritas.* The way of romantic love does not make the Christian life any easier than the other ways; like them, it only makes it possible.

The parallel here between the Beatrician vision—or any of the other modes of the Affirmative Way—and traditional Christianity is perhaps too obvious to need much pointing up. In both cases there is an intrusion of the Divine into the natural order; in the case of Christianity as such this intrusion is the historical Incarnation, in the case of romantic love an image or vision of the effect of the Incarnation. This intrusion is in both cases the "given," the *kerygma,* which is to be acted upon by some means; this "given" may be defined as that which makes salvation possible, but not inevitable. The Beatrician vision is an analogue of Christ's earthly life, which is time-bound and limited; the loss of the vision is an analogue of Christ's ascension; the desolation of the lover when the experience has passed is an analogue of the Apostles' desolation at Christ's departure. What is literally true of the Gospel story is analogically true of human experience. What Williams found in the romantic love experience was " 'an exact correlation and parallel of Christianity.' "[56] The organization of Mrs. Shideler's book points this out very well: Part I is entitled "The Imagery of Love" and is introductory to the second and third parts, "The Diagram of the Glory" and "The Co-Inherent Life." Her book, like Williams's doctrine of love, is a repetition of "holy history": first comes the experience, then the doctrines and the ways in which the doctrines are institutionalized. It follows, then, that to question or accept Williams's doctrine of the Affirmative Way is in a sense to question or accept the whole meaningful story of traditional Christianity.

Or at least this is the claim that Williams and perhaps some of his followers would advance. Wholly aside from the accuracy of the analogy, one sees immediately its advantages. The apparent deficiencies of the romantic experience will be the apparent deficiencies of the Christian teaching. The romantic failure to act on the experience will be comparable to the sinner's failure to act on grace, the romantic's success will be comparable to the accepted Christian "good life," and so on. The analogy is indeed a tantalizing one, although a devil's advocate would perhaps suggest that it is, after all, not only an analogy but a simplification.

If we ignore for a moment the fact that Williams's argument for romantic love is at least partly analogical, we see that the argument involves two different and very difficult areas of knowledge. The first is the question of love itself: what is human "romantic" love, and how does it differ from, or resemble, man's love for God and, in turn, God's love for man? The second involves Williams's use of Dante's work as the prime example of romantic love leading to beatitude, and here one must ask the old question about the function of Beatrice in Dante's work. Is she a real woman, and, if so, does she remain real throughout his work or does she become symbolic and anagogical? Is she a woman in the *Comedy,* or is she Theology? If she is both literal and anagogical, according to Dante's fourfold scale of meaning, then what becomes of Williams's prime example of the Way of Romantic Love? In what follows I shall seem to be arguing against Williams's doctrine, but in fact I am not. I am raising difficulties, and as Newman said, ten thousand difficulties do not necessarily constitute one doubt. Williams's analogy may still bear up, perhaps bear up all the better for having been scrutinized—as the larger thing that his analogy echoes has borne up under, and even fed on, the various scrutinies to which it is always being subjected.

I do not pretend to have the final answers to these questions, but some lines of approach to the answers may be sketched out. In a discussion of the nature of sexual love, most modern writers have thought it necessary to take the historical approach, on the assumption that the modern view of human love has evolved—in Barfield's terms, that human love has undergone a series of transformations correlative with the evolution of human consciousness. From this view, to paraphrase Lewis, what we call romantic love—sexual love as a thing to be respected and even sentimentalized—does not appear in classical antiquity, nor in the early Middle Ages. It is not to be found in Homer, Virgil, Ovid, St. Paul, or St. Augustine. Odysseus's love for Penelope is hardly touched on as a thing in itself; Dido's love for Aeneas is a kind of frenzy, a pathetic derangement; Ovid's *Art of Love* is a series of ironic commentaries on the sexual warfare between men and women; for St. Paul, St. Augustine, and the early Middle Ages in general, it was better to marry than burn. Every woman was, at least potentially, *Eva rediviva;* medieval marriages—or at least those of which we have many records—were marriages of convenience. It is only with the literature of courtly love, beginning in France in the eleventh and twelfth centuries, that we begin to note a change, that we begin to see woman valued for her own sake and finally idealized, that we begin to see sexual love treated as an ennobling force. Tracing this concept of love in its purely literary expression, we can watch its progress from the troubadour poetry of eleventh century France and the romances of Chrétien de Troies, up through Dante and his contemporaries, through Petrarch, and finally into English poetry in the early Elizabethan translations of Petrarch, and into English thought in such things as Castiglioni's *The Courtier.* If we continue a little further, we can see the gradual decline from the earlier sentimentalizing of woman and the idealization of love; to move from Sidney and Spenser to Shakespeare is to move from sentimentality to a form of realism; and to move from Shakespeare to Donne is to move to a grimmer and more clinical sort of realism that is frequently ironic and even cynical.

This view of romantic love, which I have largely paraphrased from Lewis's *The Allegory of Love,* has recently been severely criticized. It may well be that Lewis's view is drawn less from history than from literary history. And it may even be true that he minimizes the element of sexual love in classical literature. Penelope's love for Odysseus may simply be assumed rather than dealt with as a subject. And certainly Dido's love for Aeneas does not seem to differ essentially from that of Iseult's for Tristan, except that it is unrequited. We may not agree with Lewis that the phenomenon of courtly love marks one of the real changes in human sentiment. But most discussions of romantic love assume some sort of historical conditioning, and Lewis's view may at least serve as such an assumption.

The important part of such discussions, I think, is the attempt to distinguish the kinds of love possible to human beings, the attempt to show that there is, or is not, a relationship between man's love of woman and man's love of God. For what Williams's romantic theology claims is that love of woman can lead to love of God, in fact to beatitude. For Williams, the romantic love relationship is, in Buber's terms, a spectacular example of the I-Thou relationship possible to human beings; and in all such relationships the Divine Thou is operative. "Every particular *Thou* is a glimpse through to the eternal *Thou;* by means of every particular *Thou* the primary word addresses the eternal *Thou.*" More specifically, "He who loves a woman, and brings her life to present realisation in his, is able to look in the *Thou* of her eyes into a beam of the eternal *Thou.*"[57]

The question is, what connection (if any) is there between romantic love and love of God, between Eros and Agape? For Anders Nygren, no connection exists. Eros is one thing, agape another. Agape, the love for God, is brought about by God Himself. Where there is nothing, He puts something, and then there is human love for Him. There is no possibility of confusing the two loves; they differ in ends and in origins, and human love (eros) is not even an image or an echo of love for God (agape), for man is naturally capable of eros and naturally incapable of agape.[58] For de Rougemont, romantic love (eros) is the dark passion pictured so well in the Tristan myth. It is an analogue to the Manichean and pagan desire for utter extinction in the One. Eros, or "boundless desire," does not want earthly fulfillment; what it really wants is death. Tristan and Iseult are forever parting, forever separating, because they do not really want each other. They want the agonies of being apart, because their passion is an echo of the Manichean hatred of matter and of diversity; underneath the surface, love of eros is the urge to flee the world of daylight for the night of extinction.

> Eros is complete Desire, luminous Aspiration, the primitive religious soaring carried to its loftiest pitch, to the extreme exigency of purity which is also the extreme exigency of Unity. But absolute unity must be the negation of the present human being in his suffering multiplicity. The supreme soaring of desire ends in non-desire. The erotic process introduces into life an element foreign to the diastole and systole of sexual attraction—a desire that never relapses, that

> nothing can satisfy, that even rejects and flees the temptation to obtain its fulfillment in the world, because its demand is to embrace no less than the All. It is *infinite transcendence,* man's rise into his god. And this rise is *without return.*[59]

Christianity, according to de Rougement, has changed the whole end and direction of eros. The Incarnation both gave to man and showed to man the worth and dignity of the individual. Man no longer had to run from other men because they were diverse and imperfect manifestations of the One. It was now possible to love the other "as he or she really is." Christian love was now seen to be in imitation of Christ's love for the Church; and it is this Christian love which is agape, the love of one's neighbors, the love of one's enemies. Eros and agape, for de Rougemont as for Nygren, have no connection; in fact, it is part of de Rougemont's thesis that marriage founded on the Manichean admiration for passionate love cannot help but founder. Neither in Nygren nor in de Rougemont, then, is there anything like a Way of Romantic Love. Eros leads nowhere in Nygren's scheme; in de Rougemont's it leads only to Manicheism or hell.

M. C. D'Arcy, in a work published after Williams's death, has looked critically at the work of Nygren and de Rougemont and several others. There are, he believes, partial truths in Nygren, de Rougemont, the Existentialists, the Personalists, in Buber and Karl Heim, and he draws on all of them in order to achieve his final distinction between eros and agape. All things, says D'Arcy, exist according to two principles which will be called different things in different spheres of existence. The two may be paired on one level as dominant and recessive, on another as male and female; psychologically they may be called aggressive and regressive, or egotistical and effacing. On the level of brute creation, they will be the principles according to which the species survives: the receptiveness of the female complementing the urge of the male. On the spiritual level they will be the desire for self-perfection and the desire for self-sacrifice. On the philosophical level, they will be act and potency, form and matter, essence and existence. The human person, according to D'Arcy, like all other things, is composed of these two principles, and so is his love. One kind of love is eros, the assertive, possessing, dominating love which is associated largely with the intellect; it "has a desire to know all things," as Aristotle said, and this desire to know essences (meanings) is largely self-regarding and egotistical. This relationship is the one that Buber calls the "I-It" relation, in which the object is not regarded existentially as a "Thou" but only essentially as a thing to be understood. This is eros, or, in D'Arcy's phrase, the *animus*. Complementing this kind of love in all humans is the *anima,* the agape. This is the other side of the coin—the desire for self-sacrifice, the passivity, the desire to be done to, to be used, to be made into something else. This is the non-intellectual love which desires not essences but existence; this is the love which constitutes for Buber the "I-Thou" relationship; it does not seek to see the other person as an "It," an essence to be understood; it sees the person existentially as a being who must be received as himself.

Now these two principles of love operate together in any human love, whether it be the love of a man for a woman or the love of a man for God. "A person . . . has to include both the human essence and the existence of that essence if it is to be properly and adequately defined. The self-regarding love preserves the integrity of the self and prevents the other love from getting out of hand and being too prodigal."[60] In human affairs, that is, in love of humans for each other, the *animus,* the intellect, nearly always has to be in charge of the *anima,* lest the *anima* give itself up foolishly to something unworthy of the self. "Were our loves enlightened we could say: ama et fac quod vis. But it is not until the searchlight of truth has played upon the many shapes which hold our attention and the many loves which beckon to us, that we can give ourselves wholeheartedly to another. . . ."[61] The love of a man for a woman, then, is wary love; it has to be prudent because it is fallible and may be misinformed. But in the case of agape, love of man for God, this wariness is put away:

> in one case, and one only, that of divine love, the self may and must drop all its self-regard, strip itself and say, "all that I am and have is yours." The primary act of the creature is not to possess God but

> to belong to Him. The essential self is not, indeed, dead—that could not be so long as a person remains a person—but it is the existential self, the anima, which goes forth to greet the divine lover. No doubt that essential love prepares the way. The mind has for a long or short while to direct and fortify the anima. The true God may be hidden and have to be discovered, and when he is discovered there must be so much to be learnt about him, either by the mind's own effort or from God's own communications about himself. . . . The mind, then, will have constant work to do, but nevertheless, so far as the primary relation to God is concerned, love dictates all, and the love is one of homage and sacrifice and self-giving.[62]

In brief, then, for Nygren, eros is wholly different from agape. The finite cannot love the infinite except by a capacity specially infused by the infinite itself so that, as it were, the infinite loves itself through a finite medium. In this way God remains the Wholly Other. For de Rougemont, agape differs from eros in that the end of human love (mankind, one's neighbors) has been essentially changed by the Incarnation. To love God means to love one's redeemed neighbors in obedience to God's command. For D'Arcy, one loves both God and man by means of the same capacity for love, but the mixture of the animus and anima changes radically as the loved object is either human or divine. Man gives himself over to God as he is never safe in doing in a merely human relationship. Thus, for all three men there is some kind of distinction between the loves of man, distinction either of kind or of degree.

But no such distinction seems to exist in Williams's romantic theology. It is true that there are two kinds of love: that of Palomides (untheologized) and that of Dante (theologized). But on analysis these seem not to be so much two kinds of love, which we might call eros and agape, as simply love as distinguished from lust, or love as distinguished from passing infatuation. Where the other writers draw their distinctions is exactly where Williams does not. If Williams is right, then Dante loved, not Beatrice, or not *only* Beatrice, but God-in-Beatrice; more accurately perhaps, in view of Williams's insistence on the Athanasian creed, Dante loved Beatrice-in-God. Bluntly, he loved both woman and God at the same time in seemingly the same way. Eros and agape merge: a single human affection may encompass both God and man. Dante, it is true, saw the circle of Christ painted with the image of man; but it should be added that he saw it in heaven, and that even in heaven it was a symbol. Beatrice's eyes *mirrored* the two-natured gryphon who is Christ; her eyes did not *contain* it. The ingodding of man at the Incarnation seems, for Williams, to have blurred any distinction between the kinds and even objects of human love. One of Williams's frequent remarks is that the motto of the Affirmative Way is, "This also is Thou; neither is this Thou." All things are God's image, God's manifestation, all things participate in God—but no things are God. But *caritas* as induced by romantic love seems simply to say, "This is Thou," and drop the balancing disclaimer. Even if we distinguish as carefully as the Athanasian creed does between substance and person, the identification of Beatrice and God seems hardly avoidable.

Nor do the examples of romantic love in Williams's novels do anything to clarify romantic theology. There, where one might hope to find some sort of explication of the particular duties of the romantic lover acting in accord with the Beatrician vision, one finds generally that the union of thought and feeling with a particular vision has produced, not the good life arrived at in a new way, but sheer power. The girl in *The Greater Trumps* who created matter by holding the Tarot cards did so because she was really in love. The hero of *The Place of the Lion* saved the world because, through the power he had gained by being in love, he was able to recall the animals of the earth to their archetypes before they could devastate the earth. In short, the "occultism" of the novels prevents their being taken seriously as examples of romantic theology or of theologized true love.

Then there is the question of Dante and the function of Beatrice in his work. The question is important to Williams's view of romantic love because, for him, Dante is the prime example of the Way of Romantic Love, and, in fact, as I have said, a great part of his romantic theology reads like a gloss on Dante. So far as it may be shown that Williams finds a more explicit system of love as leading to beatitude in Dante than is really there, then so far Williams's system seems to exist without examples. Now Williams holds, as we have seen, that Dante began this system in the *Vita Nuova* and enlarged upon it in his later work; he makes much of Dante's encounter with Beatrice in the streets of Florence, and the fact that Dante said that his beatitude had come upon him. But it is a commonplace that the medieval habit of thought was incurably analogical: it saw most earthly things as analogues of heavenly things, and it saw in this way as a matter of course without, as it were, premeditation. One need only point to the microcosm-macrocosm analogy and the medieval notion of the "signatures" on things. And if Dante's *caritas* in the *Vita* was meant to be taken as serious theology, then any number of other similar protestations of the poets of the *dolce stil nuovo* must also be so taken. Cavalcanti's *ballata Veggio negli occhi,* for example, says almost exactly what Dante says in the *Vita* in the passage which Williams has quoted as the beginning of the Way of Romantic Love:

> In my lady's eyes I see a light full of spirits of love which brings wonderful delight into my heart, so that it is filled with joyous life;
>
> Such a thing befalls me when I am in her presence that I cannot describe it to the intellect: It seems to me that as I gaze at her there issues from her semblance a lady of such beauty that the mind cannot grasp it, and from this at once another is born of wondrous beauty out of which it seems that there issues a star which says: "Behold, your blessedness is before you."
>
> When this beautiful lady appears, a voice goes forth before her which celebrates her meekness so sweetly that if I try to repeat it, I feel that her greatness is such that it makes me tremble, and in my soul stir sighs which say: "Lo, if you gaze at this one you will see her virtue ascended into heaven."[63]

In short, what Williams seems to ignore in his continual citation of Dante as a teacher of the Way of Romantic Love is that Dante, in treating love philosophically and even theologically, was doing no more than the other writers of his school. Thus the image of the lady in the Cavalcanti poem just quoted would strike the poet, as Beatrice struck Dante, in the vegetative and sensitive soul, but in the rational soul it would give him

> another sort of experience, neither joyous nor sad, but wonderful. There the image of the lady was rendered intelligible as an essence of wondrous beauty and, glowing in the intellect as a celestial intelligence, a star, it foretold the salvation of the poet if he could but follow this beauty to its source in heaven. Of all the *stilnovisti*, only Dante attempted such an excursion, and that effort led into another kind of poetry, in which the beauty of the lady became a progressive revelation until at last it was quenched in a greater beauty still, the ineffable beauty of God.[64]

In other words, it was the fashion of the school of the sweet new style to prescind from the beauty of the real lady and dwell on the essence of beauty, to talk, in short, not of romantic love as a way of salvation, but of the Idea of Love. Of the ladies in the poems, Beatrice included, "We have no idea . . . where they come from or where they go; their very nature is in doubt, whether human or divine."[65]

Further, Dante was careful to insist in the *Convito* that Beatrice was not only Beatrice in the Paradiso; according to his fourfold interpretation, she was also theology. Williams seems to feel too that she is both, but that so long as she is in some sense still Beatrice, Dante is showing the way of Romantic Love. But just so far as Beatrice becomes anything but Beatrice, so far is she an assertion that Dante was not erecting a personal experience into a theological system. And if he was not doing this, then Williams's prime example of the Romantic Way is gone.

But let us suppose that Williams's analogy between the romantic experience and Christian holy history is a valid one, as it may be in spite of the difficulties I have been suggesting. Then the only real objection to it is not theological but purely natural and human: it seems disappointing, as its analogue, the Christian religion, so often seems disappointing. It seemed at the outset to promise so much for daily living—for the time being—because it deals with one of the truly unforgettable experiences in human life. But it can account for the fading of the romantic vision only by saying that it is one's duty to see all things in love, "as to the Lord." But, unhappily, that is what all Christians have always known and have always found so difficult. Worse, it is exactly what most Christians have found to be the most humdrum part of religious life. What can be drearier than to act as if you love your neighbor simply because you know you should, even when you believe that such power of loving is given to you? Romantic theology, in brief, is not exciting, though it deals with perhaps the most exciting thing in the world. Romantic love may lead to sanctity, but then so may anything else. The romantic love experience, then, seems qualitatively the same as any other experience, and thus remains as enigmatic as any other experience. In the world we know, human love, like other human experiences and emotions, may lead to obvious evil when, like the other experiences, it is not theologized, when it is not used as a religious means. We may recall that in Milton's myth of the Fall, romantic love, even in its unfallen state, played a great part in, was even the efficient cause of, the Fall itself; nor would it be difficult to point out any number of great works of Western literature that have echoed Milton in seeing human love as basically tragic. Lewis has both confirmed Williams's analogy of love to formal Christianity and indicated the disappointing quality of it that I have been trying to describe:

> In reality . . . Eros, having made his gigantic promise and shown you in glimpses what its performance would be like, has "done his stuff." He, like a godparent, makes the vows; it is we who must keep them. It is we who must labour to bring our daily life into even closer accordance with what the glimpses have revealed. We must do the works of Eros when Eros is not present. This all good lovers know. . . . And all good Christian lovers know that this programme, modest as it sounds, will not be carried out except by humility, charity and divine grace; that it is indeed the whole Christian life seen from one particular angle.[66]

However, I am less concerned with the ultimate validity of romantic theology than I am with the religious cast of mind that could produce it. And it is surely clear that this cast of mind can hardly be called anything but romantic. Both the poetry and the theology of Williams are "transcendental" in the usual sense that the term is applied to Goethe, Emerson, and Whitman: all nature, including human nature, is an image of divinity, a reflection of

God. Nothing is truly God except God Himself; yet all things imitate Him in their degrees, all things are reminders of God, like Whitman's grass, a handkerchief of the Lord designedly dropped. (It is true that most writers whom we place in the transcendental line are Idealists—Goethe, Emerson, Thoreau, Coleridge. We have seen that Barfield turned Lewis into a rather grudging Idealist on the ground that Lewis's transcendental beliefs made no sense in a dualistic world. But with Williams, as with Whitman, we find the anomalous case: the poet who insists on the mind-body dualism and who stresses the goodness of the two "parts" of man. Yet both Williams and Whitman belong to the tradition. Neither will admit to a monistic view, yet in stressing the equality of the body and the soul they allow themselves to share in the benefits of the Idealistic view.)

In any event, Williams, like Barfield and Lewis, has made a conscious attempt to bring the manner of romanticism to the matter of religion, to combine a literary bent with religious beliefs. And like Barfield and Lewis, he has succeeded to such a degree that it is impossible to separate his romanticism from his religion. Labels aside, I think it is most accurate and most useful to see Williams's work as romantic religion in the way that we see Wordsworth's *Prelude* as romantic naturalism. What both Wordsworth and Williams illustrate is the other side of the Kant-Coleridge coin—the creative side. Coleridge talks much of the creative imagination, but most of his own creative work may fairly be called assimilation rather than creation, as Lowes's monumental work has shown. What one rarely finds in Coleridge is what one often finds in Wordsworth: the belief in a kind of vision perceived by the Imagination, and a poetic attempt to be true to this vision. This is in great part the explanation of Wordsworth's best work: he had a profound faith in his vision, he tried to be faithful to it, and he tried on occasion to make it meaningful in a discursive way. He was, in Williams's terms, a true romantic, a reflective romantic. He was not content with the experience of the passionate apprehension of the divine life in Nature. He kept turning it around, observing it, trying to make it significant by speaking of it in Hartley's terms, or Plato's, or Spinoza's. And this is also the case with Williams. He too begins with the experience and the reaction to it; he too reflects upon the experience; he too is faithful to the vision and determined to make it meaningful. But where Wordsworth was naturalistic, Williams is Christian. For him, "the feeling intellect" is the union in experience of the two sacred modes of God's manifestation in body and spirit. To reflect upon the romantic experience is, for a Christian, to theologize it; it is to see in that vision the love, the co-inherence, which is the law of life: man ingodded in the body and spirit of Christ.

Chapter Five

J. R. R. Tolkien and *The Lord of the Rings*

The emergence of J. R. R. Tolkien as a public literary figure is surely one of the oddities of our times. In the 1930s and 1940s, beyond the relatively small professional world of philology and medieval scholarship, he was known only as the author of a children's story, *The Hobbit,* published in 1938. As late as 1946, he was still a shadowy figure whom Lewis referred to in his preface to *That Hideous Strength:* "Those who would like to learn further about Numinor and the True West must (alas!) await the publication of much that still exists only in the MSS. of my friend, Professor J. R. R. Tolkien."[1] This anonymity remained until 1954 when the first two volumes of *The Lord of the Rings* were published in a hardback edition, followed by the third volume in 1955. The trilogy was reviewed by such distinguished writers as Auden and Edmund Wilson, and Tolkien's public career began. For about a decade the trilogy attracted fit audience though few, and Tolkien acquired a kind of underground reputation. It was possible in those years to find passionate admirers of the trilogy—usually in the universities—but it was also possible to find very knowledgeable literary people who had never heard of it or could not abide it.

Then in 1965 the explosion occurred. Two paperback editions

of the trilogy were published in this country: one by Ace Books (an edition not authorized by Tolkien), and one (the authorized version) by Ballantine Books. Suddenly Tolkien was famous. In ten months, according to a writer for the *Saturday Evening Post,* the trilogy sold more than a quarter of a million copies,[2] and it has continued to sell at a remarkable rate. For about two years Tolkien became a campus craze, replacing Golding, who had replaced Salinger. There is a Tolkien Society of America, "800 at last count,"[3] and at least one journal devoted largely to his work.[4] I believe we have lived through the phenomenon now and are coming out the other side, but it is hard to be sure. Most of the collegiate interest in Tolkien occurred in the eastern universities and in a few in California. It is possible that there will be further demonstrations of interest in midwestern colleges, if there really is any truth to the theory that there is a kind of cultural lag in many midwestern institutions. Elvish signs may appear on store fronts in Nebraska (as they did on subway walls near Columbia University), and lapel buttons asserting that Frodo lives may spring up in Kansas. But in any case, serious critical consideration of Tolkien's work has never been limited to either the east or west coast; in fact, one of the most sustained collections of critical essays on Tolkien grew out of a symposium held in 1967 at Mankato State College in Minnesota.[5]

Nearly all the serious discussion of Tolkien's trilogy resolves itself into three basic questions (though in practice they often overlap): (1) What is the value of fantasy, of imagined worlds? Can such writing be taken seriously? Can it be anything but "escapism" of some sort? (2) What is the genre of the trilogy? What can it be compared to? (3) Does the trilogy have any relevance to human life, and if so how? In the early discussions of the work there is the widest possible variety of opinion on all these questions. More recently, though the questions of fantasy and genre are still debated, there has been general agreement that the work is to be taken seriously; or at least people who do not like Tolkien are no longer writing about him. In the following pages I shall examine these questions, and some of the answers that have been given to them, as a means of suggesting my own view: that the trilogy is best seen as an example of romantic religion, and that Tolkien's now well known essay on fairy stories is basically an argument for the kind of romantic religion that the trilogy presents.

Auden, in a review of *The Return of the King,* the final volume of the trilogy, notes that the book produces "violent arguments," that no one who reads it seems to have "a moderate opinion." And what produces the immoderate reactions is the question of the validity of purely imagined worlds. Auden supposes "that some people object to Heroic Quests and Imaginary Worlds on principle; such, they feel, cannot be anything but light 'escapist' reading."[6] He goes on to argue persuasively that both the Heroic Quest and the perfectly "realistic" or "naturalistic" novel are literary extremes. The Heroic Quest, he thinks, depicts a pattern of Good against Evil that is not readily discernible in human events as we know them, though the pattern may well be there. But at the other extreme the realistic novel also depicts man in a way that does not square with our subjective experience. We feel ourselves as "willing" creatures who at least partly shape the pattern of our lives in time; this subjective feeling is one of the basic facts of consciousness. But the usual novel, whether "psychological" or not, is forced to depict man as existing in a series of causes and effects over which he seems to have no control. Both extremes falsify life, but neither is to be damned for it.

Edmund Wilson, reviewing the trilogy about threee months later, might well have been replying to Auden. The fact that grown-up people can take seriously a work that deals with imaginary kingdoms forces him to conclude that "certain people . . . have a lifelong appetite for juvenile trash." If he must read of imaginary kingdoms, he prefers Cabell's *Poictesme.* "He at least writes for grown-up people, and he does not present the drama of life as a showdown between Good People and Goblins." For Mark Roberts, too, the trilogy has "no relevance to the human situation" largely because it is "contrived." In brief, Wilson and Roberts argue that the book is simply "escapist" because it is "made up." But Gerald Jonas, like Auden, does not see fantasy as necessarily escapist: "The only 'escape' in Tolkien is to a world where the struggle between Good and Evil is waged more fiercely and openly than our own, where the stakes are at least as great, and where the odds are, if anything, even more perilously balanced." The work, he thinks, is so little escapist that in reading Tolkien one should be somewhere where he can keep his eye "on at least one small patch of something green and growing," for "wherever there are green and growing things, there is still Hope."[7]

The disagreement about the value of imagined worlds spills over into the disagreement about the genre of the work. There have been numerous attempts to "place" the trilogy in order to make comparative judgments. I shall note them only briefly here and return to some of them later on. For Auden, the genre is "the Heroic Quest."[8] For Wilson, the work is "a philological game."[9] For William Blissett, the work is "a heroic romance," and "perhaps the last literary masterpiece of the Middle Ages." Christopher Derrick calls it a "huge and serious epic," and Bruce A. Beatie makes a strong case for its being a "traditional epic," with all the "essential elements" of traditional epic: "folk-tale, fiction, and saga." I myself have argued elsewhere that the trilogy is a fairy story in Tolkien's sense of that term. And Alexis Levitin is perhaps most nearly right when he says that the trilogy "partakes of the nature of the epic and the fairy story, as well as being, quite clearly, a quest tale." He points out that there are really two heroes in the work: Aragorn, the traditional epic hero, and Frodo, who is closer to the fairy-tale hero, a character, in Auden's words, who " 'is not recognizable as a hero except in the negative sense—that he is the one who to the outward eye appears, of all people, the least likely to succeed. . . .' "[10]

But it is the larger question of the meaning, the significance, the relevance of the trilogy to life which subsumes these first two questions. It is interesting that Wilson and Roberts should be able to dismiss the work as escapist while Jonas suggests reading it only in the presence of a symbol of Hope, and while Douglass Parker finds in it the pre-Christian fatalism of *Beowulf*. The words that Tolkien borrowed from *Widsith* to describe *Beowulf*, Parker thinks, apply to the trilogy itself—"Life is fleeting: everything passes away, light and life together."[11] We may talk all we like of "subjective truth" and "personal interpretation," but surely our critics can tell a hawk from a handsaw? I believe Mr. Levitin's idea that the work is a combination of genres is a partial answer to this question, and I shall suggest later on that the work, because it is "romantically religious," is, like formal religion, both heartening and frightening—heartening because it offers solace for the world's ills of evil and death, frightening because in order to offer this solace it must stress the existence of these ills, and the inevitability of them.

From the very beginning, the defenders of the trilogy have been denied one potentially very forceful argument: they have been unable to say that the book is relevant to life on the grounds that it is an allegory. Tolkien himself has denied that the work is allegorical, and critics such as Wilson have not let other critics forget it. But Tolkien's denial of allegorical intention leaves open the possibility of other ways by which a story can "mean":

> As for any inner meaning or "message," it has in the intention of the author none. It is neither allegorical nor topical . . . I cordially dislike allegory in all its manifestations. . . . I much prefer history, true or feigned, with its varied applicability to the thought and experience of readers. I think that many confuse "applicability" with "allegory"; but the one resides in the freedom of the reader, and the other in the purposed domination of the author.[12]

Tolkien's distinctions may perhaps be re-worded to say somethink like this: the trilogy is not allegorical; Tolkien had no distinct and settled "point" to make about the human condition or anything else, no argument—and an allegory is an argument. The trilogy is "feigned history"—by which he must mean simply "fiction," or "fiction carrying with it the illusion of historical reality," narrative which the reader accepts as "real" while he reads it. (I do not see that "feigned history" differs essentially from the created reality of James or Conrad, or even any poor realistic novelist, but that may not be relevant to the distinction.) "Feigned history," like "true history," is open to "application" by the reader; he may see the history as relevant to his own time, his own particular situation, and so on. What Tolkien has done is to bring up the old critical question, Where does the meaning of a literary work reside?, and answer it quite simply by saying, "In the mind, or freedom, of the reader." In one of the notes at the end of his essay on fairy stories, he makes the distinction clearer by contrasting the ways of pictorial art with those of fiction; the contrast is almost the reverse of the famous Jamesian dictum that fiction is analogous to both painting and drama, and that fiction succeeds best when it approaches closest to these other arts. Tolkien argues that "The radical distinction between all art (including drama) that offers a *visible* presentation and true literature is that it imposes one visible form. Literature works from mind to mind and is thus more progenitive. It is at once more universal and more poignantly particular." The example he cites is fiction in which there are occasional illustrations, literal pictures:

> If a story says "he climbed a hill and saw a river in the valley below," the illustrator may catch, or nearly catch, his own vision of such a scene; but every hearer of the words will have his own picture, and it will be made out of all the hills and rivers and dales he has ever seen, but specially out of The Hill, The River, The Valley which were for him the first embodiment of the word.[13]

On the one hand, of course, such a view seems an invitation to utter subjectivism, the view that the fictional work—that is, the trilogy, for Tolkien is talking specifically of that—is like a blot of ink in a Rohrschach test, open to any interpretation, with no interpretation any "truer" than the others because there is nothing objectively "there" in the ink blot. But really Tolkien is not so much defining a critical position as describing a psychological fact. Not only the trilogy but any piece of literature is "used" according to the condition of its reader; even when some sort of objective meaning is agreed upon by a group of readers of a Shakespeare sonnet or a James novel, there is still the question of whether the art work is relevant to each reader's life—whether it "speaks to his condition" —and that is of course a perfectly personal and subjective problem. And it may be added that even if we take Tolkien's remarks as referring specifically to "meaning" and not simply to "use," and as referring to all literature—that is, even if we suppose the critical position so much feared by every teacher, that the literary work may mean all things to all readers—there is a word to be said for such a position. We tend to talk in extremes when we deal with the problem. We suppose on the one hand the Ideal Reader, who when he reads Shakespeare is perfectly aware of the Elizabethan world-view, cosmology, physiology, theory of drama, vocabulary, and so on. On the other hand we suppose the Benighted Reader, ignorant of all the knowledge and insight possessed by the Ideal Reader; we suppose someone like the lady in the Thurber essay who thought *Macbeth* was a murder mystery and was convinced that Macbeth had not really "done it." No doubt both extremes exist, but both are very rare.

Ever since I. A. Richards's test tube experiments of several years ago we have known that students "misinterpret" poetry very frequently. At least that is the way that we usually phrase it to ourselves. But really it is more accurate to say that they react differently to a given poem or story. It is true that very often a student cannot "reduce" a poem or story to a statement of its meaning; but if the New Critics have taught us nothing else they have taught us the fallacy of this approach to literature, this "heresy of paraphrase." To the extent that a poem or a fiction is an "experience" or a "world," then the student's reaction to it is in its own way valid, just as his reaction to the real world in which he lives is also valid. If he hunts for morals in literature, it is because he hunts for morals in life, because he is a certain kind of person. We seem afraid sometimes that literature will not survive unintelligent approaches to it, but it has survived Gosson and Rhymer and countless local censors. It has even survived *intelligent* disagreement about approaches and meaning: witness the differing views of *Paradise Lost* to be seen in Dryden, Blake, Shelley, Lewis, Douglas Bush, and Eliot. We are inclined to be fretful if a student does not agree with our interpretation of a poem—when all the evidence argues that the meaning of any art work lies in the relationship between the art work and the perceiving subject; when depth psychology has shown that there exist potential levels of meaning in a work which the writer himself and no one else of his time could know; when, as Lewis has pointed out about the famous scribal error in Virgil ("the tears of things"), a meaning can never be intended at all, either consciously or unconsciously, but simply occur by accident;[14] when all would agree that the general import of an art work changes over the years, so that Moliere's *The Misanthrope* or Shakespeare's *The Merchant of Venice* simply do not mean for us what they meant for their contemporary viewers. In short, what Barfield says about language itself, I should say for language constructs: we tend to see the meaning of an art work as fixed and constant, when all the evidence indicates that it is variable and shifting, a reflection of the growth and change of the human mind and outlook.

In any case, Tolkien has left the meaning of the trilogy "open," and there has been no lack of interpretation, or applicability. William Blissett, who views the work as heroic romance, believes that Tolkien's "fable" is to be seen as "a parable of power for the atomic age."[15] And Douglass Parker, who sees it as imitating many of the qualities of *Beowulf,* believes that Tolkien has gone to fantastic lengths to make his world "a prodigious and . . . unshakable construct of the imagination" in imitation of the Beowulf poem because Tolkien feels "that only in this way can he attain what the author of *Beowulf* (also an antiquary) attained: a sense of man's Vergänglichkeit, his impermanence, his perishability." And for Parker this imaginary world has relevance to the real one. Tolkien's borrowings from, or re-workings of, myths from the Anglo-Saxon, Celtic, and Norse provide a bridge from his world to ours; they make "the implicit statement that our world, in the Age of Man, the Fourth Age, is a *continuation* of his, and will recapitulate its happenings in new terms, as the Third Age recapitulated the Second, and the Second the First."[16]

For many critics the trilogy is above all else a moral construct. Michael Straight, who regards the work as one of the "very few works of genius in recent literature," argues that the major theme of the trilogy is essentially a moral one: personal responsibility, as symbolized by Frodo and his relationship to the Ring. "In the presence of limited good, and of corruptible man, what is the responsibility of the ring-bearer? Is it to use present evil on behalf of present good and thereby to ensure the continuation of evil? Or is it to deny present gain in an effort to destroy evil itself?" Thus the work is not escapist; it "illuminates the inner consistency of reality."[17]

Patricia Spacks, too, stresses the ethical character of the work. It does not present the war of good and evil as a matter of Good People against Goblins, as Wilson says; rather "the fundamental power" of the work derives from "the force and complexity of its moral and theological scheme." Frodo and Sam are clearly endowed with free will, and free will "entails a necessarily structured universe." The overall pattern of the work illustrates one of man's fundamental problems, his relation to the universe. Frodo and Sam's sense of dedication to the quest shows a sense of duty not merely to themselves; it shows also a "cosmic responsibility, justified by the existence of some vast, unnamed power for good." Tolkien has rejected realism in order "to talk more forcefully about reality."[18]

Lewis sees the meaning of the trilogy as heroism, the heroism of a man if he is simply to live. He does not like to extract a moral from a work that he finds "good beyond hope," but if there must be a moral, then that is it, "that our victory is impermanent." The work serves to recall us "from facile optimism and wailing pessimism alike, to that hard, yet not quite desperate, insight into Man's unchanging predicament by which heroic ages have lived."[19]

Finally, in one of the most interesting of the recent analyses of the book, Dorothy K. Barber argues that, though the work is not allegorical, it has an "anagogical structure,"[20] that there is "a coherent and consistent significance which is largely Christian" (p. 38). I have remarked in connection with Lewis's trilogy that he used the natural metaphors of height and depth and light and darkness to good advantage to suggest good and evil in his depiction of the interplanetary battle. Dorothy Barber's contention is that Tolkien has done this kind of thing much more thoroughly and subtly in the trilogy, that the structure and meaning of the trilogy in fact exist because of Tolkien's "profound understanding of the creative power of words" (p. 38). He has let language carry the meaning of his story:

> By turning primary world figurative language into secondary world literal language, Tolkien has incorporated metaphysical Christian qualities into the physical nature of Middle-earth and into the physical and mental qualities of its peoples . . . I hope to show that the story turns on these religious qualities, that the contending qualities of Good and Evil, as we know them from the Bible, constitute the motives for action and the patterns for action. Tolkien has done this largely by allowing such words as light, darkness, part and chance to operate in all of their possible meanings. (pp. 38–39)

After an analysis of the religious implications of Tolkien's essay on fairy stories—an analysis that I wholly agree with and to which I shall return later on—she goes on to document her argument in the most convincing way possible. The basic contrast is between Light and Darkness, of course, and she meticulously notes the variety and degrees of the contrast. Light seems to issue from the elven center of Lorien; Gandalf "cancels the Hounds of Sauron by light from his staff"; the great spider Shelob is "wounded by the pristine light from the phial of Galadriel"; light is painful to Gollum; after Frodo is wounded by Gollum in the struggle for the Ring he is "removed or translated to another land whose light has a stronger healing power than the light of Lorien" (p. 43). But there is more than this, and more than Sauron's being named the Dark Lord who lives in the Land of Shadows; the Light-Dark dichotomy extends through all the physical and moral nature of Middle-earth. Darkness, for example, suggests lack of being, or lack of substance, and all the evil beings of the trilogy illustrate this. Sauron has no body, and like the orcs, and Gollum, and Shelob, and Saruman, and the Ringwraiths, he is voracious, literally lusting after substantiality. "Once again, Tolkien has let a physical quality, lack of substance, develop into a nonphysical quality, the feeling of incompleteness, the greed, which causes Sauron and all evil creatures to devour all they can reach" (p. 45). The fact that Frodo and Sam often see themselves as figures in a "story" suggests Providence, a Christian pattern in the events of the book, and Miss Barber concludes that "because of the nature of figurative language and the many connotations carried by the words light, darkness, part and chance, Tolkien has been able to let a Christian anagogical significance arise from the story, if the reader chooses to look for it" (p. 49). This rough summary does not do justice to the brilliance of the essay; it is an excursion into philological interpretation that Tolkien himself might have written.

Because of the forceful arguments of critics such as Professor Bruce Beatie I should no longer argue that the trilogy is "only" or "simply" a fairy story in Tolkien's terms. Mr. Levitin's comment that it is a combination of epic, fairy story, and quest tale seems to me a better description and, incidentally, a good means of ending the whole argument about genre. But I still maintain, as Miss Barber does, that Tolkien's essay on fairy stories throws much light on the trilogy and, what is much more important, that the essay indicates a view of literature and life that is both romantic and religious.

Tolkien's essay attempts to determine the nature, origin, and use of fairy stories. As to the nature of them, no definition can be arrived at on historical grounds; the definition must rather deal with "the nature of Faerie: the Perilous Realm itself, and the air that blows in that country."[21] But this is exactly what cannot be either defined or accurately described, only perceived. Faerie may be roughly translated as Magic, but not the vulgar magic of the magician; it is rather magic "of a particular mood and power" (p. 43), and it does not have its end in itself but in its operations. Among these operations are "the satisfaction of certain primordial human desires" such as the desire "to survey the depths of space and time" and the desire "to hold communion with other living things" (p. 44). Travellers' tales are not fairy stories, and neither are those stories which utilize dream machinery to explain away their marvels; if a writer attaches his tale of marvels to reality by explaining that it was all a dream (as in the medieval tradition, for example), "he cheats deliberately the primal desire at the heart of Faerie: the realization, independent of the conceiving mind, of imagined wonder" (p. 45).

These remarks throw much light on the trilogy. It is a fairy story in the sense just described: it concerns itself with the air that blows through the Perilous Realm of Faerie. It attempts to satisfy "certain primordial human desires." It surveys the depths of time, as Lewis's trilogy surveys the depths of space (and in Tolkien's sense, Lewis's trilogy is thus a fairy story). The story itself is of the Third Age, but the story is full of echoes out of the dim past; in fact, the trilogy is in great part an attempt to suggest the depths of time, "which antiquates antiquity, and hath an art to make dust of all things." The Third Age is, for the reader, old beyond measure, but the beings of this age repeatedly tell stories out of ages yet deeper "in the dark backward and abysm of time," and in fact often suggest that these stories recount only the events of relatively recent times, and that the oldest things are lost beyond memory. All this is to satisfy that primordial desire to explore time, for "antiquity has an appeal in itself" (p. 57). Fairy stories, Tolkien's among them, "open a door on Other Time, and if we pass through, though only for a moment, we stand outside our own time, outside Time itself, maybe" (p. 57).

And the trilogy attempts to satisfy the other desire, "to hold communion with other living beings," just as Lewis's trilogy does. The Ents, for example, are the great trees of the Third Age, and are among the oldest living things. They speak to the hobbits in a language as old, as slowly and carefully articulated, as the earth itself. And when Tom Bombadil speaks, it is as if Nature itself—non-rational, interested only in life and in growing things—were speaking. The elves, the dwarfs, even Gollum and the orcs, are gradations—either up or down—from the human level; they are "other living beings" with whom the reader holds communion in the trilogy world of imagined wonder.

Lewis, we recall, had much to say of the books of Beatrix Potter; it was in these that he found early traces of the thing he called Joy. And Tolkien finds something in them of Faerie. They are mostly beast fables, he thinks, but they "lie near the borders of Faerie" because of the moral element in them, "their inherent morality, not any allegorical *significatio*" (p. 46). Here, perhaps, is a partial answer to the question which, as we have seen, all the critics of the trilogy have dealt with: the relevance of the work to human life. It is not only through allegory that invented characters and actions may have significance. Allegory is ultimately reducible to rational terms; and in this sense there is no allegory in *The Lord of the Rings*. But there runs throughout the work an "inherent morality" which many critics have discerned, and which some have tried to reduce to allegory. It is the element of the numinous that is to be found throughout the work of George Macdonald and in Lewis's novels. It is the sense of a cosmic moral law, consciously obeyed or disobeyed by the characters, but existing nowhere as a formulated and codified body of doctrine. Patricia Spacks has commented that Tolkien has included in the trilogy "all the necessary materials for religion."[22] It is even more accurate to say that he has included Conscience, which may be defined, for the purposes of the trilogy, as an awareness of natural law. But it is not a rational awareness; that is, rationality plays almost no part in it. It is rather an emotional or imaginative awareness; the doctrine does not exist, but the feeling normally attached to the doctrine does. The value of this inherent morality, as we shall see, comes under Tolkien's heading of "Recovery," which is one of the uses of the fairy story.

Fairy stories, then, are those which utilize Faerie, "the realization of imagined wonder," and which have, or may have, an "inherent morality." Their nature is "independent of the conceiving mind," or, as Lewis said of Macdonald's myth-making, it comes to us on a level deeper and more basic than that of the conceptual intellect, and must be perceived by the imagination.

Tolkien's views of the origins of fairy stories take us a step closer to the heart of the matter. The history of fairy stories is "as complex as the history of human language" (p. 49). In this history three elements have figured in the creation of "the intricate web of Story" (p. 49): invention, diffusion, and inheritance. The latter two lead ultimately back to the first and do nothing to clear up the mystery of invention. For diffusion is merely "borrowing in space" (p. 50) from an inventor, and inheritance is merely "borrowing in time" (p. 50). Both presuppose an inventive mind, and it is to the nature of the inventive mind that Tolkien now turns.

> The incarnate mind, the tongue, and the tale are in our world coeval. The human mind, endowed with the powers of generalization and abstraction, sees not only *green-grass,* discriminating it from

> other things, . . . but sees that it is *green* as well as being *grass*. But how powerful, how stimulating to the very faculty that produced it, was the invention of the adjective: no spell or incantation in Faerie is more potent. And that is not surprising: such incantations might indeed be said to be only another view of adjectives, a part of speech in a mythical grammar. The mind that thought of *light, heavy, grey, yellow, still, swift,* also conceived of magic that would make heavy things light and able to fly, turn grey lead into yellow gold, and the still rock into swift water. If it could do the one, it could do the other; it inevitably did both. When we can take green from grass, blue from heaven, and red from blood, we have already an enchanter's power—upon one plane; and the desire to wield that power in the world external to our minds awakes. It does not follow that we shall use that power well upon any plane. We may put a deadly green upon a man's face and produce a horror; we may make the rare and terrible blue moon to shine: or we may cause woods to spring with silver leaves and rams to wear fleeces of gold, and put hot fire into the belly of the cold worm. But in such "fantasy," as it is called, new form is made; Faerie begins; Man becomes a sub-creator. (pp. 50–51)

Barfield might well have written this passage; but, more important, behind the passage, as behind the work of Barfield, there is the romantic doctrine of the creative imagination. Faerie is a product of the "esemplastic" imagination, a product of the Secondary Imagination, which is an echo of the Primary Imagination that creates and perceives the world of reality.

Nor is the creative imagination to be taken lightly, or metaphorically, in Tolkien's theory of the fairy story. The writer of the story is really a sub-creator; he creates a "Secondary World" (p. 60) which the mind of the reader really enters. Further, the reader's state of mind is not accurately described in the phrase "willing suspension of disbelief," which indicates a kind of tolerance or tacit agreement. When the story is successful, the reader practices "Secondary Belief" (p. 60), which is a positive thing. So long as the artist's art does not fail him, "what he relates is 'true': it accords with the laws of that world. You therefore believe it, while you are . . . inside" (p. 60).

Tolkien elaborates, and slightly qualifies, the doctrine of the creative imagination in his discussion of the use of fairy stories. He begins with a dictionary distinction between the Fancy and the Imagination. According to this distinction, the Fancy is the image-making faculty, what Coleridge called "a mode of memory emancipated from the order of time and space";[23] the imagination is "the power of giving to ideal creations the inner consistency of reality" (p. 66). Coleridge thought of the two capacities as wholly distinct faculties, the Fancy being analogous to the understanding, and the Imagination analogous to the Reason. Tolkien would re-combine them because he believes "the verbal distinction philologically inappropriate, and the analysis inaccurate. The mental power of image-making is one thing, or aspect; and it should appropriately be called Imagination. The perception of the image, the grasp of its implications, and the control, which are necessary to a successful expression, may vary in vividness and strength; but this is a difference of degree in Imagination, not a difference in kind" (p. 66). What gives "the inner consistency of reality" or Secondary Belief is not properly Imagination but Art, which is "the operative link between Imagination and the final result, Sub-creation" (p. 67). Needing a term to express both the "Sub-creative Art" and "a quality of strangeness and wonder in the Expression, derived from the Image" (p. 67), he chooses to use the word *Fantasy*. For the term, in the sense in which he means it, "combines with its older and higher use as an equivalent of Imagination the derived notions of 'unreality' (that is, of unlikeness to the Primary World), of freedom from the domination of observed 'fact,' in short of the fantastic" (p. 67).

He is aware, he says, of the implications of the word *fantastic*, that it implies that the things with which it deals are not to be found in the "Primary World." In fact, he welcomes such implications, for that is exactly what he means by the term, that the images which it describes are not extant in the "real" world. That they are not "is a virtue not a vice" (p. 67). (We are reminded of Barfield's use of Shelley's lines: "Forms more real than living man, / Nurslings of immortality.") Just because Fantasy deals with things which do not exist in the Primary World, Tolkien holds, it is "not a lower but a higher form of Art, indeed the most nearly pure form, and so (when achieved) the most potent" (p. 67). It is relatively easy to achieve "the inner consistency of reality" in realistic material. But good Fantasy is very difficult to write. Anyone, Tolkien points out, can say "the green sun," but

> To make a Secondary World inside which the green sun will be credible, commanding Secondary Belief, will probably require labour and thought, and will certainly demand a special skill, a kind of elvish craft. Few attempt such difficult tasks. But when they are attempted and in any degree accomplished then we have a rare achievement of Art: indeed narrative art, story-making in its primary and most potent mode. (p. 68)

The fairy story, then, of which the trilogy is a partial example, uses Fantasy, and so far as it is successful is "story-making in its primary and most potent mode." That is to say, in dealing with fantastic things rather than with real ones it attempts the purest form of narrative art, and succeeds to the extent that it induces in the reader the state of mind called Secondary Belief. In short, invented or created stories, if successful, are better than, on a higher level than, stories which merely manipulate the materials of the Primary World. Now this is so not only because such invented stories are harder to make but because they offer certain things to the reader which realistic stories do not offer, or do not offer to the same degree. These things Tolkien calls Recovery, Escape, and Consolation.

"Recovery (which includes return and renewal of health) is a regaining—re-gaining of a clear view" (p. 74). Recovery is a means of "seeing things as we are (or were) meant to see them . . ." (p. 74). All things become blurred by familiarity; we come to possess them, to use them, to see them only in relation to ourselves. In so doing we lose sight of what the things themselves really are *qua* things—and "things" here includes people, objects, ideas, moral codes, literally everything. *Recovery* is recovery of perspective, the old Chestertonian lesson which Tolkien calls "Mooreeffoc, or Chestertonian Fantasy" (p. 74), which Chesterton borrowed from Dickens. Fantasy provides the recovery necessary to those of us who do not have humility; the humble do not need Fantasy because they already see things as not necessarily related to themselves;

their vision is not qualified by selfishness or egotism. Lewis, as I have said, defends the trilogy's relevance to life, and he does so in terms of what Tolkien means by Recovery:

> The value of the myth is that it takes all the things we know and restores to them the rich significance which has been hidden by "the veil of familiarity." . . . By putting bread, gold, horse, apple, or the very roads into a myth, we do not retreat from reality: we rediscover it. As long as the story lingers in our mind, the real things are more themselves. This book applies the treatment not only to bread or apple but to good and evil, to our endless perils, our anguish, and our joys. By dipping them in myth we see them more clearly.[24]

We re-discover the meaning of heroism and friendship as we see the two hobbits clawing their way up Mount Doom; we see again the endless evil of greed and egotism in Gollum, stunted and in-grown out of moral shape by years of lust for the ring; we recognize again the essential anguish of seeing beautiful and frail things—innocence, early love, children—passing away as we read of the Lady Galadriel and the elves making the inevitable journey to the West. We see morality *as* morality by prescinding from this or that human act and watching the "inherent morality" to which all the beings of the Third Age—the evil as well as the good—bear witness. And, perhaps, the devouring nature of time itself is borne in on us, as it was for the Elizabethan sonneteers, and we learn again from the trilogy that all things are Time's fools, that all comes within the compass of his bending sickle.

If Tolkien is right, if Recovery is what he claims it is, and if Fantasy provides Recovery, then it follows that Fantasy, far from being irrelevant to reality, is in fact terribly relevant to moral reality. And the trilogy, so far as Tolkien's art does not fail him, is an example of the dictum, so favored by the Renaissance critics and the ancients, that literature is both *dulce* and *utile,* that Spenser, as Milton said, could be a better teacher than Aquinas.

Finally, the fairy story, by the use of Fantasy, provides Escape and Consolation, two elements which are, as Tolkien notes, very closely connected. In fact, Escape brings about Consolation as its end or effect. Now the fact that the fairy story is "escapist" is the very crux of most of the accusations brought against it (as we have seen in regard to the trilogy). But Tolkien will not admit that Escape is a bad thing. The word, he thinks, has fallen into disrepute because its users too often confuse "the Escape of the Prisoner with the Flight of the Deserter" (p. 76).

> Why should a man be scorned, if, finding himself in prison, he tries to get out and go home? Or if, when he cannot do so, he thinks and talks about other topics than jailers and prison-walls? The world outside has not become less real because the prisoner cannot see it. (p. 77)

Thus Escape from Hitler's Reich is not desertion, it is really rebellion, a refusal to be identified with Hitler. And, Tolkien thinks, this is often the nature of Escape. A man may refuse to write about the world in which he lives not out of cowardice (which is the usual accusation) but because to write about it is in a sense to accept it. He may, like Thoreau, simply secede. And this, for him, is not desertion; it is war, "real Escape, and what are often its companions, Disgust, Anger, Condemnation, and Revolt" (p. 77).

But fairy stories provide other Escapes, and these bring about Consolation of various kinds. Fairy stories, like other kinds of literature and like many other things as well, can provide a kind of solace in a world of "hunger, thirst, poverty, pain, sorrow, injustice, death" (p. 79). And this kind of solace or respite is necessary; it is not refusal to face reality, it is a time needed to regroup one's forces for the next day's battle. Thus the poets talk of "Care-charmer sleep" and the sleep that knits up the ravelled sleeve of care; but they do not advocate sleeping one's life away. Further, fairy stories, as we have seen, provide a kind of Consolation in their satisfaction of "primordial human desires."

But the major Consolation that the fairy story has to offer is one which it contains to a degree that no other kind of literature can equal. It is "the Consolation of the Happy Ending":

> Almost I would venture to assert that all complete fairy-stories must have it. At least I would say that Tragedy is the true form of Drama, its highest function; but the opposite is true of Fairy-story. Since we

> do not appear to possess a word that expresses this opposite—I will call it Eucatastrophe. The eucatastrophic tale is the true form of fairy-tale, and its highest function. (p. 81)

What the fairy story pre-eminently presents is "the joy of the happy ending" (p. 81), and it is in this respect that the fairy story, for Tolkien, is related to reality. But the reality is not the reality of this world, the world of flux and opinion; rather the eucatastrophe "denies . . . universal final defeat and in so far is *evangelium,* giving a fleeting glimpse of Joy, Joy beyond the walls of the world, poignant as grief" (p. 81). The good fairy story, by means of its eucatastrophe, gives the reader "a catch of the breath, a beat and lifting of the heart, near to (or indeed accompanied by) tears" (p. 81), for in the eucatastrophe, or happy ending, the reader has "a piercing glimpse of joy, and heart's desire, that for a moment passes outside the frame, rends indeed the very web of story, and lets a gleam come through . . ." (p. 82). The relevance of the fairy story to reality lies in this "gleam," which is a "sudden glimpse of the underlying reality or truth" (p. 83).

Thus there are two answers to the question, Is the fairy story true? The first, and obvious answer is, it is true if it induces Secondary Belief, if the Art has successfully translated the image of the "created wonder." But that is merely a question of art. The nature of eucatastrophe suggests that the second answer is infinitely more important, for "in the 'eucatastrophe' we see in a brief vision that the answer may be greater—it may be a far-off gleam or echo of *evangelium* in the real world" (p. 83). It is in this second truth that the fairy story, for Tolkien, ceases to be merely literature, and becomes explicitly a vehicle of religious truth, becomes what Man is for Barfield, Joy is for Lewis, and Love is for Williams.

God has redeemed man in all his capacities, and one of his capacities is that of telling stories, especially fairy stories. As Redemption has once more made man in the image and likeness of God, so the capacities of man to some degree echo the capacities of God. In this sense, this second truth of the fairy story is "only one facet of a truth incalculably rich" (p. 83), for in all spheres of human activity there is necessarily something like the signature of

God. The eucatastrophic fairy story, a product of redeemed man, echoes the Gospels, which contain a story "which embraces the essence of all fairy stories" (p. 83). For the Gospels contain not only marvels, as the fairy story does; they contain the birth of Christ, which is "the greatest and most complete conceivable eucatastrophe," "the eucatastrophe of Man's history" (p. 83). And they contain the Resurrection, which is "the eucatastrophe of the story of the Incarnation" (p. 83).

The joy which the ending of the fairy story gives, says Tolkien, is of the same quality, though not the same degree, as the joy which we feel at the fact that the great fairy story of the Gospels is true in the Primary World, for the joy of the fairy tale "has the very taste of primary truth" (p. 84). This is the justification of the fairy story (and, in part, of the trilogy), that it gives us in small—in the beat of the heart and the catch of the breath—the joy of the infinite good news. For "Art has been verified. God is the Lord, of angels, and of man—and of elves. Legend and History have met and fused" (p. 84).

I am gratified that Miss Barber explicitly agrees on this point. Citing the same passage from Tolkien's essay that I have just referred to, she comments: "We may then propose from this passage that in *The Lord of the Rings* Tolkien is creating a story in which one can detect the *Gloria,* an echo of evangelium."[25] Professor Beatie argues that the trilogy cannot be a fairy story in Tolkien's terms because it does not provide the needed happy ending and thus does not provide Consolation:

> Sauron is destroyed, but he is only the servant of a greater evil that still exists to plague the following ages. Frodo returns to the Shire; but like Moses . . . he who saved his age is unable to enjoy the fruits of what he has achieved; with Bilbo and the Elves, he passes away over the sea. Most important, however, is the fact that *The Lord of the Rings* does not really *end.* . . . Frodo and Sam, resting during the climb up to the pass of Cirith Ungol, discuss the nature of tales. "Take any tale you're fond of," says Frodo. "You may know, or guess, what kind of tale it is, happy-ending or sad-ending, but the people in it don't know. And you don't want them to." Sam, considering this, realizes that their own journey is only a small part

> of the immense tale of the Ring, and asks: "Don't the great tales ever end?" "No, they never end as tales," answers Frodo. "But the people in them come, and go when their part is ended."[26]

It seems to me there are several objections to Professor Beatie's argument. First, he is blurring two levels of perceived reality—that of the hobbits and that of the reader. Frodo's remark that the people in the tale do not know the kind of tale they are in is exactly right—but the reader (as Frodo implies) knows. Second, as Miss Barber has noted, Frodo, though he leaves the Shire, leaves it for a better and "brighter" place, like Ransom at the end of the Lewis trilogy. Third, Tolkien has never said that fairy stories deny the realities of evil and death, only that they provide the "good turn" that suggests ultimate victory and peace. The phrase "and they lived happily ever after" surely was never meant to imply that "they" lived forever on earth. If the story of Christ is for Tolkien the archetypal fairy story, with the eucatastrophe consisting of the Resurrection, then it should be added that though Christ "defeated" death, even He did not return permanently to the land of the living, or at least not in His previous historical body. "To be a man," as Tolkien has said elsewhere, "is tragedy enough." Human life ends in human death, and fairy stories do not change this essential fact of the Primary World. What they do is hint at the *Gloria* that follows death. In *The Tolkien Reader,* Tolkien's essay on fairy stories is followed by one of his own fairy stories, "Leaf by Niggle," a story (according to the Publisher's Note) "which illustrates the ideas suggested." In the story, Niggle dies and goes to a better world than ever he imagined.

In any case, I do not believe it too much to say that Tolkien's view of the fairy story has made explicit and Christian Coleridge's claim for the worth of the creative imagination. The Secondary Imagination, which created literature, was an "echo" of the Primary Imagination, which is "the living Power and prime Agent of all human Perception, and . . . a repetition in the finite mind of the eternal act of creation in the infinite I AM."[27] For the fairy story, as Tolkien insists, is sheer creation, the making of a Secondary World out of, and by means of, the Imagination. That is the special activity of the fairy-story maker, and the one by which he becomes, not a writer, but a sub-creator of a kind of literature analogous—or more than analogous—to the universe created *ex nihilo* by the true Creator. In his degree he creates joy—or creates what gives joy—as God, in the purposeful drama of creation, has created what also gives joy, the world with the Christian happy ending. Tolkien's defense of Fantasy is also a defense and, it may be, the last defense of the doctrine of the creative imagination, which brings the making of God and the making of man so close that they nearly touch:

> Although now long estranged,
> Man is not wholly lost nor wholly changed.
> Dis-graced he may be, yet is not de-throned,
> and keeps the rags of lordship once he owned:
> Man, Sub-creator, the refracted Light
> through whom is splintered from a single White
> to many hues, and endlessly combined
> in living shapes that move from mind to mind.
> Though all the crannies of the world we filled
> with Elves and Goblins, though we dared to build
> Gods and their houses out of dark and light,
> and sowed the seed of dragons—'twas our right
> (used or misused). That right has not decayed:
> we make still by the law in which we're made. (pp. 71–72)

Chapter Six

Conclusion

I said at the beginning of this study that I intended to present a phenomenon called romantic religion: a construct in which literary and religious ideas and attitudes fuse. I said also that Frye and Wellek seemed accurate in describing romanticism as a homogeneous movement centering around the powers of the creative imagination—the synthesizing and reconciling qualities of the imagination, as Wellek calls them. I believe the preceding chapters bear out both these contentions.

For Barfield, as we have seen, religion is romanticism come of age. In the temporal polar relationship that exists between God and man, the imagination is the means by which God and man interact. God's progressive creation of the world, in fact, occurs through the human imagination. No one, I submit, can make the doctrine of the creative imagination more important than to say that it is man's link with God and that God creates by means of it. Barfield's creative imagination is not merely a "finite echo" of divine creation; it is the agent of this creation. Such a position necessarily emphasizes the immanence of God in man, and involves, for a Christian, the doctrines of the Incarnation and Redemption. Barfield's esoteric Christianity retains these doctrines by seeing them as parts of the cosmic transformation of God's consciousness into man in the form of man's unconsciousness. The historical Incarnation is the turning point in time, the moment at which God's ineffable consciousness of Himself (through the agency of Christ) becomes partially knowable to man, by means of the imagination. As man becomes more and more self-conscious, able to probe ever deeper into his own unconscious mind, he is able to participate ever more consciously in his relationship with God (again, through the agency of Christ, or grace). This progressive self-consciousness, the actuating of the potential matter of the unconscious mind, is the redemptive process. Thus it is possible for man to speak of his relationship to God in superlatives, as we have seen: Theosophia becomes Anthroposophia. God is not the "wholly other" or the "unimaginably other," as Lewis calls Him. He is, in fact, precisely the "imaginable other," whose nature (so far as man can ever know it) will be known through the human imagination.

None of the other three men, being more orthodox Christians, will travel the road of Anthroposophy with Barfield. But the doctrine of the creative imagination clearly implies the awful closeness of man to God. Thus as we have noted, both Lewis and Williams make much of the Athanasian creed, which stresses, not so much that God was made man as that manhood has been taken up into the Godhead. Lewis, we recall, agrees that our logic must participate in the Word; Williams holds, in effect, that the lover sees Christ in his beloved, seeing in the Beatrician vision the "ingodding" of man; and Tolkien calls the fairy story writer a subcreator who makes by the same laws by which he is made. None of the three will say categorically what Barfield sees as the ultimate implication of the creative imagination: God's immanence in man. Thus all three must (in one way or another) maintain the efficacy of the Secondary Imagination without attempting to specify the real nature of the Primary Imagination. And it is in the Primary Imagination (according to Barfield), in the realm of formulation and figuration, in the realm where language is born, that God's immanence is to be found.

But if Lewis, Williams, and Tolkien hesitate over Barfield's argument for God's immanence in man, they do not abandon certain positions which Barfield sees as following from it—positions difficult to maintain on grounds other than Barfield's. Thus, according to Williams, it is possible to establish relationship with God through man, or through woman. Something like the beatific vision occurs in romantic love, Williams thinks; something like the immanence of God in man becomes apparent to the romantic lover in that moment of vision. It is this which puts the lover in a state of *caritas,* in which he sees all things in love. For Barfield, the relationship between man and God is simpler and clearer. When man begins truly to know himself, he begins truly to know God, though always within the severe limitations of his human nature. By the traditional means of the creative imagination, Barfield has lessened the emphasis on God's transcendence. Williams, like most orthodox Christians, is at pains to preserve both the immanence and transcendence of God, but, as I have suggested, his near identification of *eros* with *agape* leads him very close to Barfield's position.

Again, in the matter of myth, Barfield has much to say, and his view of myth follows from his basic religious position, or helps to verify it. Myth is "the ghost of concrete meaning." And by "concrete meaning" Barfield means the cosmic spirit which is God and which is extending its self-consciousness in man's imagination. Barfield sees both myth and language itself as existing in the form of unconscious meaning before the existence of any individual thinker. On examination, both myth and language point backward to the pre-human time when all that existed was spirit, undividuated meaning, the original phase of the cosmic evolution. Thus myths—the Paradisal myths, for example—suggest truth in a quite literal sense; they allude to the original "way things were." Lewis, we have seen, adopted from Barfield a "more respectful" attitude toward myth, and speaks of myth as "a real if unfocused gleam" of truth, a theory which I have compared to the theory of scriptural accommodation. And both Lewis and Tolkien speak, rather more than wistfully, of the possibility of all myths being "true" in some other existence than our own. Williams, too, feeling the call of myth, goes so far as to adapt the Arthurian myth as a kind of objective correlative for his religious views. But, quite plainly, Barfield has explained the origin and force of myth (whether we accept his total view or not) in a way that the others have not. They have *used* myth in various ways and with varying degrees of effectiveness, but they have not really said why. Or, rather, they have used myth, or made up "new" myth, as a means of avoiding conceptual argument, as a means of speaking symbolically rather than rationally. There is nothing wrong with this, of course, so far as it works. But to the extent that it can be interpreted, or reduced to a set of rational propositions, it must strike the reader as artificial, as something closer to allegory than to true myth. True myth—in Barfield's terms and (I believe) in reality—is nearly impenetrable; there are no "ideas" in it for the reader to penetrate *to,* for it is the closest thing in man's mental life to pure pre-logical thought, meaning which the rational intellect has not yet ordered—more of an experience than a thought at all. Thus, to try to construct "new" myth must really be an impossible task, for the new myth will always contain, no matter how deeply buried, a set of intellectual presuppositions. Lewis's *Till We Have Faces,* I think, is more forceful than his other fiction precisely because it comes closest to myth in Barfield's sense, and is thus less easily reduced to allegory. And it is worth noting that in this case Lewis was dealing with a "real" myth, even though it is a late and comparatively rationalized version. And in the same way, part of the force of Tolkien's trilogy comes from its echoes of and borrowings from real myths out of the Teutonic and Celtic past.

Barfield's most recent remarks about symbolism and imagination should be recalled in this connection. In both "Imagination and Inspiration" and *Unancestral Voice,* we have seen him arguing that the function of the imagination in the future will be to discover "clear and distinct ideas"; it may discover them as "beings" rather than as concepts—in the form of the Blakean beings, or forces, in *Unancestral Voice*—but the beings will be explainable in "monosemous" language, in something like the way that the beings of the old allegories like *Pilgrim's Progress* are explainable. In other words, the function of future imagination will be to go *beyond* rational argument, to go forward to new, decipherable meaning, not backward to buried rational argument, not backward to the ambiguity of "mythic thinking."

I believe it is at this point that Barfield's work moves most sharply away from that of the others, this insistence on movement forward to new truths. I do not mean that the others are simply defenders of the Old, as one critic has called them,[1] though they are obviously more orthodox and conservative than Barfield. I mean that, in Emerson's terms, Barfield is Man Thinking, while the others are rather what Emerson might have called Man Feeling. It is true that Barfield begins with an experience—the aesthetic experience of reading certain kinds of poetry—but from that experience he tries to construct a theory of knowledge. The others also begin from experience, but try to validate or "theologize" that experience in terms of their religious and literary convictions. Lewis, Williams, and Tolkien are not really concerned with new knowledge as such; they are concerned with the romantic experience which in various ways brings them closer to God. If we accept some kind of distinction of the elements within a religion—such as von Hügel's, or more recent versions of it[2]—and assume that every religion is composed of personal religious experience (sometimes mystical), conceptualization, and some form of institution, then Lewis, Williams, and Tolkien may represent the personal element and Barfield the conceptual. The institutional element remains the formal church to which the writers belong—in all four cases some form of Christianity.

Here I should stress again that by "personal religious experience" I mean the romantic experience, not a mystical experience; Lewis, Williams, and Tolkien do not claim to be mystics, though, as we have seen, Williams's friends attributed to him both sanctity and various states of mystical vision. None of the three men claims to have experienced the kind of state which Edwyn Bevan describes:

> in the mystical experience a man's ordinary consciousness of temporal sequence is suspended and he seems to apprehend by direct contact, or even by identification, some tremendous Reality which is above, or below, or behind, the multiplicity of things or psychical events, a Reality which reduces this multiplicity of things to an unreal appearance. It involves an apprehension which seems knowledge in a supreme degree, even if it is knowledge without any conceptual content.[3]

Williams especially talks often of the unity behind the multiplicity of things, and of the unity of man; but when he does so he does not speak of his own experience but of that of the Lady Julian, of Evelyn Underhill, or of the author of *The Cloud of Unknowing.* And Lewis's fictional hero, who undergoes a kind of mystical experience at the end of *Perelandra,* describes his experience in terms borrowed from Ezekiel or from any of a number of mystics who have described the ultimate reality as a great dance. The experience that Lewis, Williams, and Tolkien are concerned with is not the mystical experience, and they are too honest to try to confound them. Their concern is with the value and meaning of the romantic experience, an experience undergone by everyone at some time or other. In their various ways, all three writers see in this experience some sort of religious and moral significance.

Lewis has spelled out explicitly both what the romantic experience is for him and the meaning he has attached to it. His phrase "the baptism of the imagination" is a perfectly accurate description of the phenomenon. The romantic experience is for him spilt religion; it is God-sent. A great part of his character and life was formed for him by the visitation of a longing over which he had no control, which he did not make for himself, and which he could not explain until he had been reconverted to Christianity. The painful pleasure of this thing he called Joy took on meaning for him only when he found that it was to be gained from reading Macdonald, in whose work Joy and holiness were nearly indistinguishable. Ultimately, from within the framework of Christianity, he could see that the romantic longing—the stab and pang felt at the ideas of far-off lands and remote pasts—was really longing for God. The romantic desire for fairy land mantled the real desire for heaven; fairy land was, when seen rightly, a preview of the land of spices. In the last analysis, all longing has God for its final cause. In Aquinas's words: "In the perfect happiness of heaven nothing more will remain to be desired; in the full enjoyment of God man will obtain whatever he has desired in other things."[4]

Williams, too, has tried to make the romantic experience meaningful, to make it, like Lewis's Joy, the beginning of a religious way of life. He has tried, as Lewis said, to theologize the romantic experience, to make of it the basis for the "romantic theology" we have examined. He has tried to make the experience of falling in love a beginning of the Positive or Affirmative Way, the way of life which consists, not in withdrawal from the world, but in acceptance of the world, the way by which one who has been granted grace by the falling-in-love experience may affirm the goodness of God's creation. The lover is awarded the power of seeing all things in *caritas,* in effect of seeing them as God sees them. Further, the love experience is only one mode of the romantic experience. The romantic experience of Nature, as Wordsworth lived it, is another of the modes; and from that experience, as from the love experience, the spiritual power or grace proceeds. What the romantic experience provides is an awareness of the relationship between God and man and between God and Nature. But the awareness is not knowledge; it is a feeling, an intelligible emotion "felt along the heart," a thought "steeped in feeling,"[5] an awareness of

> the sentiment of Being spread
> O'er all that moves and all that seemeth still;
> O'er all that, lost beyond the reach of thought
> And human knowledge, to the human eye
> Invisible, yet liveth to the heart. . . .[6]

The romantic lover and the lover of Nature, in the moment of the romantic experience itself, see all things as unfallen, see all things reflecting God, all things looking

> Towards the Uncreated with a countenance
> Of adoration, with an eye of love.[7]

Finally, Tolkien, combining the religious value of the romantic experience with an explicitly Christian interpretation of the creative imagination, sketches out with clarity and boldness a form of romantic religion which in some ways sums up and brings into focus the beliefs of both Lewis and Williams. The version of the romantic experience that he is concerned with is the peculiar throb and thrill felt at the "good turn" in the eucatastrophic fairy story. This Joy is qualitatively the same as the Christian *Gloria,* the beatitude of the blessed; and this Joy is brought about primarily by a kind of literature which is wholly the work of the Secondary Imagination. Man, the sub-creator, creating in the image of and as an echo to the primary creator, brings into being essentially the same spiritual state as does the Almighty when he bestows the gift of final beatitude. This qualitative identity between Tolkien's Joy and beatitude is, I believe, the position which Lewis's Joy and Williams's *caritas* assume when they are set down in explicit terms. Longing, love, the joy of the man-made eucatastrophe—in short, the romantic experience as these men define it—these are best explained by the fact that the romantic experience is in quality, but not in duration, identical with Christian beatitude. The lesser experience is not an echo of the greater; it is not analogous to the greater; it is not a reflection or a shadow of the greater. The romantic experience *is* beatitude, in however small a portion. It is a tiny room, but it belongs to the many-mansioned house of bliss.

In brief, what Lewis, Williams, and Tolkien have done is to defend the romantic experience by showing it to be religious experience, and have done so by traditionally romantic means. The experiences have been set within the framework of their formal religious beliefs by means of "mythologizing" those religious beliefs. Not only Tolkien, but Lewis and Williams too, have prescinded from the Primary World and have in effect built their churches in the imagined world of fairy land—the Third Age, Perelandra, Logres. And what they are defending is very precious to them: not class-room romanticism, not self-pity, or sentimentality, or gushiness, or any of the thousand other things that romanticism is often accused of. What they are holding is the last bastion against the enemy; it is the experience itself—longing, love, the thrill of the "good turn"—seen *sub specie aeternitatis,* as Vaughan saw Sundays:

> The milky way chalked out with suns; a clue
> That guides through erring hours; and in full story
> A taste of Heav'n on earth; the pledge, and cue
> Of a full feast; and the out courts of glory.

Now no one would deny, I think, that there has been a genuine and wide-spread resurgence of interest in romanticism in the past several years, both in England and America. The debunking of the romantics by Hulme, Eliot, Pound, and some of the Marxist and Freudian critics is out of date. In its place we have serious scholarly and critical work on both the English and American romantic writers: the work of M. H. Abrams, Kathleen Coburn, Frye, Wellek, and others on the English romantics; the work of Gay Wilson Allen, Sherman Paul, Walter Harding, Leon Howard, and others on the American romantics. At the same time we see Wallace Stevens—the modern poet most concerned with a doctrine of the creative imagination—emerging as one of the major figures in American poetry. The four men I have been discussing have all in various ways contributed to this resurgence, but they have also benefited from it. In defending romantic poetry and romantic theory they have helped to shape the climate of opinion that makes mythological fiction and mythological poetry acceptable. Williams's poetry and the fiction of Lewis and Tolkien can be taken seriously now because Shelley and Keats are once again respectable, and because the great discussions of myth and mythology are still in full swing—because, in short, serious criticism has turned to the past with a new kind of curiosity and respect.

But the question I want to advance and try to answer concerns not so much the literary as the religious implications of the phenomenon I have been describing. If the work of the four men is not only literary but religious—implicitly in the case of Tolkien, explicitly in the case of the others—then their religious views are unique, or they are anomalous, or they are a recognizable part of the current religious situation. I know that the phrase "current religious situation," so far as it can be said to refer to anything at all, refers to a vast, complicated, perhaps amorphous combination of religious, social, and cultural forces. But I am simply pointing to it as something we all recognize as being there: the extraordinarily fluid condition of formal Christianity in Western Europe, England, and America. One cannot pick up a newspaper or magazine without coming across some reference to change (desired or dreaded) in rite or dogma or tradition. We have seen the situation described variously as upheaval, turmoil, ferment. For some, it seems the end of formal religion, for others a fresh start. In Barfield's terms, for some the fluidity seems to be true evolution—transformation of a persisting unity into new form; for others, it seems to be substitution, the replacing of something dead by something essentially different—religion by secularism, order by chaos. We are deluged by news of inter-faith dialogues, inter-denominational communion, all sorts of ecumenical activity that suggests new recognition on all sides of the validity of all sects and churches involved. Non-religious writers have seen the whole situation as the final, predictable movement toward total skepticism in religious matters, the inevitable triumph of profane values over sacred. Worried religious people have often seen the situation as leading to a kind of tepid unity of minimal belief, something like an extreme form of Lewis's "mere" Christianity, in which there will be almost no serious commitment to any kind of dogma. Throughout Christendom Aeolus's bag seems to have been untied and the winds of change blow everywhere. Martin Buber is taught in Roman Catholic high school religious classes; all shades of Christian theologians seriously discuss Bultmann and the necessity of demythologizing the scriptures; Rome admits the ultimate liberty of the private conscience in religious matters; alternatives to Christianity seem more and more to be "live options"—Zen Buddhism, for example, and the so-called psychedelic religions based on the use of "mind-expanding" drugs. On a different level, the work in comparative religion of William James (still highly thought of), Otto, and Eliade have made it impossible for the sophisticated Christian to be parochial any longer. He simply cannot draw the sharp line between Christianity and "heathenism" that it was possible for him to draw even a few years ago. He can no longer talk of the "one true religion"; at best he can only talk of the "truest" religion among many true religions. He is driven to a kind of tolerance that is for many Christians unsettling, as if they were being forced to say, like the pigs in Orwell's *Animal Farm,* that all animals are equal but some are more equal than others.

I shall not try to evaluate the religious phenomena I have been citing, but I believe we can detect a quality or flavor that is common to many of them. The "current religious situation" is strongly, if only half-consciously, "existential." The term has been abused and overworked; yet, in the usual imprecise meaning that it carries, it is the most accurate term available. Sartre's sharp statement that existence precedes essence has filtered down—in the language game —to mean a distrust of tradition and institutions, a reluctance (as Burgeon told Chevalier) to believe only on authority, a turning within one's own mind and conscience for final answers. Within the Roman church the doctrine of papal infallibility and the teaching authority of the Magisterium are seriously challenged. Within all Christian churches, increasing numbers of both clergy and laymen are revealing a general suspicion about traditional theology, a view close to Bacon's: that traditional theology is not only hair-splitting but that it is largely a construct of the theologians' own minds and has little to do with life as it has to be lived. I cite one prime example of this seeming irrelevance of theology to everyday life: the proclamation by the Roman church with all solemnity that the Jews are no longer to be held guilty of "deicide." The religious press made much of this proclamation, but outside of formal theological circles it was received with a collective yawn. The word itself was new to most laymen, and the concept it referred to seemed simply silly. One is reminded of Barfield's description of the Reformation in *History in English Words*. Historically, it was a splitting up of the Christian church, but psychologically it was a draining away of individual belief in the power and efficacy of traditional rites and symbols. In the same way, any kind of "immanent life" seems to have left traditional theology. In the popular mind it has simply lost its importance.

In fact, in trying to assess the current religious situation, in trying to find some meaning or pattern to it, we find that Barfield seems to describe it very accurately, and in fact that it is Barfield who in a sense predicted it. We may not feel able to accept all the Anthroposophical implications of his view that history is divine history, a series of conflicts between the impulse toward true evolution and the impulse toward substitution. But, more than many of the other analyses of the current situation, it saves the appearances. It explains on the one hand the decline of the institutional church and on the other the subjective anxiety so prevalent among religious people. More and more, according to Barfield, we are moving beyond the institutional church which has meant for us "fatherhood," regularity, law. We are moving toward something, not different, but new, a transformation of that father-law into subjective law, or "son-law," the dictates of the individual conscience. Surely something like this process—if not the precise process that Barfield describes—is evident in such things as "situation ethics" and the necessity so many people feel to "commit" themselves to social causes for personal, moral reasons (the Negro cause, the pacifist cause, the cause of the poor). Surely such things suggest some sense of personal morality almost detached from institutional operation—and suggest also the private and subjective agony of choice, the *angst* or isolation that we hear so much of.

In answer to the question posed earlier—whether the religious views of Lewis, Williams, Tolkien, and Barfield reflect aspects of the current religious situation—I should answer yes. The peculiar attractiveness that Tolkien's trilogy has for so many people seems to me explainable by the very fact that has caused so much critical comment: the fact that it is a moral drama without reference to anything beyond itself, particularly without reference to a formal moral code or to any kind of religious institution. Its characters are faced with existential moral choices of the same quality as those the readers of the trilogy are faced with. Thus, though it is not "realistic" in the usual literary sense, it is a realistic depiction of the current religious climate, whether Tolkien intended it to be that or not.

As for Lewis and Williams, at first glance they would seem to be only conservatives, preservers of traditional Christianity, and I am sure they saw themselves in this role. But in an age of change even conservatives will show evidence of this change. Thus both men mythologized traditional Christianity as well as defended it. Milton retold the traditional Christian myth. They did not. This does not mean that they rejected the myth (Lewis defends it very specifically in *Letters to Malcolm*); but it does mean that they saw it as no longer sufficient to carry the "tenor" of religious truth. And this is the same premise from which Bultmann and the other demythologizers start. In addition, both men have revealed that the personal religious life involves a practice of private substitution and exchange of pain and guilt, a literal bearing of others' burdens, that has little or no connection with institutional religious life. More important, Williams's notion of all human beings as inter-dependent—exchanging and substituting, whether consciously or not—is relevant to, even a description of, the current movement of much theology toward Christology, and the growing preoccupation with social duty to one's neighbor. Any theological position that argues for the essential unity of mankind seems relevant now. The notion of co-inherence—the image of the city—suggests the growing humanitarian feeling of our time. The late Martin Luther King spoke of the black man as the white man's conscience. If Williams were alive and aware of the present racial turmoil in America, he might well speak of the black man's suffering as a kind of unconscious and certainly unwilling substitution for the white man, the white man's happiness made possible by the black man's misery. *Fuimus ille unus*—we were one; we are one. In one way or other, I think, all three men testify to the erosion—or transformation—of traditional religion and the consequent turning inward that, with Barfield's help, I have been describing.

But Barfield has done more than describe the religious situation, and his work does more than reflect certain aspects of that situation. It bears directly on it. I have said that much current "liberal" theology is really Christology. It is certainly true that the theology being most widely discussed today—liberal and "radical" theology and Death of God theology and "Christian atheism"—assumes the absence in contemporary consciousness of any traditional feeling for God the Father. These theologies argue in various ways that if man is to come into contact with divinity it must be through Christ—not even God the Son, but God become man, or God *in* man. In technical language, what these theologies assert is God's "radical immanence" in man and the consequent irrelevance of any notions about the Creator-God of the Old Testament, Who is by definition transcendent. However Christians may view the arguments of liberal and radical theology—whether they simply assert that in some way they are a part of the Mystical Body of Christ, or whether, like some of the radical theologians, they use the word *kenotic,* and speak of God as "emptying Himself into Christ"—it seems to me that Barfield has much to say to them. For especially in *Saving the Appearances* and *Unancestral Voice,* Barfield, speaking in non-theological language, has dealt with the terrible mystery that all Christians must come to terms with, or else remain practicing Deists whose God exists forever beyond and above them. He has dealt with the mystery of the Incarnation, what I have called the qualitative connection between God and man. The phrase "radical immanence" frightens most of us: we do not want to *be* God. And it also suggests the sort of blurry pantheism of such writers as Salinger, whose character in *Franny and Zooey* saw Christ in the fat woman out front in the theatre. (We have seen Lewis, in *Letters to Malcolm,* struggling to retain both God's immanence and His transcendence, and as a result wondering, rather pathetically, whether he had ever really loved God, because God was still, in some sense, outside himself and incomprehensible.) Barfield speaks to those afraid to be God, to those glad to be God, and to the uncertain ones like Lewis. He is not a "kenotic" theologian, but his argument suggests why the kenotic theologians should have come into prominence in our time. His argument for a polar relationship between God and man suggests at once the awful closeness of God and man but also the fact that they are not one being. It retains God's transcendence while at the same time stressing His immanence, and thus His approachability by means of the imagination. It suggests the divinity in man as his unconscious source of power but also the humanity in him as both his limitation and his necessity to choose.

To object that, for Barfield, God and man are simply entities who exist only by interaction, not of themselves, is to advance the older Theosophical and pantheistic argument of occultists like Angelus Silesius: "I know that without me God can live no instant; if I become nothing, He must of necessity give up the ghost."[8] But Barfield's position does not blur time and eternity, as that of Angelus Silesius does. Man's relationship to God is indeed polar (a matter of interaction), but it is also temporal. Angelus Silesius's sentence describes the relationship among the members of the Trinity, a relationship among eternal equals. Barfield's argument more subtly (and more truly, I think) insists on the veil of time which all

Platonists have insisted is but the shadow of eternity. We may participate in the polarity of the Trinity only as we utilize the Christ in us, with the help of grace and by means of the imagination. Barfield's Christianity is esoteric, but it remains Christianity. Potency need not become act. The light shines in the darkness, but the darkness may or may not comprehend it.

I should like to make one point about the discussion of religion and romanticism which is the subject of this study. I said in the Introduction that I believed any deeply held literary belief implies a religious point of view. The discussion of "romantic religion" has, I hope, been an illustration of this belief. In a sense, then, this study is an addition to the old humanistic argument that literature is the handmaiden of religion and philosophy, that in its own way it includes them, that it is not only sweet but useful, uniquely relevant to human life.

Notes to the Text

Notes to Chapter One

1. Christopher Derrick, "Nightly Intelligence," *The Tablet,* CCXIX (June 5, 1965), 636.

2. T. J. J. Altizer and William Hamilton, *Radical Theology and the Death of God* (New York, 1966), p. 148.

3. T. J. J. Altizer, review of *Worlds Apart, Journal of Bible and Religion,* XXXII (1964), 385.

4. Carl Michalson, "The Ghost of Logical Positivism," *Christian Scholar,* XLIII (Fall 1960), 223.

5. John Wilson, *Language and Christian Belief* (London, 1958), p. 16.

6. Ibid., pp. 17–19.

7. Northrup Frye, ed., *Romanticism Reconsidered,* Selected Papers from the English Institute (New York, 1963), pp. 1, 10–11, 14.

8. Ibid., pp. 113, 121, 129–30.

9. C. S. Lewis, ed., *Essays Presented to Charles Williams* (London, 1947), p. xi.

10. John Heath-Stubbs, *Charles Williams,* Writers and their Work, no. 63 (London, 1955), p. 13.

11. C. S. Lewis, ed., *George Macdonald, An Anthology* (New York, 1947), p. 18.

12. George Macdonald, *Phantastes* (London, 1923), p. 237.

Notes to Chapter Two

1. John J. Mood, "Poetic Language and Primal Thinking: A study of Barfield, Wittgenstein, and Heidegger," *Encounter,* XXVI (August 1965), 417–33; Robert W. Funk, *Language, Hermeneutic, and Word of God* (New York, 1966), esp. pp. 113 ff; Owen Barfield, "The Rediscovery of Meaning," reprinted in Richard Thruelsen and John Kobler, eds., *Adventures of the Mind, Second Series* (New York, 1961), pp. 311–26; see also G. B. Tennyson, "Owen Barfield and the Rebirth of Meaning," *Southern Review,* V (January 1969), 42–57.

2. C. S. Lewis, *Surprised By Joy* (London, 1955), pp. 189–90.

3. Owen Barfield, *Romanticism Comes of Age,* New and Augmented Edition (Middletown, Conn., 1967), pp. 17–19. The original edition was published in London in 1944 by the Anthroposophical Publishing Co. (now the Rudolf Steiner Press). My references are to the later edition.

4. Lewis, *Surprised By Joy,* p. 195.

5. Rudolf Steiner, *The Philosophy of Spiritual Activity* (London, 1949), p. 67.

6. Ibid., p. 160.

7. Barfield, *Romanticism,* pp. 189, 176, 199.

8. Rudolf Steiner, *Mystics of the Renaissance* (New York, 1911), pp. 27–28.

9. Barfield, *Romanticism,* p. 228.

10. W. B. Yeats, "Magic," in *Essays* (London, 1924), p. 33.

11. Barfield, *Romanticism,* pp. 230–31.

12. Steiner, *Spiritual Activity,* p. 17.

13. Barfield, *Romanticism,* pp. 84–85.

14. T. J. J. Altizer, Review of *Worlds Apart, Journal of Bible and Religion,* XXXII (1964), 384.

15. Owen Barfield, *Poetic Diction,* 2nd ed. (London, 1952), p. 36.

16. Owen Barfield, *Speaker's Meaning* (Middletown, Conn., 1967), p. 25.

17. Owen Barfield, *History in English Words* (London, 1954), pp. 14, 21. Succeeding references to this book are shown in the text.

18. Ibid., p. 89. Lewis's discussion of Roman Allegory in *The Allegory of Love* (New York, 1958) is clearly much indebted to Barfield on this point. Lewis cites *Poetic Diction* at the beginning of his discussion (Chapter II, "Allegory").

19. Barfield, *Poetic Diction,* 2nd ed., p. 14. Succeeding page references to this book are shown in the text.

20. Owen Barfield, *Saving the Appearances* (London, 1957), p. 51. Succeeding page references to this book are shown in the text.

21. Cf. Robert Redfield, *The Primitive World and its Transformations* (Ithaca, N.Y., 1957), esp. Chapter IV, "Primitive World View and Civilization." Redfield quotes D. D. Lee as saying that, for the primitive, "man is *in* nature already, and we cannot speak properly of man *and* nature" (p. 85). Cf. Also H. and H. A. Frankfort, *et al, Before Philosophy: The Intellectual Adventure of Ancient Man* (Baltimore, 1954).

22. Barfield, *Romanticism,* pp. 14–15.

23. Ibid., p. 253. The next few page references to this book are shown in the text.

24. Barfield, *Appearances,* p. 137. The succeeding page references to this book are shown in the text.

25. Charles S. Sherrington, *Goethe on Nature and on Science* (Cambridge, 1949), p. 11.

26. Owen Barfield, *Worlds Apart (A Dialogue of the 1960's)* (Middletown, Conn., 1963), p. 7. Succeeding page references to this book are shown in the text. Burgeon reappears as the "hero" of *Unancestral Voice* (1965). He made what I believe is his first appearance in a little-known book by Barfield (under the pseudonym of G. A. L. Burgeon) called *That Ever Diverse Pair* (London, 1950). The book, now out of print, is very difficult to find. The Library of Congress lists it under Burgeon's name and classifies it as "Law-Miscellaneous." In the book Burgeon is the idealistic alter ego or "sleeping partner" of the practical minded solicitor named Burden. Together they form an amusing and ironic picture of the tension Barfield must have felt over the years between the demands of his profession and his need to live in the larger world of thought and letters. Burden reappears briefly in *Unancestral Voice,* but Burgeon dismisses him at once when he voices skepticism over Burgeon's mystical visitor.

27. Owen Barfield, "Imagination and Inspiration," *Interpretation: The Poetry of Meaning,* ed. Stanley R. Hopper and David L. Miller (New York, 1967), p. 70.

28. Ibid., pp. 72–73.

29. Ibid., p. 75.

30. Owen Barfield, *Unancestral Voice* (Middletown, Conn., 1965), p. 16. The succeeding page references to this book are shown in the text.

31. In *Essays Presented to Charles Williams* (London, 1947); reprinted in *The Importance of Language,* ed. Max Black (Englewood Cliffs, N.J., 1962).

32. In *Essays and Studies,* n.s., III (1950).

33. In *Metaphor and Symbol,* eds. L. C. Knights and Basil Cottle (London, 1960).

34. Barfield, *Speaker's Meaning,* p. 37. The succeeding page references to this book are shown in the text.

35. Walter Jackson Bate, *Coleridge,* Masters of World Literature Series (New York, 1968), p. 218.

Notes to Chapter Three

1. J. A. W. Bennett, "'Grete Clerk,'" in *Light on C. S. Lewis,* ed. Jocelyn Gibbs (New York, 1965), p. 49; Neville Coghill, "The Approach to English," ibid., p. 65.

2. C. S. Lewis, *Surprised By Joy* (London, 1955), p. 12. The next several references to this book are shown in the text.

3. C. S. Lewis, Preface to *George MacDonald, An Anthology* (New York, 1947), pp. 20–21.

4. C. S. Lewis, *The Pilgrim's Regress* (New York, 1935), p. 11. Succeeding page references to this book are shown in the text.

5. C. S. Lewis, "Psycho-Analysis and Literary Criticism," *Essays and Studies,* XXVII (1942), 7.

6. Lewis, *Surprised By Joy,* p. 196.

7. Lewis accepts this process explicitly. An appendix to his *Allegory of Love* refers the reader to *Poetic Diction* for further explanation. The process is also assumed in Lewis's "Bluspels and Flalansferes: A Semantic Nightmare," in *Rehabilitations and Other Essays,* reprinted in *The Importance of Language,* ed. Max Black (Englewood Cliffs, N.J., 1962).

8. Owen Barfield, *Poetic Diction,* 2nd ed. (London, 1952), pp. 91–92.

9. Lewis, *Surprised By Joy,* p. 221.

10. Ibid.

11. G. K. Chesterton, *The Everlasting Man* (New York, 1955), p. 266.

12. E. Schillebeeckx, O. P., discusses this "anonymous revelation" in some detail in *Revelation and Theology,* Vol. I (New York, 1967), pp. 6–10.

13. C. S. Lewis, Preface to *The Pilgrim's Regress,* 3rd ed. (Grand Rapids, Mich., 1958), p. 11.

14. Charles Moorman, *Arthurian Triptych* (Berkeley, 1960), p. 18.

15. Lewis, *Surprised By Joy,* p. 222.

16. C. S. Lewis, *The Problem of Pain* (New York, 1946), p. 64.

17. C. S. Lewis, *Miracles* (New York, 1947), p. 161. The next three references are to this book and are shown in the text.

18. Kathleen Nott thinks that Lewis's monism is superficial, that he is often "troubled . . . by the old difficulty of Cartesian dualism." *The Emperor's Clothes* (Bloomington, Ind., 1958), p. 259.

19. C. S. Lewis, *Letters to Malcolm* (New York, 1964), pp. 68–69.

20. Ibid., p. 73.

21. G. K. Chesterton, *St. Thomas Aquinas* (New York, 1933), p. 139.

22. Second of "Two Songs For A Play."

23. Lewis, *Problem of Pain,* p. 124.

24. C. S. Lewis, *Of Other Worlds* (New York, 1966).

25. Lewis, *Pilgrim's Regress,* p. 218.

26. Lewis, *Pilgrim's Regress,* 3rd ed., p. 171.

27. Lewis, *Pilgrim's Regress,* pp. 219–20.

28. I am indebted to Professor Howard W. Fulweiler of the University of Missouri for his remarks to me on this point.

29. Lewis, Preface to *George Macdonald, An Anthology,* pp. 14, 16–17.

30. Lewis, "Christianity and Literature," in *Rehabilitations,* p. 196.

31. Robert Graves, Introduction to *The Golden Ass of Apuleius* (New York, 1954), p. xvi.

32. Ibid., p. 130.

33. C. S. Lewis, *Till We Have Faces* (New York, 1956), p. 313. Page references are shown in the text.

34. B. R. Redman, "Love Was the Weapon," *Saturday Review,* XXXX (January 12, 1957), 15.

35. T. F. Curley, "Myth into Novel," *Commonweal,* LXV (February 8, 1957), 495.

36. Lewis, *Pilgrim's Regress,* 3rd ed., p. 15. Barfield, in his introductory essay in *Light on C. S. Lewis,* also insists that it is a myth, not an allegory.

37. Lewis, *Problem of Pain,* pp. 70, 65, 71.

38. The term is Mircea Eliade's. See *Cosmos and History* (New York, 1959), p. 35.

39. C. S. Lewis, *Out of the Silent Planet* (New York, 1943), *Perelandra* (New York, 1944), and *That Hideous Strength* (New York, 1946).

40. Lewis, "Bluspels and Flalansferes," in *Rehabilitations,* p. 158.

41. Hoxie N. Fairchild, *The Romantic Quest* (New York, 1931), p. 251.

42. W. H. Auden, *For the Time Being,* in *Collected Longer Poems* (New York, 1969), p. 196.

43. C. S. Lewis, Preface to *Mere Christianity* (New York, 1957), p. vi. The next several references to this book are shown in the text.

44. C. S. Lewis, "Transposition," in *The Weight of Glory and Other Addresses* (New York, 1949), p. 28.

45. Nott, *Emperor's Clothes,* p. 255.

46. C. S. Lewis, *The Abolition of Man* (New York, 1947), p. 11.

47. Ibid., p. 32.

48. Coleridge, *Aids to Reflection, Complete Works,* I (New York, 1871), p. 215. The next three references are to this book and are shown in the text.

49. Lewis, *Problem of Pain,* p. 83.

50. Lewis, "The Weight of Glory," in *Weight of Glory,* pp. 12, 8, 13.

51. Lewis, "Transposition," in *Weight of Glory,* pp. 17, 28, 25.

52. C. S. Lewis, *Reflections on the Psalms* (New York, 1958), pp. 7, 2, 112, 113, 113–14.

53. Lewis, *Letters to Malcolm,* p. 13.

54. C. S. Lewis, *The Four Loves* (New York, 1960), p. 191, 191–92.

55. Austin Farrar, "The Christian Apologist," in *Light on C. S. Lewis,* p. 40.

56. Lewis, *Letters to Malcolm,* pp. 52, 101–2, 102, 103, 121, 124.

57. See C. T. Sanders, *Coleridge and the Broad Church Movement* (Durham, N.C., 1942).

58. Stephen Neill, *Anglicanism* (Baltimore, 1958), pp. 422, 429.

59. Coleridge, *Aids to Reflection,* p. 195.

60. Lewis, *Letters to Malcolm,* p. 103.

61. C. S. Lewis, Preface to *The Great Divorce* (New York, 1946), p. vii.

Notes to Chapter Four

1. John Heath-Stubbs, "The Posthumous Career of Charles Williams," *New Republic,* CLIV (June 11, 1966), 19; C. S. Lewis, "Williams and the Arthuriad" in *Arthurian Torso* (London, 1948); Charles Williams, *The Image of the City and Other Essays,* edited by Anne Ridler (London, 1958); *Charles Williams: Selected Writings,* edited by Anne Ridler (London, 1961); Alice Hadfield, *An Introduction to Charles Williams* (Lon-

don, 1959); Mary M. Shideler, *The Theology of Romantic Love: A Study in the Writings of Charles Williams* (New York, 1962).

2. C. S. Lewis, Preface to *Essays Presented to Charles Williams* (London, 1947), p. xiv.

3. T. S. Eliot, Introduction to Charles Williams, *All Hallows' Eve* (New York, 1948), p. xi; W. H. Auden, Introduction to Charles Williams, *The Descent of the Dove* (New York, 1956), p. v; Ridler, Introduction to *Image of the City,* p. xxii.

4. Auden, Introduction to *Descent of the Dove,* p. v; Lewis, *Arthurian Torso,* p. 123; Nevill Coghill, "The Approach to English," *Light on C. S. Lewis,* ed. Jocelyn Gibbs (New York, 1965), p. 63.

5. T. S. Eliot, Introduction to *All Hallows' Eve,* p. xvii.

6. George Every, *Poetry and Personal Responsibility* (London, 1949), p. 41; Heath-Stubbs, "The Posthumous Career of Charles Williams," p. 19; V. de Sola Pinto, Review of *Charles Williams: Selected Writings, Notes and Queries,* n.s., IX, No. 8 (August 1962), 319.

7. John Heath-Stubbs, *Charles Williams,* Writers and Their Work, no. 63 (London, 1955), p. 15.

8. Charles Williams, "The Son of Lancelot" in *Taliessen through Logres and The Region of the Summer Stars* (London, n.d.), pp. 55–56.

9. Charles Williams, *The Forgiveness of Sins* (London, 1950), p. 119. The volume also includes *He Came Down From Heaven.*

10. The doctrine that the Incarnation would have occurred even had there been no Fall, Williams attributes to Duns Scotus. See *Descent of the Dove,* p. 122.

11. Williams, *Forgiveness of Sins,* pp. 119–20.

12. Williams, "The Vision of the Empire" in *Taliessen,* p. 6.

13. Williams, *Descent of the Dove,* pp. 69–70.

14. Williams, "Anthropotokos" in *Image of the City,* p. 112.

15. Williams, "Taliessen on the Death of Virgil" in *Taliessen,* p. 32.

16. Ridler, Introduction to *Image of the City,* p. xlix.

17. Williams, *He Came Down From Heaven,* pp. 17, 19, 20.

18. Williams, *The Forgiveness of Sins,* p. 123.

19. Williams, "The Vision of the Empire" in *Taliessen,* pp. 10–11.

20. Williams, *The Forgiveness of Sins,* p. 129.

21. Williams, "The Son of Lancelot" in *Taliessen,* p. 55.

22. Charles Williams, *The Figure of Beatrice* (London, 1943), p. 8.

23. Antony Borrow, "The Affirmation of Images," *Nine,* III (1952), 327, 329.

24. Lewis, Preface to *Essays Presented to Charles Williams*, p. vi.

25. Williams, "Blake and Wordsworth" in *Image of the City*, p. 60.

26. Heath-Stubbs, *Charles Williams*, pp. 18–19.

27. Charles Williams, *Many Dimensions* (London, 1947), p. 58.

28. Ridler, Introduction to *Image of the City*, p. xxv.

29. Heath-Stubbs, *Charles Williams*, p. 36.

30. Williams, "The Vision of the Empire" in *Taliessen*, p. 8.

31. See Denis Saurat, *Milton: Man and Thinker* (New York, 1925), Part IV, Section II, pp. 281–328. See also Saurat, *Gods of the People* (London, 1947), pp. 140–41.

32. Ernest Beaumont, "Charles Williams and the Power of Eros," *Dublin Review*, CCXXXIII–CCXXXIV, No. 479 (Spring 1959–Winter 1960–61), 71.

33. Charles Williams, *The Greater Trumps* (New York, 1950), p. 51.

34. Eliot, Introduction to *All Hallows'* Eve, p. xv; Beaumont, "Charles Williams," p. 74; Evgveny Lampert, *The Divine Realm* (London, 1944), n.1, p. 93 (quoted by Beaumont, p. 74).

35. Williams, "The Index of the Body" in *Image of the City*, p. 85.

36. "Sensuality and Substance" in ibid., p. 75.

37. "The Index of the Body" in ibid., p. 84.

38. Ibid., p. 85.

39. Ibid., pp. 86–87.

40. Williams, "Taliessen in the Rose Garden" in *Taliessen*, pp. 26–27.

41. Charles Williams, *Religion and Love in Dante* (Westminster, 1941), p. 5.

42. Ibid., p. 3.

43. Williams, *He Came Down From Heaven*, p. 65.

44. Ibid., p. 66.

45. Williams, *Religion and Love in Dante*, pp. 6–7. The next several references to this book are shown in the text.

46. Williams, *He Came Down From Heaven*, p. 70.

47. Williams, *Figure of Beatrice*, p. 232.

48. Williams, *He Came Down From Heaven*, p. 79.

49. Lewis, *Arthurian Torso*, p. 126.

50. Williams, "The Coming of Palomides" in *Taliessen*, pp. 35–37.

51. Charles Williams, "Seed of Adam" in *Seed of Adam and Other Plays* (London, 1948), p. 11.

52. Williams, *He Came Down From Heaven*, p. 80.

53. Ibid., p. 81.

54. Williams, "The Star of Percivale" in *Taliessen,* p. 46.

55. Williams, *He Came Down From Heaven,* p. 85.

56. Shideler, *Theology of Romantic Love,* p. 1.

57. Martin Buber, *I and Thou,* tr. R. G. Smith (New York, 1958), pp. 75, 106.

58. For my summary of Nygren's views I am indebted to M. C. D'Arcy's *The Mind and Heart of Love* (New York, 1956), *passim.*

59. Denis de Rougemont, *Love in the Western World,* tr. M. Belgion (New York, 1957), p. 52.

60. D'Arcy, *Mind and Heart of Love,* p. 365.

61. Ibid., p. 367.

62. Ibid., p. 368.

63. Quoted from Maurice Valency, *In Praise of Love, An Introduction to the Love Poetry of the Renaissance* (New York, 1958), p. 229.

64. Ibid.

65. Ibid., p. 210.

66. C. S. Lewis, *The Four Loves* (New York, 1960), pp. 159–60.

Notes to Chapter Five

1. C. S. Lewis, Preface to *That Hideous Strength* (New York, 1946), p. viii. Dr. Dimble, the authority on Arthurian myth in the story, may be partly modeled on Tolkien.

2. Henry Resnik, "The Hobbit-Forming World of J. R. R. Tolkien," *Saturday Evening Post* (July 2, 1966), p. 91.

3. Ibid.

4. *Tolkien Journal,* published by the Tolkien Society of America, 159 Marlborough Rd., Brooklyn, N.Y., 11226; Richard Plotz, ed.

5. *Mankato State College Studies,* II, No. 1 (February 1967).

6. W. H. Auden, "At the End of The Quest, Victory," *New York Times Book Review* (January 22, 1956), p. 5.

7. Edmund Wilson, "Oo, Those Awful Orcs," *Nation,* CLXXXII (April 14, 1956), 313–14; Mark Roberts "Adventure in English," *Essays in Criticism,* VI (January 1956), 458; Gerald Jonas, "Triumph of the Good," *New York Times Book Review* (October 31, 1965), p. 78.

8. W. H. Auden, "The Hero Is A Hobbit," *New York Times Book Review* (October 31, 1954), p. 37.

9. Wilson, "Oo, Those Awful Orcs," p. 312. Wilson quotes with great relish some of Tolkien's remarks made in a statement to his publisher: "The invention of languages is the foundation. The 'stories' were made rather to provide a world for the languages than the reverse. I should have preferred to write in 'Elvish' " (p. 312). In the Foreword to the Ballantine edition, Tolkien modifies these statements. The book "was primarily linguistic in inspiration and was begun in order to provide the necessary background of 'history' for Elvish tongues" (p. viii). But he adds later: "The prime motive was the desire of a tale-teller to try his hand at a really long story that would hold the attention of readers, amuse them, delight them, and at times maybe excite them or deeply move them" (p. ix). The Foreword is in vol. I, *The Fellowship of the Ring* (New York, Ballantine Books, 1965).

10. William Blissett, "The Despots of the Ring," *South Atlantic Quarterly,* LVIII (Summer 1959), 449; Christopher Derrick, "From An Antique Land," *The Tablet,* CCXVI (December 15, 1962), 1227; Bruce A. Beatie, "Folk Tale, Fiction, and Saga in J. R. R. Tolkien's *The Lord of the Rings,*" *Mankato State College Studies,* p. 4; R. J. Reilly, "Tolkien and the Fairy Story," *Thought,* XXXVIII (Spring 1963), 89–106 (reprinted in *Tolkien and the Critics,* ed. Neil D. Isaacs and Rose A. Zimbardo [Notre Dame and London, University of Notre Dame Press, 1968]); Alexis Levitin, *Mankato State College Studies,* p. 27.

11. Douglass Parker, "Hwaet We Holbylta . . . ," *Hudson Review,* IX (Spring 1956-Winter 1956–1957), 609.

12. Tolkien, Foreword to the Ballantine edition, p. xi.

13. J. R. R. Tolkien, "On Fairy-Stories," in *Essays Presented to Charles Williams* (London, 1947; photographic reprint, Grand Rapids, Michigan, 1966), p. 87. This essay has been reprinted in *Tree and Leaf* (London, 1964), and in *The Tolkien Reader* (New York, 1966).

14. C. S. Lewis, *The Personal Heresy* (New York, 1939), p. 16.

15. Blissett, "The Despots of the Ring," p. 450. Tolkien explicitly denies this intention in the preface to the Ballantine edition (pp. x–xi), but presumably he cannot deny Mr. Blissett his "application."

16. Parker, "Hwaet We Holbylta," pp. 605, 608, 606.

17. Michael Straight, "The Fantastic World of Professor Tolkien," *New Republic,* CXXXIV (January 16, 1956), 26, 24, 26.

18. Patricia Spacks, "Ethical Pattern in *The Lord of the Rings,*" *Critique,* III (Spring-Fall 1959), 30, 34, 35, 41.

19. C. S. Lewis, "The Dethronement of Power," *Time and Tide,* XXXVI (October 22, 1955), 1374.

20. Dorothy Barber, "The Meaning of *The Lord of the Rings,*" *Mankato*

State College Studies, p. 38. The next several references are to this essay and are shown in the text.

21. Tolkien, "On Fairy-Stories" p. 43. Page references to the essay are shown in the text.

22. Spacks, "Ethical Pattern in *The Lord of the Rings,*" p. 36.

23. *Biographia Literaria,* Chapter XIII.

24. Lewis, "The Dethronement of Power," p. 1374.

25. Barber, "Meaning of *The Lord of the Rings,*" p. 40.

26. Beatie, "Folk Tale, Fiction, and Saga," pp. 5–6.

27. *Biographia Literaria,* Chapter XIII.

Notes to Chapter Six

1. Roger Sale, "England's Parnassus: C. S. Lewis, Charles Williams and J. R. R. Tolkien," *Hudson Review,* XVII, No. 2 (Summer 1964), 203–25.

2. See Robert A. McDermott, "Religion As An Academic Discipline," *Cross Currents,* XVIII, No. 1 (Winter 1968), 17–24.

3. Edwyn Bevan, *Symbolism and Belief* (Boston, 1957), p. 349.

4. *Summa Theologica,* 2a–2ae. xxviii. 3.

5. Wordsworth, *Prelude,* II, 399.

6. Ibid., 401–5.

7. Ibid., 413–14.

8. Rudolf Steiner, *Mystics of the Renaissance* (New York, 1911), p. 43.

Index